W9-BTN-210

To Joe

Stay on Purpose

TRANSFORMATIONAL CHANGE

How to transform Mass Production Thinking to meet the challenge of Mass Customization

by

THOMAS K. WENTZ

Copyright © 1999 by Corporate Performance Systems, Inc.

All rights reserved. No part of this publication may be reproduced, distributed, or transmitted in any form or by any means, including photocopying, recording, or other electronic or mechanical methods, without the prior written permission of the publisher, except in the case of brief quotations embodied in critical reviews and certain other noncommercial uses permited by copyright law. For permission requests, write to the publisher at the address below.

ORDERING INFORMATION

Transformational Change may be purchased for educational, business, or sales promotional use. For information please write:

Corporate Performance Systems, Inc.
5001 Pine Creek Drive
Westerville, Ohio 43081
Tel: (614) 890-2799 Fax: (614) 890-6760

or visit our web site at:
www.transchange.com

Cover design by Faith Leibowitz and Robin Becker
Printed by Boehm, Inc.

The paper used in this publication meets the requirements of the American National Standard for Permanence of Paper for Printed Library Materials Z39.49-1984.

Library of Congress Catalog Card Number: 99-90364
Wentz, Thomas K.
    Transformational Change: How to transform Mass Production Thinking to meet the challenge of Mass Customization / by Thomas K. Wentz – 1st ed.

    Includes bibliographical references
    ISBN 0-9668435-0-9

Acknowledgments

This book represents the collective experience of hundreds of people who are trying to find meaning and fulfillment in their work. As I wrote the book, I knew people and organizations were achieving dramatic results by being aligned on purpose. Peter Benson and all my friends at Solidstate Controls Incorporated served as a brilliant model of Transformational Change.

Mike Corbo, Dave Voris, Barb Beath, and Jean Hilliard constantly stressed the Mass Production Thinking models. Their experiences revealed important messages about surviving and growing within the Mass Production organization. My son, Bill, helped me realize that my golf game was limited by mass produced golf clubs. My daughter, Pam, served as a model of how a person can choose to be different and quickly become "world class."

During the first ten years of my consulting career, I was fortunate to work with three very talented and supportive colleagues: Mary Doyle, Kathy Hoyt, and Jill Schultz. Our experiences together are beyond acknowledgment. Without them there would be nothing to write. Gregg Spieth challenged me to experiment and was the collaborator who helped me extract meaning from the experiments. My other colleagues, Lynne Joyce, Tom Panek, Tom Corroto, and Terry Ainsworth, all helped to transform experiments into client experience. The collective intelligence of these people is reflected in every chapter. My thanks to all of you for your contribution and support.

Commitment to write the book was inspired by Brad, known to us as *Beaker*. Mass Production Thinkers failed to accurately diagnose his illness, and his gradual demise gave me clarity that burn out can be terminal.

Acknowledgment must go to many senior leaders who played the Mass Production Thinker game every day, yet privately admitted to me they were burned out. Some of the most insightful learning occurred behind closed doors and after hours in emotional discussions about the burned out and still shining phenomenon. I won't mention your names here or in this book, but I give you sincere appreciation for revealing the trauma of contextual blindness at the executive level.

To the graduates of empowerment and advanced leadership experiences, I acknowledge your shift from compliance to commitment. It was exciting to watch the transformation. You proved unequivocally that alignment on purpose is a powerful force.

Many people contributed to the finished product. Special thanks go to Penny, Michelle, Lynn, Sally, Bob, and the people at Boehm, Inc. for transforming ink into graphic communication.

Finally, never forget that today is the day, after the day that ends in "y." Don't defer the experience of living today. Fulfillment is a state of being. I acknowledge those who know this reality.

Table of Contents

Introduction

Transformational Change is the conscious and intentional change of a substance, object, organization, or mechanism to create a *different* form of matter, process, or relationship. Transformational change, therefore, brings into being new and different products, services, processes, and organizations.

While the process of Transformational Change is very complex, it happens routinely around and within us every day. Examples abound. Trees are transformed into paper, and your body easily transforms food into energy. People's lives are transformed through educational, marital, and religious experiences. Countries are transformed when new political approaches are adopted. The shift from communism to democracy is a massive transformational undertaking.

We have entered a time when many old models of business, government, education, and society are being transformed. The Industrial Age has been replaced with the Information Age, and the Human Potential Age is emerging. Hierarchical organizations have been dismantled in favor of flatter, more responsive networks. The control mechanism of middle management has been swept aside by a new model called self-directed teams. There are many books about this type of change, and I promise that *Transformational Change* will not bore you with the history of this evolutionary process.

Everyone knows that change is happening. There are many excellent books that prescribe specific advice concerning the challenges ahead. Yet, many organizations continue to struggle. One senior leader recently told me his company had been through 30 different change initiatives and "We still aren't world class."

Key Point:
- **The old models of business are built on Mass Production Thinking.**
- **Reorganization and reengineering don't guarantee that rethinking will occur.**
- **To be world class is an illusion within the *Context* of Mass Production Thinking.**

I wrote *Transformational Change* to help you realize that Mass Production Thinking does not inspire or motivate people. Every executive wants motivated employees, but Mass Production Thinkers get caught up in the numbers and believe that change is a function of control. Workers at all levels have been blamed for a lack of work ethic. Mass Production Thinkers truly believe that the problem is one of productivity. People who are experiencing blame are psychologically unable to commit their creative talent to those who blame. *Transformational Change* will help you eliminate blame and release the human potential that is waiting to be applied.

Transformational Change will help you understand why people resist change. The very word *change* drives fear into the hearts of many people because the result of the change is not desired or known. Have you been involved in a change initiative where the intention was to downsize; do more with less; or work smarter, not harder? The announced intention is about reorganizing the organization and effectively reducing the number of people in the organization. Confronted with this type of message, people immediately speculate about their role in the process and the desirability of the end result. People cannot embrace change when the end result is not known or the intention appears to eliminate their jobs.

Transformational Change will help you formulate and communicate a *vision of a desired end result* even within the most difficult change situations. The leadership message must be carefully crafted. The announced intention must always be about the customer and how *the Business of the BUSINESS* must change.

The Mass Production Thinker will tend to communicate a vision in terms of measurements. For example, let's suppose I told you I was going on vacation next week. What would be your logical next question? "Where are you going?" Just suppose I tell you, "I'm going to drive 1,000 miles, at 60 miles per hour, and average 30 miles per gallon." How's that for an answer? You would ask me again, "Where are you going?" I would say, "1000/60/30." This is a strange answer to your question, but I hear this answer every day. Executives frequently confuse measurements and vision. I attended a national sales meeting recently where the president showed a screen entitled "Our Vision–$200 Million, 12% net bottom line and a stock price at 20 times earning." How many times have you been told, "We're going to be a $200 million company in five years?" Why not $201 million?

Transformational Change is about establishing new ways to measure success within the *Context* of Mass Customization. The cost-plus mentality of Mass Production does not lead to innovation. It is an illusion to believe that *the Business of the BUSINESS* will be transformed using a linear measurement mentality. The accounting group of a very large financial services organization quietly admitted to me that they had no clue how to measure Mass Customization and would never embrace such a change in thinking.

Transformational Change will help you transform your personal life. Simply stated, personal transformation is about creating what you *want to be* and doing what you *want to do*. A world of abundance will become your playpen and you will be able to transfer this awareness to those you love.

Transformational Change will also help you become a proper advocate for change. Many people today want to be effective change agents, but most people don't know how. Many Transformational Change advocates are perceived as crazy or radical thinkers because their ideas challenge the *Context* of the existing environment. A *Context* is how people see the world, interpret circumstances, and explain behavior. The *Context* is well-embedded in belief systems and will cause people and nations to tenaciously defend their existence.

Being an effective change agent is difficult because the change ideas always make people "wrong" for their beliefs. People confronted in this manner will typically eliminate the messenger rather than change the *Context* of current reality. Let me give you several examples.

It's 1492 and you are Brian Jones, President of Aztec Flat World Boats. The stock market is booming and shares in Aztec have experienced a 70% increase over the past year. The unique maneuvering system invented by Aztec makes your boats much easier to dock in crowded harbors.

You have just met a man named Christopher Columbus who wants to know why your boats only have a 30-gallon water tank on-board. Your answer is "That's all people need for a day." You proceed to tell Christopher about the new maneuvering system and why Aztec stock would be a great investment.

Can you feel the tension Christopher would feel? To Brian the question appears to be about the Content features of the boat, but the real issue is one of *Context*. Christopher sees the world as round; Brian sees the world as flat. Christopher's message challenges the *Context* of Brian's thinking. Is there any wonder they gave Christopher Columbus prisoners to pilot his ships?

It's 1912 and you are Fred Burke, president of Wagon Masters, Inc. You have just been awarded a patent on a new shock-absorbing device that makes your stagecoaches more comfortable. You have heard about the horseless carriage, but Wagon Master stock has doubled with the announcement of the patent. A young man by the name of Henry Ford came by recently to see how you build coaches. You told him they are all custom built by the world's finest craftspeople. Mr. Ford is an entrepreneur who is looking for investment capital to build horseless carriages. He has concluded that "crafting" will not produce carriages fast enough. You told him nothing will replace the horse and comfortable carriages and Wagon Master stock would be a good investment.

The question Mr. Ford is asking is about *Context*. He wants to shift from crafting to Mass Production. Mr. Burke is arguing for the Content that is designed into his coaches. A challenge to the existing *Context* always brings an argument for embedded Content.

Key Point: • **The investment in Content in today's business environment is enormous, and business owners are committed to realizing a return on that investment.**

Consider President Kennedy's speech about landing a man on the moon by the end of the decade. It's the early 1960s and space travel is still the fantasy of Buck Rogers and Captain Video. The aviation industry has just finished transforming commercial aircraft from propellers to jets. Some people could easily believe that a jet plane could be modified to fly faster and arrive in space. The sound barrier has been broken. Why not the gravitational barrier?

We all know that an entirely new and different vehicle had to be created for space travel. Astronauts would experience the threatening, weightless environment of space. In 1960, aeronautical engineering textbooks did not contain the technology of space vehicles. The investment in new technology was massive, and creative talent had to be consciously and intentionally applied to transform aviators into astronauts.

| Key Point: | • **The engineering knowledge to operate in the new business environment is totally new in the past 10 years. Many Mass Production methods are technologically obsolete.** |

Leap ahead to 1972 and you are a consumer asking General Motors why their cars guzzle gas and why their engines fail at 50,000 miles? Their answers are about the styling and comfort of the new models and how your next purchase should be a car of higher quality. In 1972, quality was a Content feature afforded by upper class buyers.

Once again, your question is about *Context* and their answer is about Content. The embedded design features assume that you are not entitled to quality unless you are affluent. In 1972, quality was directly proportional to price. The higher the price, the higher the quality. The *Context* of quality was defined by the affluence of buyers. The *Context* of seeing buyers within mass market segments led to the marketing strategy of planned obsolescence. If companies like General Motors could create a predictable interval of product failure, new and improved models could be planned and introduced to sustain consumer demand.

Recall how Ralph Nader and the consumerism movement challenged the *Context* of quality in the 1970s. Many companies thought that consumerism was a fad and tried to ignore and eliminate Ralph. Like Christopher Columbus and Henry Ford, Ralph Nader challenged the *Context* and companies defended their Content.

Let's explore one more example. It's now 1998 and you just bought a personal computer to connect to the Internet. The salesperson likely did not tell you about the quality differences between brands. Quality is not defined by how long it will last or how well it is styled. You don't have to pay more for quality. All computers have the same processor. You pay more for speed, connectivity, and customization to meet your needs. You actually may pay less to get exactly what you need. It has all changed. The questions now are will it connect and can it be upgraded. A computer doesn't wear out with use. It is, however, technologically obsolete before you buy it.

Key Point:	•	The *Context* has changed and the Content of products today is different.
	•	Technological obsolescence has replaced planned obsolescence as a dominant business strategy.

Welcome to *Transformational Change*. What you are about to read can be as frustrating as the dialog contained in the pervious examples. As you read this book, you must consciously think about key words, such as *Context* and Content. These words look alike and will easily confuse the casual reader. Throughout the book, you will encounter words such as *structure, purpose, alignment, capability,* and *collective intelligence*–all of which have very different meanings in the new business environment. I apologize in advance for the contextual differences, but the water tank capacity question Christopher Columbus presented is important. The answer will determine the success of his journey.

In this book, I frequently talk about your journey into the new business environment. The journey is happening. It isn't optional. Whether you like it or not, we are all loaded on the boat, plane, or rocket to a new *Context* of doing business. As with Christopher Columbus, the world was round and everyone had to transform their thinking. Mr. Ford created a new *Context* of serving massive numbers of people with affordable products. Foreign competitors proved that quality was not an affluence issue, and the Internet has proven that the business environment is truly global. To be *local* and *global* is called Mass Customization. The new *Context* is here to stay. The only question to answer is, "Can you transform *the Business of Your BUSINESS* to meet the new requirements?"

This book describes the process of Transformational Leadership. The major contextual issue that limits your journey is Mass Production Thinking. In 1922, Mass Production Thinking did not exist. In 1972, it was well embedded in every executive's mind. In 1992, it became obsolete to think that way. As with a three-year-old computer, an executive that is programmed with Mass Production Thinking is technologically obsolete. Likewise, managers who grew up in the 1960s, 1970s, and 1980s are in need of significant upgrades. I call this phenomenon *burned out and still shining*.

Many of the chapters in *Transformation Change* will challenge you to *think about what you think about*. This is not an insult to your intelligence; rather, it is a challenge to your *awareness*. People are not aware of how they think or why they constantly repeat predictable behavior patterns. The *Context* of your existence makes your thinking patterns instinctive and comfortable. While you read this book, you can be easily frustrated thinking outside your existing *Context*.

Experience this example. Draw a Roman numeral five. Pick up a pen and do it. Now, with one line make it a six. Simple. Now draw a Roman numeral nine. Come on, do it. Now, with one line make it a six. If you are stuck, the issue is contextual. I will give you the answer, but try to find the answer and you will feel the frustration of contextual blindness.

Transformational Change is frustrating because it always involves a shift in *Context*. This book was neither easy to write, nor will it be easy to read. Most people read and think within the *Context* of Mass Production. I am writing in the *Context* of Mass Customization. Consider the Roman numeral nine again and think about the S IX you are trying to create. Can you see it yet? The word *line* does not mean straight line just as a *network* does not define the lines of authority within the new business environment.

I have chosen to embed my credibility as an author in the book rather than documenting it here in the "Introduction." I prefer that you not judge my credibility as an author or consultant, rather as a consumer, who like you, is confronted by Mass Production Thinking every day of our lives. It is amazing how many times a day we tolerate being over-promised and under-delivered. After I determined that Mass Production Thinking would always over-promise me as a customer, I concluded that Mass Production Thinking is *not* based on serving customers.

As you read, try to separate yourself as a leader, parent, manager, or executive from the Mass Production organization or mechanism that constrains you. This isn't easy. It is so logical to argue for the way you have always managed and look for ways to do it better. The level of awareness about Mass Customization is less than 10 years old. Many executives don't even know the term. Some who have heard it believe that Mass Customization is a new strategy within the *Context* of Mass Production.

Please read carefully because contextual awareness is blinding. To help you, I have intentionally included many statements as Key Points. While these statements seem redundant at times, they all contain contextual shifts in thinking.

Finally, for those who clearly see the world of Mass Production Thinking and choose to believe it will always be that way, *you are right*. A return on investment formula will drive your decision making and this is also right. To set goals and measure progress is important and critical to success. This book is not about what's *right* or *wrong*. That approach would reduce the book to a polarized debate within Mass Production Thinking. The new business environment is *possible*. It is neither right nor wrong. It is *different*.

If you get confused by what appears to be semantics or doubt the validity of the statements I make, you have two choices: read on or find a Mass Production Thinking book to read. You can easily eliminate me and ignore the message. They tried to ignore Christopher and Ralph and you too can throw this book away. If you read on, you will come to the answer. Please rest assured I mean no harm to you as a Mass Production Thinker or to your company. The examples I provide are real; the actual company names don't matter. Companies that are caught in the snare of Mass Production Thinking all behave the same way. It's all a matter of structure. Please be clear that the choice to create what you want to *be* within the new environment is yours.

Chapter 1
Burned Out and Still Shining

What you are about to read is true. I have not included company or individual names to maintain privacy. We have all been participants in the Mass Production revolution. We have all learned to manage and lead organizations using Mass Production Thinking. We have implanted Mass Production Thinking in our sons and daughters, and most of them are carrying on the family tradition. Vast fortunes have been made using Mass Production Thinking, and it is important that we all protect our investments.

Over the past 17 years, I have served as an organizational performance consultant, helping clients meet the challenges of change. In the beginning of my consulting career, it was easy to diagnose performance issues. I have an Industrial Engineering degree, a Masters of Business Administration, and 17 years of actual sales management experience. I am, like you, well grounded in Mass Production Thinking. Organizational performance problems could always be diagnosed as poor planning, ineffective organization, and lack of control over *things*. If you know the principles of Mass Production Thinking, you too can be a consultant.

It was easy to design performance systems with feedback loops that revealed cause and effect relationships. Every consultant has a model or matrix that explains performance deficiencies, and I had several good ones. It was easy to identify the attributes of effective leaders and managers and determine that those attributes were missing in every organization. It was easy to find someone to blame for the problems.

My work produced results for my clients, but—and here's the main issue— the performance improvement was *never good enough*. My work with one client involved changing the selling process. Ninety sales people were trained in a new high-performance sales process. It paid big dividends, quickly. At the year-end sales awards banquet, the president handed out the sales achievement awards and ended his speech saying, "We've had the best year ever, *but* it's still not good enough!" The salespeople were crushed. They had exceeded quota by 38%. What is good enough?

I began to wonder *what is enough* and why are executives universally unfulfilled by year-end results? It was easy to improve performance, but it was almost impossible to satisfy the insatiable appetite of senior management. People were exhausted trying to produce *enough*.

As a consultant, I began to ask myself if I understood what was happening to my clients and if I had the necessary tools to help them change. It was easy to find fault in what was visible—mainly people. Then I realized that the same *performance problems* existed everywhere. I heard the same speech from Jack, Dick, Sue, Jane, Carl, Rick, and Ed. I finally realized that the leaders were trying to improve performance by fixing people and *people can't be fixed*. You can't fix the performance if the performance you want has never existed—fixing is the wrong work.

This book is about the rest of the story. We have arrived at a time when something different is happening, and explaining what's happening using Mass Production Thinking just doesn't work.

What's Happening?

Companies, businesses, organizations, universities, and institutions of all sizes and types are confronted with change. Following are the common themes of what's happening:

- They all *want* to change.

- Many *have* changed to survive.

- Many *have* changed to grow.

- Many *change initiatives* have been implemented, but results are still not good enough.

- They all want to be *different* from what they *are*.

- They all want to do something *better*.

- They all want *more* of something.

- New *visions* describe the future in terms of excellence or world class.

- Many *don't know how* to change.

- Some think they know *what* to change, but they aren't sure *how*.

- They are all embroiled in a contest trying to defeat *time*.

- They all think the answer lies in finding the *cause of the problem* and eliminating it.

- They all *blame* some amorphous thing for their problems, such as the culture, government, foreign competition, labor, or management.

- They all have embraced *information technology* as the answer.

- The *speed* of business has accelerated beyond tolerable levels.

- *Chaos* is everywhere.

- *Buzzword* solutions have been tried and proven ineffective.
- The *global marketplace* appears to be the opportunity. The gold rush is on.
- The *journey* appears to be sustainable in economic terms.
- The time to attack is *now* and big, hairy, audacious goals are being set.
- *Teamwork* is necessary to produce results and *team* initiatives aren't working.
- Customers are being called *partners*.
- The *distribution channel* is now called a *supply chain*.
- Everything must be *connected* with *information*.
- The organization is now on a *network*. The organization chart doesn't explain anything.
- Business books and articles offer *solutions* that all sound alike.
- There are more *consultants* today then ever before. The Big Six have more consultants than accountants.
- Everything works for a short time, but nothing *gets fixed*.

Sound familiar?

One of my new clients, after reading this list said, "Been there, doing all of the above, still can't figure it out." His biggest concern was how to achieve 35% growth for next year to keep his job. The company had never grown at that rate, yet his boss had committed to a big, hairy, audacious goal of 35% growth to the board of directors. When he translated 35% growth into capital, resources, and people, he was exhausted just thinking about it. Yet, his boss told him it wasn't optional and he just needed to figure it out.

After lengthy discussions about what *it* is, why grow, how to grow, and limitations to growth, we again identified the villain as *not enough!* Everything he said started with *not enough*. He didn't know where he would get enough time, people, customers, and commitment. The items on the what's happening list were all happening simultaneously, and he wanted me as a performance consultant to help him *solve the problem*.

I suggested that the growth opportunity ahead was not *a problem to be solved* but rather an *opportunity to create*. He was totally confused. I'll save the rest of the story for later in this book.

After you see a pattern of behavior repeatedly, you would think people would try something different. I'm sure you know the definition of insanity:

Insanity: • **Doing the same thing over and over again, expecting different results.**

If you want different results, you must first define what *different* looks like. This is such a simple statement, but it is obviously not easy to do.

I have watched companies spend millions of dollars with consulting firms of all kinds, trying to define *different*. One client spent $10.7 million on a study with a very prestigious Big Six consulting firm. The financial projections were ambitious. The process redesign plan required a major change in strategy and the elimination of hundreds of jobs. Everyone appeared to agree to the plan *except* as it affected their division. The plan was abandoned within 30 days.

Why?—What's the answer?

Let's look at a statement from the December 8, 1997, *Fortune* magazine article entitled, "How Toyota Defies Gravity."

> Anyone want to read more about Japanese management techniques? I thought not. Last year's management fads are about as appetizing as yesterday's sushi, and ideas such as just-in-time inventory and continuous improvement feel shopworn, to say the least. TPS itself is hardly an unknown quantity. GM formed a joint venture with Toyota to study its production techniques back in 1984, and *The Machine That Changed the World,* which effectively anointed Toyota the world's productivity leader, was published in 1990. But why is it, exactly, that nobody has been able to imitate TPS, much less duplicate its results? GM, Ford, and Chrysler have all borrowed bits and pieces, and Honda's system resembles Toyota's in many areas, but nobody has been able to match the master.

What a great question—why is it, *exactly*? I have been asked this question by my clients over and over again. They want to know, "Why is it that it's never good enough?" There are many answers to why General Motors can't copy Toyota, but the exact answer is

Exactly: • **You cannot copy what you cannot see.**

This book *is not* about why General Motors cannot copy Toyota. It *is* about the answers to questions, such as

- Why is it that leaders develop plans for change and can't implement the plan?

- Why is it that companies talk about empowerment and practice control?

- Why is it that team initiatives are stalled or failing in 90% of the places where they were started with fanfare?

- Why is it there *isn't enough* when *growth* is occurring everywhere?

- Why is it that people with very little money create businesses *from nothing?*

Here is the *exact* answer to *why?*

Exactly: • **Mass Production Thinking doesn't contain the answers, and very few executives and consultants know any other way to think.**

Before you stop reading, consider the following statement by Fred Smith, CEO of Federal Express:

> Over the past twenty years, apart from the medical revolution and the microprocessor, the most significant thing to happen to the world has been the ability to take mass out of production. The inventory-to-sales ratio of the whole industrial world has dropped like a stone during the last two decades.
>
> *WIRED*, December 1996

Exactly: • **Mass is being decoupled from Production at alarming rates. There isn't any inventory behind many large organizations today. More importantly, Mass Production Thinking no longer works. You cannot plan, organize, and control the new business environment.**
          • **Mass Customization is a reality. Companies who embrace Mass Customization are achieving results that cannot be explained within the *Context of* Mass Production.**

As a consultant, I watched executives struggle through the Quality revolution and TQM initiatives, trying to change their organizations. Management consultants were explaining everything in terms of attributes of leadership. Everyone got sick of reading about the participative leader, Japanese management techniques, and all the habits of successful people. While habits and attributes matter, the answers that come from this thinking are insufficient to explain *exactly?*

Exactly: • **The answer does not lie in the visible habits or attributes of people**.

The *Fortune* article about Toyota further says,

> Remember how Vince Lombardi always said he would share his playbook with anyone, but nobody could execute like the old Green Bay Packers? It is the same thing with Toyota. Everybody has techniques and practices, but nobody has a system like Toyota's.
>
> *Fortune*, December 8, 1997

It became very clear to me that we are in a new *Context* of existence, the key ingredients of which cannot be seen (see Chapter 2, "*Context* and Content").

Exactly: • **What is seamlessness, organic, partnering, creativity, alignment, integration, empowerment, and responsiveness?**

Mass Production handbooks do not contain definitions for these terms. I did not study seamlessness or alignment in school. I studied statistical quality control, time and motion technologies, and market penetration strategies.

Mass Production Thinking is about management *control* over land, labor, and capital. The new environment is not driven with control. It is driven with *creativity, empowerment,* and *alignment.* Even more important, *alignment* and *control* are not opposite states. The challenge isn't to reverse the polarity of the existing *Context.* Creating alignment is an entirely different approach.

If the new environment is entirely different, why hasn't someone pointed this out before?

Exactly: • **The new environment has been accurately documented and is actually working in many places. You can't interpret what you can't see within the *Context* of Mass Production Thinking.**

Mass Production Thinking is the only way you know how to think. You likely tried behaving in a participative way, but it slowed-down decision making and there wasn't *enough time* to do it that way.

Exactly: • **The barriers to change are enormous. The imbedded muscle memory of Mass Production Thinking is addictive. It is a debilitating disease.**

How can you argue against 70 years of success? Mass Production Thinking is still taught in all of our most prestigious business schools. How can it be wrong?

Exactly: • **Mass Production Thinking isn't wrong. It's technologically obsolete.**

It isn't a wrong or right issue. The *Context* of the new environment is different. The challenge is similar to what astronauts experienced in the past 30 years. The *Context* of space travel is *different* than travel on earth. The *Context* of space is weightlessness. Similarly, the *Context* of the new business environment is *effortlessness*. What are partnerships and teams? People working together to make the process of work effortless.

How can you predict what will happen in the new environment? You must do the same thing the astronauts did.

Exactly: • **You must *simulate* the new environment to *experience* it before you go.**

It was impossible to predict exactly what would happen on the flight to the moon, but the astronauts simulated the journey hundreds of times to experience weightlessness.

Weightlessness? That's a non-earthbound term. It is not in the physics book of the early 1900s. Likewise, *seamlessness* is not in the Mass Production managers handbook.

Is it possible to simulate *seamlessness?* The astronauts simulated weightlessness by practicing underwater. What if it's not *exactly* right? What if it's only approximately right? A simulation prepares you to make the decision to go regardless of the risk. If the simulation proves humans cannot survive space travel, choose not to go.

You can simulate a *seamless, empowered, partnering, team-based* organization that has *innovative relationships* with customers! Yes, it is possible. Is it *exactly* right? No! However, it is approximately right.

Early in my consulting career, I realized that all the attribute training and leadership habits people were learning were being applied to make Mass Production processes and systems go faster, cheaper, quicker, better, or some other word that ended in "ER." This approach was improving many Mass Production processes, but companies still weren't achieving *enough*. I will tell you about my experiences in the following chapters of this book. In general, the ability to speed up the Mass Production environment was significant, but many companies were still falling behind.

Exactly: • **Repeating an existing process does not lead to innovation.**

People are exhausted trying to do more with less. Many companies today are financially strong and emotionally bankrupt.

Exactly: • **Mass Production Thinking is about making things go faster to reduce cost.**

As I said, I have a degree in industrial engineering. Years ago, my time and motion mentality was alive and well. With a little statistical knowledge, I could figure out how to make an assembly line move faster toward the upper limits of human endurance. People could be given incentive to exhaust their bodies in pursuit of a piece work bonus. If the job required right-handed work, I could find a thing to perform right-handed work. If people were a limiting factor in achieving speed, we could automate the process.

Exactly: • **Mass Production Thinkers are brilliant thinkers. They do not want anything to slow down; however, it must remain in *control*.**

Authority to decide is the domain of management. "Doers must do as they are told." The vital element of Mass Production is *controlled behavior.*

As the new environment came into view, the ingredients of *empowerment, seamlessness, partnering,* and *teamwork* were as foreign to the Mass Production Thinkers as weightlessness was to astronauts. The astronauts had to learn to let go and not over-control the weightless environment. A very small force translated into massive action in space. The same is true in the new business environment.

Exactly: • **The first step in learning to exist in the new environment is to let go of control.**
                   • **The new environment is not about effort. All the concepts are about *effortlessness*.**

Many Mass Production Thinkers are control freaks. If something exceeds the statistical control limits, quality experts will bring things under control.

Exactly: • **Alignment must replace control.**

Another fact became very apparent to me as I continued to consult with clients. Entrepreneurs were creating new and different ways of doing things, but most of the large Mass Production organizations could not apply the techniques of the entrepreneur within their organizations.

Exactly: • **The Content of the new environment is visible. It will not work in the *Context* of Mass Production.**

This book examines how Content must follow *Context*. It is an illusion to believe that your children can behave like adults. Don't confuse obedience with being adult. The *Context* of the child cannot accommodate the Content of adulthood. They do not appreciate opera. They would rather be at a rock concert.

The same is true in business. You can't build round world boats with a flat world mentality. You cannot embrace empowerment if you practice control.

The new environment requires a totally different customer service process than what exists in the typical Mass Production organization.

Exactly: • **You can't give away what you don't own.**

You can't give me $100 if you don't have $100. Neither can you promise customers to be responsive, innovative, and seamless if the people who must fulfill this promise don't know how to deliver these results. Mass Production organizations are notorious for over-promising and under-delivering to customers. Frankly, customers lived with this phenomenon until Ralph Nader led the consumerism revolt.

Exactly: • **Today the customer is able to get *exactly* what they want, when they want it, and how they want it. The entrepreneurial revolution has replaced Mass Production alternatives with a Mass Customized reality.**

In 1987, Stanley Davis, in his famous book *Future Perfect*, predicted that customers would experience service any time, any place, no matter, and Mass Customized. Today that reality is called an ATM machine. As a customer, you are now conditioned to expect this reality with everything you buy. The processes that deliver this reality exist within many entrepreneurial businesses. Mass Production Thinkers continue to deny that there is a market for this level of service. They are still trying to be the low cost producer!

The economics of the new environment are different. New measures of success are being recognized. Many Mass Production giants have been replaced on the Dow Jones Industrial Average with companies that didn't exist 20 years ago. What did Fred Smith say about the past 20 years? Mass has been removed from production. By who? The entrepreneur.

As I watched many of my clients struggle to achieve the new realities, I realized that telling them about Toyota or giving them articles about teamwork didn't work. Many of them had already read the articles.

Exactly: • **Knowing about a weightless environment doesn't permit you to do weightless things.**

The answer is to simulate the experience to learn what to do once you begin the journey.

I was very lucky to experience two simulations as I was looking for ways to help my clients. The first was by Dr. Barry Oshry, entitled *Tops, Middles, and Bottoms*. The second was about high-commitment work systems by Dr. William Lytle. Both simulations helped me experience the enormous barrier that Mass Production Thinking imposes on an organization.

The pivotal event in my consulting career came when one of my clients was confronted with 62 union grievances after starting an employee involvement initiative. I was challenged to explain to the union why they should cooperate with the company directive. I had to draw upon a power that is very difficult to explain, but it is a known skill described in Chapter 4, "Change," and Chapter 7, "Leadership." I had to stop dealing in attributes and start dealing with *structure*.

When we left Columbus for the assignment, my colleague, Gregg, asked, "What are we going to do with these people?" We were about to mix the management team and the union bargaining committee in a session to examine structure. We were going to put the people through a simulation that would help them experience the transformation from Mass Production to Mass Customization. The simulation was a piece of Dr. Oshry's work, some of Dr. Lytle's work, and much of my own creation. (We paid all the royalties to Dr. Lytle and Dr. Oshry.) Gregg asked if I thought it would work? I said, "I don't know, but it won't be any worse than what they have now."

It worked! From that point forward, I realized that it's not the people causing the problem. Mass Production Thinking is obsolete. To help our clients, we created our own simulation that illustrates the dynamics of Transformational Change. We have conducted the simulation hundreds of times over the past nine years, and we have watched people of all types extract meaning from the experience.

Exactly: • **Mass Production systems lack wholeness.**

The *Fortune* article on Toyota confirms:

> Toyota realizes that its cars are only as good as the weakest link in its extended enterprise. It has consciously institutionalized a set of practices for transferring knowledge between itself and the suppliers, so that the whole group learns faster.
>
> *Fortune*, December 8, 1997

It is not the purpose of this book to deify Toyota. Many companies are built on wholeness. Many entrepreneurial businesses start this way and continue the practices today. Thousands of great examples in addition to Toyota exist. Rather than wholeness, I will call it Alignment on Purpose.

Using a simulation is the only way I have found to break the stranglehold of Mass Production Thinking. Even after experiencing the simulation, many Mass Production Thinkers immediately return to their old ways.

Exactly:
- **Convinced against your will is of the same opinion still.**
- **If you aren't open to possibilities, the realism of your current reality will dominate your existence.**
- **Argue for your weaknesses and you will own them.**

I examine these phenomena many times throughout this book. I am often cynical as I write about the Mass Production Thinker. The cynicism is intended to reflect the frustration I hear expressed by people who must work for Mass Production Thinkers. I have been invited to hundreds of pity parties where people engage in "oh ain't it awful how" discussions. It is real. It won't go away by telling people to change their attitude. Frankly, it is a deep-rooted addiction to Mass Production Thinking.

Exactly:
- **Mass Production is the only way we have been trained to think and behave. It has worked for years. "If it ain't broke, it doesn't need to be fixed."**

You are a Mass Production Thinker. I am a Mass Production Thinker. Mass Production Thinking isn't wrong any more than earthbound travel is wrong. Mass Production Thinking doesn't need to be *fixed*. It isn't broken! Mass Production Thinking just doesn't apply in the new environment.

Exactly:
- **Fixing is the wrong work.**

This statement was made by James Bleasco and Ralph Stayer in their book *The Flight of the Buffalo*. It is very important to realize that the new *Context* requires organizations to live with that misery.

The second point is that you are an organic organism that functions beyond the logical explanations of human intelligence. For the religious community, I appreciate how impossible it is to explain, in human terms, how God's creation works. People, however, need a human context of conscious choice, and helping people understand how to make choices is the purpose of your work and mine.

Third, there are many philosophical approaches to life. Wars have been fought to prove who is right and wrong. To me, what I am describing is not a new philosophical approach to life or living. I am clear that your knowing self can be very different from mine; that is not an issue for Transformational Change.

Finally, and as important, the concepts that follow can be applied to any organic organism, whether it's your company, your business, your organization, or yourself. Most of this book is about transforming the Mass Production Thinking that controls your business, but be open to the opportunity to transform the lives of those you love most.

The Mass Production Thinker in you will be frustrated by the complexity of this book. You will want something simple. You will want to *fix it now!* You will want to blame the culture. You will want a new strategic approach that inspires people to produce a profit for the company. The time frame of Transformational Change will drive you crazy.

Let this frustration be real for you as you read this book. It is not my intent to give you a prescription for alleviating your pain. No one can make the frustration go away. Your imbedded muscle memory has been there for years. You learned it well. You were rewarded for knowing it. Your first promotion caused you to teach it to others.

Exactly: • **The Mass Production Thinker in you isn't wrong. However, it is technologically obsolete.**

You have heard about the stars in the heaven that still shine, but astronomers say they may no longer exist—they are burned out. Many executives have privately admitted to me that they are burned out and still working. I see sales people in workshops who emphatically claim that it's just a matter of price. They have been pounding the pavement and calling on purchasing agents for years. I ask them, "If it's just price, what value do you personally add to the process?" These people are burned out and still selling.

Burnout can occur at any level of the organization. On a recent trip, weather had delayed the scheduled departure of my flight. Many people were going to miss their connections. One of the gate attendants said to an angry passenger, "I've been in this business for 20 years and late planes are the way it is." A lack of empathy? Yes, but burned out and still working.

The frustration you will experience trying to apply Mass Production Thinking to the new business environment will cause you to age prematurely.

Exactly: • **The Context of Mass Production Thinking is burned out and still shining.**

There are many devastating examples of how Mass Production Thinking affects the ability of an organization to address the future. We will examine many of them throughout this book. The most important conclusion you can draw from reading this book is that you must be the creative force in your own life and that you have the potential to *be different*. Don't wait until your light goes out to begin the transformational process. That will confirm you are permanently obsolete.

Chapter 2
Context and Content

You can't do things differently until you see things differently.

The business environment is changing. This is a well-known fact. Every executive is *aware* that dramatic change is impacting their company, their industry, our country, and the world. If they are aware that change is occurring, why are so many companies struggling to implement change initiatives? What is the gulf between awareness and effective change? Is it a matter of interpretation, perception, skill, ability, or willingness? These are not casual questions. It is a serious issue. We see major banks, insurance companies, electric utilities, and manufacturing companies embroiled in change initiatives that aren't working. Yet, their financial results remain strong. Maybe change isn't necessary? Are they changing because it's the thing to do? Maybe it's an illusion?

The entrepreneurial revolution that has occurred over the past 20 years gives us a clue as to why organizational change is so difficult to implement. Creative people left the hierarchical model of plan, organize, and control for the freedom to dream, innovate, and inspire. The *icons* of the Industrial Age are being replaced in the Dow Jones Industrial Index with modern era companies that were created within the last 20 years. Why? What is the message we can extract from this experience?

Change is happening. There are as many explanations as there are consultants. Some use buzzwords or habits to explain what to do. No one needs to be reminded that *it's* happening, but there are very few people who can accurately explain *what's* happening and *why*. Many high-profile leaders are announcing change initiatives with devastating consequences on the people who must implement the changes. That can't be the right approach.

The purpose of this chapter, therefore, is to ban the buzzwords and help you see change in a different way.

Recall the quote from Fred Smith, CEO of Federal Express:

> Over the past twenty years, apart from the medical revolution and the microprocessor, the most significant thing to happen to the world has been the ability to *take mass out of production*. The inventory-to-sales ratio of the whole industrial world has dropped like a stone during the last two decades.

What's happening? *Mass is being removed from production!* Is this just another buzzword approach to management? Is Mass Production obsolete? If it is true, this is shocking news. There are trillions of dollars invested in Mass Production systems. It's hard to imagine that the Mass Production *Context* that has sustained our business environment for 60 years is obsolete. Mass Production processes and systems still work and remain the basis of most of our industrial giants. The clue is that the entrepreneurial companies are thriving on a totally different *Context* of existence. The internal and external dynamics of the entrepreneurial businesses are very different. Could it be that the *Contextual blind spot* of Mass Production Thinking causes change initiatives to fail?

Let's first define the terms:

Context:
- **The framework that gives meaning to experience**
- **The larger view within which everything exists**
- **The perceptions that appear as reality**
- **Your world view (for example, the world is flat)**

Content:
- **The behavior within the *Context***
- **The rules and regulations that define boundaries of behavior**
- **The principles that support life within the context**
- **The methodology that resolves tension**
- **The processes that support performance**
- **The interrelationships of people and things**
- **The expertise to support growth within the *Context*.**

It is important to know the difference between *Context* and Content. Change initiatives must impact both *Context* and Content. Many companies rush to change the Content of the business–products, processes, and systems– without changing the *Context*. Likewise some executives change the *Context*–a new vision is announced–and expect the old Content to produce different results. During times of Transformational Change, *both* the *Context* and Content must change.

Context is always a *seeing* issue. Consider how everyone initially struggles to see a hologram. When your eyes cross and you are able to achieve the trance-like stare, you *can see* the *picture* behind the *chaos*. You have achieved a change in *Context*.

The Content of the hologram is the landscape that is visible behind the chaos. When your eyes adjust, you can see it. The hologram of the current business environment is entitled *world class*! It is difficult for your engineering and manufacturing departments to create the world class landscape if they can't see it! If they see only *chaos,* they are afflicted with *Contextual blindness*. They will try to create what you describe, but the translation process is tedious.

There are times that the people in an organization can *see* the landscape within the hologram and management only sees *chaos*. *Contextual blindness* in management is oppressive and demoralizing. This scenario spawned the entrepreneurial revolution. Mass Production Thinking poses a formidable barrier to *seeing* new *possibilities*.

The Content of the Past

The *Context* of our business environment has been Mass Production for 60 years. We have all been trained in Mass Production Content principles by highly sophisticated institutions of advanced learning. The Content of Mass Production works. Many people make a living as Mass Production Content experts.

If Fred Smith is correct, we are experiencing a change in the *Context* of Mass Production. Let's assume that Mass is being removed from Mass Production. After Mass is removed, what will remain–Production? *Or*, what word will replace Mass as the adjective for Production? People are not only *unaware* that this is happening, they don't know how to describe the ultimate *Context* of their existence.

If the *Context* of Mass Production changes, will the Content of Mass Production be obsolete? Will Content experts lose their jobs? How fast will this occur? Has this ever happened before? Does anyone have experience with the changes it will bring?

Can you feel the *chaos* of this hologram? It is traumatic.

To understand the magnitude of this issue, let's step back to a time when a dramatic change in the *Context* occurred. Remember "the world is flat" and "the world is round" controversy?

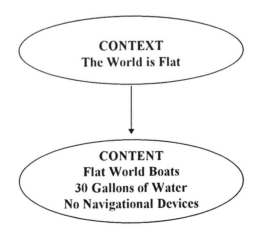

There was a time when the *Context* that drove manufacturing activity was that the world was flat. If you were the owner of Aztec Boats Inc., you would design and build boats within that *Context*. The Content experts of your organization would design and produce the boats, but the *Context* that dictates the overall orientation of the company is the world is flat.

Consider the dilemma Christopher Columbus must have had trying to buy boats to sail around the world. It is safe to say that Chris probably could neither use a flat world boat nor find people who wanted to sail around a flat world.

Once the *Context* changed from flat to round, Aztec Boats could choose to change their customer offering to reflect the requirements for round the world travel. It's doubtful whether round world boats could be built by flat world thinkers. Consider the huge differences in technology.

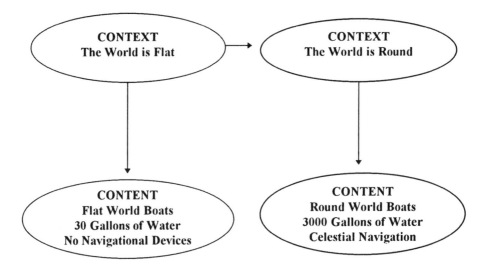

The key is that Aztec Boats owners can *choose* to change. It is not absolutely essential because the flat world markets probably remained strong. Aztec flat world boats could still dominate the market for flat world travel.

Key Point: • **It is important to separate Context from Content and understand the dynamics that both impose on the organization.**

Context always determines Content. Lets leap ahead to the 20th century. Once it was proven that the world was round, it was centuries before manufacturers produced vehicles that enabled world travel. Progress was slow because the *Context* of production was *crafting*.

Then, Henry Ford introduced the *Context* of Mass Production. This *Context* shift enabled the Content of the factory to change. The craftspeople were split into hundreds of pieces, and specific parts of the total work to be performed were assigned to a workstation. Industrial engineers, with a time and motion mentality, determined how many pairs of hands were needed to operate the workstations. The *Context* and Content shift was complete. When craftspeople were replaced with things, large quantities of standardized products could be produced.

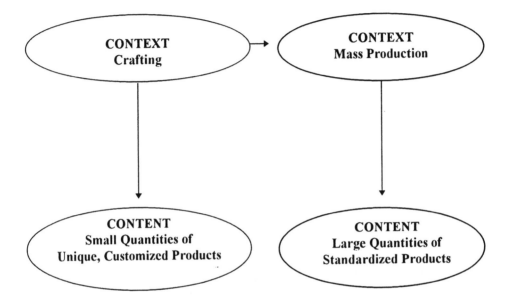

It is important to remember the old *Context* and Content can remain viable as a basis of business. The market for crafted goods remained. Just as flat world boats could still be sold for intercoastal travel, a demand remained for high quality, crafted products made by the local craftsperson.

The *Context* of Mass Production was a dramatic success. It was called the industrial revolution. We all have been the benefactors of its success.

Continuous Improvement of Content

Over the years, the Content within the *Context* of Mass Production has been dramatically improved. All the engineering professions have made exponential improvements in Mass Production processes and systems. Without Mass Production Content skills, the cost of products would be beyond the affordability of the masses.

CONTINUOUS IMPROVEMENT

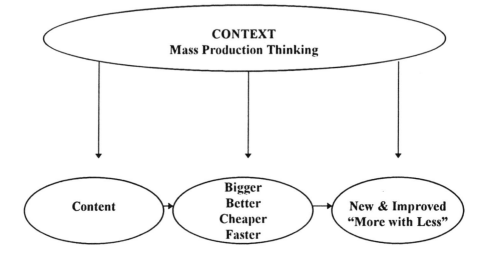

It is very important to note that the *Context* of Mass Production has remained constant for 60 years. The Content has been continuously improved. To provide orderliness to the Content, we learned to organize and control it. Content is frequently out of control. MBA schools teach aspiring young business people the skill of Content management. Because the *Context* remained constant, Content skills have become very sophisticated. Mass marketing, for example, has reached subliminal sophistication. The emphasis on Content improvement within the *Context* of Mass Productions is incredible.

Consider the development of the computer. What was the logical application of the computer? The obvious answer is to improve the Content within the *Context* of Mass Production. Computers replaced manual computations and quickly displaced the hands that were hired to run workstations. Computers were used to automate Mass Production systems and replace the hands that moved materials through the Mass Production factories. Automation gave Mass Production an exponential increase in both efficiency and effectiveness.

Key Point: • **The Information Age changed the Content of the work–but the *Context* of Mass Production remained unchanged.**

The change in the Content of work has been the focus of most change initiatives in the past 20 years. Initially, the changes were within functional entities. Computers revolutionized finance, engineering, manufacturing, and marketing. All the functions improved dramatically within the *Context* of Mass Production.

Management Means Control

The Change in Content, enabled by the computer, brought new meaning to the word *management*. Nothing could escape the scrutiny of accounting. Auditing procedures could locate the slightest budget variations. Statistical quality control procedures could pinpoint quality variances and quickly avoid producing large quantities of defective goods. Computers gave new definition to the word *control*.

Control was transformed from personal observation by supervisors to observation of numbers. Running a business became a numbers game. The computer enabled sophisticated managers to know the numbers by the third working day after the end of the month. If things were out of control, things could be *changed*.

Key Point: • **If things are in control, nothing needs to change.**

Controlling the Content within the *Context* of Mass Production is facilitated by negative feedback. When operations are within commonly accepted control limits, there is no need for feedback to the people. If things are out of control, whistles blow and sirens sound the alert. Something *must change*.

Within the *Context* of Mass Production, the word change has earned a terrifying connotation. It means something was out of control. This type of change, as we will discuss in Chapter 4, is at the observable behavioral level. It is easy to find the problem and fix it. The "out of control" mentality leads to a fix-it management style that is known for hard-nosed determination to bring things under control. It isn't surprising that the word *change* strikes fear into the hearts of many people.

Key Point: • **Until someone declares that the *Context* of Mass Production must change, all change initiatives will be perceived as improvements or fix-it approaches to the Content of Mass Production.**

The Change in Context

Please don't misinterpret the validity of Mass Production Content change initiatives. It is often very positive, useful, necessary, important, and life sustaining. We all must learn to be effective Content change agents both within our companies and within our lives.

Key Point: • **The entrepreneurial revolution declared the *Context* of Mass Production obsolete.**

As Fred Smith points out, the entrepreneurs started taking "Mass out of Production" 20 years ago. The explosion of entrepreneurial companies serving niche markets was the inception of the *Context* of *Mass Customization*. Many Mass Production companies are just now starting to recognize the *Context* of it. They are now starting to see the Content behind the hologram. It is now very visible.

Key Point: • **When the Context changes, entirely new Content will be created.**

In 1972, I worked for an air-conditioning company that *Contextually* was in the *comfort* business. The Content of the entire engineering, manufacturing, and sales organizations was designed to maximize comfort. Our sales literature talked about the comfort of an air-conditioned home. Our dealers were experts in selling comfort.

Then, the energy crisis hit! Energy had *never* been a design criterion for our equipment. Our engineers weren't concerned about the energy efficiency ratio (EER) of compressors. Energy was cheap! Our Content was technologically obsolete! Our Engineers would not change the Content, however, until our president declared, "We are now in the *energy* business." That *Context* change drove the creation of an entirely new Content. Today the air conditioning industry is dominated by companies that are primarily energy management companies. Comfort remains a key criterion of design, but it is secondary in consideration to energy.

Consider the U.S. auto industry in 1972. The *Context* about energy was that "it would always be cheap." The emphasis of automobile design was styling. The big gas-guzzlers looked great and got six miles per gallon. We all know how the *Context* of energy changed, and the Content of the auto industry was transformed.

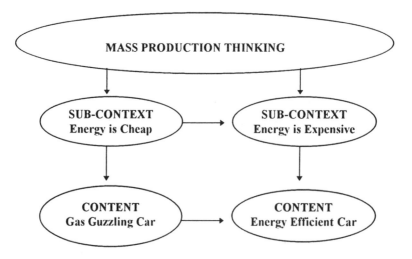

There have been many sub-*Context* changes within the larger *Context* of Mass Production. Throughout the past 60 years, however, the Mass Production *Context* has been invincible.

What if the *Context* of Mass Production is truly obsolete? Are the new tools like the Internet just improvements to the Content within Mass Production? Some people believe that the Internet is merely a sub-*Context* change. It's like the energy crisis! We will adjust the Content, using the Internet, and the *Context* of Mass Production will remain. Some executives want to know who is the authority that can tell them that the *Context* has changed? Until the authority appears, they will continue to improve the Content of the *old Context*.

The reaction to this issue is often irrational. Kill the messenger. The management mind-set of the Mass Production *Context* is based upon problem solving and control. To suggest that the *Context* of Mass Production is obsolete makes people berserk.

Gauge your emotions. The enormity of this leadership challenge is beyond comprehension. Millions of dollars are invested in Mass Production plants. The imbedded investment is trillions. The *Context* of Mass Production can't be obsolete!

Key Point:	• **The fact that people can't see the hologram doesn't mean that it doesn't exist.**
	• **The new Content for the new Context cannot be fixed into existence.**
	• **New Content has already been created. It has application in the Context of Mass Production.**
	• **The challenge is to see the new Context.**
	• **True leverage is to combine the new Content with a new Context.**
	• **Entrepreneurs have been pioneering this change for 20 years.**
	• **Your company is likely way behind.**

The *Context* Changed

The *Context* has changed. The authority on the subject is the customer. It is not a matter of whether it has changed; instead, "Can you see it yet?" Many people perceive that what's happening is more Content change within the *Context* of Mass Production. They continue to manipulate the Content to do more with less. The truth, however, is the *Context* has changed. Mass Production is being replaced with Mass Customization.

Key Point: • **Mass Customization is a permanent change in**
Context. It is not a linear extension of Mass
Production. The Content to support this _Context_ is
now being created.

This is a shocking statement to the leaders of Mass Production companies. It is tantamount to proving to the president of Aztec Flat World Boats that the world is round. The president can doubt it and continue to build technologically obsolete boats or recognize the new _Context_ and begin to transform the Content of the company to build a round world offering.

TRANSFORMATIONAL CHANGE

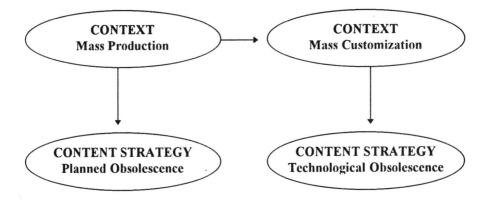

I remember the day that we found out that our warehouses were full of obsolete air-conditioning equipment. The State of California passed a law requiring an 8EER for all condensing units. Our warehouses were full of 4EER units. They were new and unused and technologically obsolete.

Chrysler had 600,000 cars that began to rust before they were sold. General Motors practiced planned obsolescence for years. Today, a car that will fail in a planned time frame is technologically obsolete. When foreign competition changed the _Context_ of the automobile, a dramatic change in Content occurred.

Key Point: • **After the Context changes, the technical revolution**
in Content will make the old Content
technologically obsolete.

It is important to remember that Aztec Boats could still market flat world boats. General Motors continued to market the gas-guzzlers. IBM continued to make mainframe computers. The markets for these products can remain strong until the technological revolution in Content within the new _Context_ makes them obsolete.

Key Point: • **Technological obsolescence is rampant within the Context of Mass Customization.**
    • **Planned obsolescence is an obsolete strategy.**

Mass Customization must be perceived as a new *Context* of business. Many Mass Production people see it as an improvement in Mass Production Content. This is not true.

The Contextual Difference

The Content of the Mass Production *Context* is built upon seeing everything from the factory-out to the market.

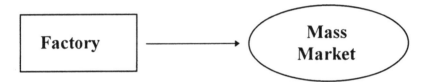

The view from the factory is of a Mass Market with *predictable* numbers of people needing *predictable* numbers of standardized products that will need to be replaced within a *predictable* time frame. The key to Mass Production efficiency is *predictable control*. Remember, Mass Production is a numbers game. This view is not wrong. It's just a way of seeing the world. The view from the factory is very logical. Making effective choices within the realm of predictability is the science of management.

The view from the factory leads to very *logical choices* of how to *organize* the factory to *penetrate the market*. Operations are centralized or decentralized. The channel of distribution that connects the factory to the market is very logical. Formulating *strategies* about how to *deploy* resources to serve the market is called *strategic thinking*. Strategic planning is a science of predictability and control.

The factory-out view leads to an "at war" mentality within the factory. The market is something to attack and penetrate. Extended over time, the defensive mentality leads to predictable thinking about how to protect the factory and its investment from erosion. The stockholders must be served.

Again, there is nothing wrong with this approach. It has worked for years and will continue to work. The predictable consequences of this approach are well known.

Key Point: • **Customer service is not the same as a process designed to serve a customer.**

The *Context* of Mass Customization is different. The view of the factory is from the customer back to the factory.

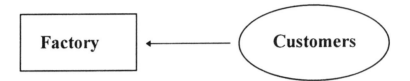

In this *Context*, the factory is designed to serve the customer. Most Mass Production Thinkers talk about serving the customer as long as the customer fits the factory. It falls apart when the factory must fit the customer. The key difference is the design of the customer service process. In the Mass Production Context, customer satisfaction is a hoped for result. Everyone knows, however, that you can't please them all. In the Mass Customization Context, customer satisfaction is the basis for process design. Satisfying a customer is not optional. It is the purpose for being in business.

We all know that the mass market has exploded into thousands of niche markets. The entrepreneurial revolution is a shift in both *Context* and Content. Entrepreneurs design the factory to fit the customer. Mass Production companies scoff at the entrepreneur as not being a player in the big game. "We're General Motors; we have 52% of the U.S. auto market. Let the *foreigners* have their 1%. They'll never be a major player."

Mass Customization is *not* a return to crafting, as many Mass Production Thinkers believe.

Key Point: • **Mass Customization is truly what it says, "creating a customized offering for the customer with speed and doing business one-to-one."**

It is difficult for Mass Production Thinkers to see the possibilities of Mass Customization. In some industries, there is nothing to see–*yet*. The Content is just now being created.

New Content and Measurement

The most visible Content at this time is the Internet. The Internet is a Content tool for the Mass Customizer. Federal Express is becoming the channel of distribution for the Internet. Behind the *Context*, the Content is being created as you read. The infrastructure of the Mass Customizer is a network, not a hierarchy. The manifestation of Mass Customization is becoming very visible and making Mass Production Content specialists technologically obsolete.

The toughest dilemma facing leaders today is to recognize that the *Context* has *changed*. It is no longer productive to make choices using a Mass Production, factory-out view. It is critical to *see* the *world as round* although it still appears to be flat! It is critical to begin to design the processes of the factory to serve customers although it appears logical to design them to be more efficient and effective in serving stockholders.

Key Point: • **Share of customer is a very different measurement than share of market.**

Mass Production Thinkers talk about customer satisfaction, but they measure market share. Customer service is the reactive aftermath of a Mass Production process that was not properly designed. The failure of a standard product requires customer service! The ultimate measure for Mass Production success is not, however, customer satisfaction. It is bottom line profit and market share. Acceptable market penetration figures assume that customer satisfaction is within acceptable limits.

In the new *Context*, measurement shifts to share of customer. Share of customer thinking would suggest that an insurance company should provide your homeowner, auto, and life insurance coverage; plan your investment strategies; and secure your retirement. Insurance companies can think share of customer, but they can't change the Mass Production Content to produce this result.

Many share of customer companies have been created in the past 20 years. Consider Wal-Mart–one-stop shopping. They can fulfill *all* your needs. A large shopping mall is another example. The mall contains all the stores that can meet your shopping needs.

The marketing process behind share of customer thinking is database management. Count the number of catalogs you receive in the mail and you will realize how many databases contain your name. Yet, share of customer measurement systems are just now being created by the accounting profession to support the process.

The fatal flaw in the reengineering revolution was to adopt reengineering to improve Mass Production processes. In many cases, the reengineering initiative merely automated existing processes using information technology. The intended purpose of reengineering is to invent *new processes* designed to serve customers; then, and only then, enable them with information technology.

I could give you clear examples of companies who embraced the reengineering revolution to improve the Content of the Mass Production *Context*. When I asked the tough questions about the intent of the initiative, it was quickly evident that the *Context* of the customer had not changed and the initiative would ultimately fail.

The Paradox of the Hologram

The *Contextual* blind spot of Mass Production Thinking is the biggest barrier to successful organizational transformation. The challenge is enormous. The resistance of the Mass Production *Context* is formidable. The imbedded investment in Mass Production, factory-out channels of distribution is staggering.

The terrifying truth is that executive bonus plans will keep many companies chained to the Mass Production *Context* for many years to come. Many executives will survive until their planned obsolescence (retirement) as Evolutionary Leaders are finished. In some places, 30-year veterans of the strategy "wars" are still being promoted to senior leadership positions.

A new *Context* always presents a paradox to those with the old view. A hologram appears to be paradoxical; either you can see it or you can't. The truth however, is *both* views of the hologram exist. It is you who cannot *see*. Mass and Customized appear mutually exclusive to the Mass Production mind. The paradox is unresolvable within the Content of the Mass Production *Context*. The new Content within the new *Context* appears to be an opportunity to fix the old *Context*. Doing more with less will increase the bottom line, increase the executive bonus, and keep stockholders happy. Pleasing Wall Street is an enormous priority.

What is the correct name for the new *Context*? It appears to be Mass Customization. It may be Mass Customerization.™ Whatever the name, it has arrived. Want proof? Ask yourself, "What do I want from companies that serve me?" Do you want products and services customized to meet your exact needs? Are you satisfied with standardized commodities and experiences? Our expectations as customers are way beyond the deliverable of a Mass Production, factory-out system. We have created the opportunity. It is now time to transform the organizations we work in to meet our own expectations.

The good news is a world of abundance lies ahead. Within the new *Context*, new Content is being created. The next millennium will experience a dramatic change. Mass Production processes and systems will be replaced with totally new Content. The Content experts of the future are starting to graduate from colleges.

The following chapters of this book will help you understand how to begin the journey. New perspectives on change, leadership, structure, and forces must be developed. Enjoy the ride. It will be exciting.

Chapter 3
The Customer

Over the past 15 years, our experience as customers has changed dramatically. It has changed from being victimized to being the driving force for the new business environment. It all started when we rebelled at being told "you must buy our cars" when we knew they were designed to fail at 50,000 miles. The planned obsolescence strategy of General Motors had conditioned us to expect products to fail and accept the fact that the failure was our fault. Appliances were designed to fail in predictable intervals to prepare us to buy the next new and improved model. *New and improved* was the mantra of marketing experts everywhere.

Consumer advocate Ralph Nader entered the scene and consumerism became a full-fledged movement. In 1972, General Motors proclaimed that consumerism is a fad and continued to believe that planned obsolescence would dominate the market.

I won't chronicle what has happened since then. You know the history. The change in consumer behavior has been beyond Ralph's dreams and expectations. The question isn't has it changed, but why?

Key Point:
- **Working in the monolithic, standardized, hierarchical Mass Production business is boring.**
- **Creative talent is stifled within the Context of plan, organize, and control thinking.**
- **The innate ability to create a business within our capitalistic Context is a free choice.**
- **As consumerism spread, entrepreneurs stepped forward to fulfill the new consumer expectations.**
- **The customer expectations today are quantity, quality, and responsiveness.**
- **The entrepreneurial revolution is spreading around the globe.**

The entrepreneurial revolution started in the early 1970s and, propelled by information technology, continues unabated today. Coupled with the consumer revolt, the entrepreneurial business revolution is transforming consumer expectations all over the world.

Try It, You'll Like It

The transformation of consumer expectations took 25 years. The customer relationship with an entrepreneurial business starts with trial and error. Entrepreneurial businesses begin with a niche orientation and a genuine purpose of helping customers solve a unique problem.

Key Point: • ***Try it, you'll like it* replaced new and improved.**

Entrepreneurial businesses must under-promise and over-deliver to survive. Try it, you'll like it is the only promise the entrepreneur can make. Entrepreneurs are committed to inventing new solutions to old problems by creating products that never existed. The products aren't improved versions of old models; they are unique.

In the beginning of the entrepreneurial revolution, consumers were wary. Buyer beware was well ingrained in our thinking. We were tired of being over-promised and under-delivered. The imbedded distrust of the planned obsolescence strategy of Mass Production initially caused consumers to be cautious about try it, you'll like it appeals.

Trial and error relationships are strange at first, but in most situations the consequences of the error aren't life threatening. I bought a new calculator to augment my slide rule, not replace it. The risk factors were low and the potential rewards were high.

Key Point: • **The entrepreneurial revolution took on almost any challenge.**

The bottom line is that customer expectations about quantity, quality, and responsiveness have accelerated exponentially over the past 25 years. Today, the Mass Production model of over-promise and under-deliver is still there, but the cynicism about this approach has caused the collapse of many of the Industrial Age giants.

Trial and error relationships spawned another revolution that is not inherent to Mass Production organizations. The entrepreneur and client realized that the process of working together was just as important as the products that were being created. Built on trust in intention, the permanent partnership for innovation was born. The just in time revolution of Japanese competitors appeared to be the cause, but the seeds were planted in the trial and error revolution.

Trial and error relationships and process partnerships are accelerating exponentially. Every software company starts with a trial and error beta site partner. Computer networks are created by partners building systems together. Software sales are on a try it, you'll like it basis. The ongoing relationship is a continuous upgrade, not planned obsolescence. In many instances, the process relationship is just as important as the product being provided. The key to this revolution is alignment on purpose.

Mass Customization

The entrepreneurial revolution, complete with try it, you'll like it and process partnerships, has brought us to a new *Context* of business called Mass Customization. Stanley Davis first coined the term Mass Customization in his famous book *Future Perfect* in 1987. B. Joseph Pine continued the theme in his book *Mass Customization*: *The New Frontier in Business Competition*. The reality of Mass Customization is here to stay.

Key Point: • The entrepreneur starts with customization within a niche and develops the ability to do it in mass.

It is very important to see that the natural growth of the entrepreneurial business is from customization within a niche to Mass Customization. Entrepreneurs are connected to their customers in unique and innovative ways. It would be very foreign for them to abandon this thinking and embrace the over-promise and under-deliver orientation of Mass Production. Most entrepreneurs left the *Context* of Mass Production Thinking to create something different for customers. It is blasphemy for them to return to the old game.

I'm sure you know an entrepreneurial company that has reverted to Mass Production Thinking. Many have, but in almost every case, the original entrepreneur is gone. Many entrepreneurial companies have been purchased by Mass Production Thinkers and quickly ruined by switching them back to the old game. In most cases, the entrepreneur, equipped with the proceeds from the buy out, has moved on and is creating another try it, you'll like business.

Mass and customization are paradoxical to the Mass Production Thinker. For years, we have been programmed to think that standardization is the only way to achieve low cost producer status. Large lot runs of standardized products spread setup costs over a broad base, and planned obsolescence gives the manufacturer a predictable time frame within which to develop the next model. "Keep it simple, stupid! Plan, organize, and control. We have 52% of the U.S. auto market! Why should anything be produced in mass *and* customized?"

As the "Competitive Advantage" chapter of this book reveals, Mass Production models are based on new and improved offerings of the core competency. Mass Customization challenges the core competency model and places Mass Production Thinking at great risk. A Mass Customization approach combines competency with a capability to achieve competitive advantage. Inherent in all Mass Customization opportunities is a standardized process that is based upon interdependent relationships between functional entities. Interdependent relationships demand integrated, seamless, effortless processes enabled by information technology.

Key Point: • **You must *start* with *customized* and extend to *mass*. You cannot start with mass and extend to customized.**

To the Mass Production Thinker, anything that is customized is called a *special*. Specials require extra engineering and special handling by manufacturing. Specials disrupt the efficient flow of the Mass Production system. Sales people are told to sell standard units and avoid specials at all cost.

Customers, on the other hand, want everything customized in some way to meet their needs. "Hold the onions and bring the dressing on the side." Simple requests for customized service annoy Mass Production Thinkers. Many Mass Production Thinkers believe that Mass Customization, if it is to exist, is a linear improvement of Mass Production. Many people believe that Mass Customization is a limited strategy that, like the entrepreneurial revolution, will be limited to niche markets. The big boys aren't concerned, "We're going to compete on price and be the low cost producer." The most arrogant Mass Production Thinkers claim that, "Consolidation will occur; there will only be three major players in the end."

Key Point: • **There may only be three major players in the end, but those who remain will be Mass Customizers.**

The best I can say to those who are unaware of the reality that Mass Customization will bring is good luck. I hope your company doesn't fail on your watch.

The acid test is to examine your own consumer experience. How many items were on the shelves of the local drug store 15 years ago? Where is that drug store today? How many types of pain medication are offered by the Drug Emporium today?

Visit the newsstand. Look at all the magazines. Fifteen years ago, there were 10. Today there are thousands. They even arrive at your door customized with your name inside.

My wife counted the number of catalogues that arrived in the mail three weeks before Thanksgiving. One hundred and twenty-two different catalogues just in time for holiday shopping. You don't need to leave home to buy anything. You can shop all around the world from home. You are no longer limited to your hometown department stores.

Consider Wal-Mart. How big is the central warehouse that supplies the Wal-Mart stores? If Wal-Mart was a true Mass Production phenomenon, they would have huge warehouses to store vast truckloads of finished goods. Think again. Instead, the questions are what is a cross-docking system and how do the thousands of suppliers supply it?

Key Point:
- **The key to successful Mass Customization is logistics.**
- **Mass producers call it supply chain management.**
- **A process is not a chain. It is a network.**
- **Mass Production Thinkers cannot resolve the paradox of mass and customized.**

You experience mass customized buying every day. How do you buy a gallon of paint? Select the color, mix it, and it's delivered—mass customized.

Key Point:
- **What are Wendy's and Burger King? Two hundred and fifty-six ways to have your burger—with speed.**
- **What is an ATM machine? Banking done anytime, anyplace—mass customized just as Stanley Davis predicted.**
- **What is a shopping mall other than a massive complex of customized shops to help you have a customized shopping experience?**

Mass Customization is not limited to customization of the product. Consider the Hertz Gold Club Service or Frequent Flyers Clubs. As a consumer you can experience the trip anyway you want it—mass customized.

It's foolish, therefore, for the Mass Production Thinker to think that Mass Customization is a fad. Like consumerism, it will not go away. It's also foolish to continue to develop Mass Production business strategies that lead to standardized banking when the ATM is evidence of mass customized banking. It's foolish to believe that a low cost producer strategy will bring market domination when the market has exploded into thousands of niches that can't be dominated.

Key Point:
- **Mass Production Thinking is the only way many executives know how to think. Mass Customization is appealing to them, but they cannot let go of plan, organize, and control to achieve it.**

As a consumer, start to think about how companies that serve you think. Ask how they are aligned—to make a profit or to help you get what you want?

Nothing suggests that Mass Production manufacturing will vanish soon. There will still be economies of scale associated with large lot runs. Baby Shampoo by Johnson & Johnson will continue to be made in large quantities, but how it is delivered to Wal-Mart has already changed. The executives at Johnson & Johnson must think Mass Customization. They can't serve Wal-Mart without a logistics partner.

The Partnership Revolution

Mass Customization is driving the need for seamless processes. Many of my clients are confronted with requests to create *partnerships* where adversarial vendor relationships currently exist. Many of these requests are coming from staunch Mass Production Thinkers—"Lower your prices and we'll give you all our business." Beware, this is nothing more than advanced vending. It appears to be win-win until you lower your price and don't get all the business. Remember, Mass Production Thinkers over-promise and under-deliver. They aren't likely to put all their eggs in one basket.

On the other hand, there are legitimate partnerships being formed every day. A partnership is based on the concept of effortless effectiveness. If a company can outsource a technology to someone who specializes in that technology, the partnership concept has tremendous economic leverage for both parties. The key is *alignment on purpose*. It is impossible to sustain a partnership if the alignment between the parties is to make a profit.

Many partnerships are initially created with profit-making strategies as the aligning force. Many of them work for a period, but the partnership will always arrive at the point where more for one is less for the other. At this point, win-win turns to win-lose.

Have you ever been on a teeter-totter? Were you ever held up in the air by your win-win partner? We've all been there. Most of us have experienced win-win relationships that quickly turned into win-lose. Why does it happen?

A partnership in business always begins as trial and error. "Let's try it and see if we like it." It's like dating in a personal relationship. You don't start by getting married. Never forget, a true partnership is always about *process integration*. Because the process doesn't initially exist and must be created, it takes time for every partnership to form. Potential partners must experiment with the process to make it work.

Partnerships that are formed to lower the cost of one company and increase the volume of the other are vendor relationships disguised as partnerships. These types of relationships can be productive, but seldom do they reach the partnership level.

True business partnerships are always based on innovation and process continuity between the two partners. If either partner fails to fulfill their part of the process, the whole process fails. The intended result of process continuity must be defined by the *purpose* rather than the economic benefit to be derived.

Mass Production Thinkers are confused by this entire issue. They announce the desire to create partnerships with customers and continue to practice vending with suppliers to their own organization. Companies that sell their products through manufacturers representatives frequently treat their representatives in adversarial ways and profess to want partnerships with the ultimate consumer.

Key Point: • **It is impossible to create a partnership with the ultimate customer unless the process of serving that customer is integrated.**

Within the *Context* of Mass Customization, the role of the Mass and the role of the Customizer often reside in two separate economic entities. These two entities must form a partnership if both are to realize the benefits of Mass Customization.

Key Point: • **Mass Customization is not a new Mass Production strategy. It is a new *Context* of business requiring new interdependent relationships called partnerships and teams.**

The important point to be made is that The Mass *and* The Customizer are often independent economic entities working together within the process of serving customers. If the two entities don't become interdependent partners in process, aligned on purpose, the *Context* of Mass Production will dominate the customer experience.

After you can see *"the business of your business"* as customizing the experience for every customer, everything will change for you. Initially, it will scare you to death. The need to break the stranglehold of Mass Production Thinking will be an obvious barrier to success.

Key Point: • **Take time to see your company from the customer's point of view. Think about how what you do can be perceived as customized.**

There have been hundreds of customer-focused initiatives started by Mass Production Thinkers. Being customer focused and retaining your Mass Production mentality will not cause you to change. Rather, be the customer of your own company. If you sell heating and cooling products, how would you heat and cool your own home? If you sell computers, how would you want them to be configured or enabled? Eat in your own restaurant. Bank at your own bank. Insure your own life and home. Are you confident you are in good hands?

Key Point: • **The issue is integrity.**

The next time a stockbroker calls to pitch his recommendations, ask him to prove that he owns what he recommends. I know a bank where nearly two-thirds of the employees don't have their personal accounts at that bank. I know an insurance company where many of the executives are insured by the competition. Don't you find that fascinating?

> **Key Point:** • **Mass Production Thinking is based on "do as I say, not as I do."**

There are many interesting dilemmas facing the Transformational Leader. The most important issue is how to transform the over-promised and under-delivered experience of the customer. Define what *"the business of your business"* would be if you under-promised and over-delivered. Think about what is customized and what is mass. Don't start with mass and try to extend it to customized. That won't work.

The Sales Interface

The customer experience will never change until there is a transformation in thinking about how and what the salesperson must sell. Traditional Mass Production salespeople are trained to sell product features and benefits. The competency must be sold and the buyer must be forced to buy. You've seen the ads; "Closers only need apply." For years, salespeople have been trained how to prospect, probe, qualify, handle objection, and close. The *Context* is to fit the customer to the factory. Said another way, salespeople must convince the customer that what the factory makes meets their needs. This factory-out mentality has been the backbone of sales rallies and sales training seminars for years.

I've conducted hundreds of sales training seminars to help my clients break the stranglehold of Mass Production Sales Thinking. It is incredible how many sales executives are still trying to win the Mass Production battle. Mass Production sales managers are convinced that everything has been reduced to a commodity. They defend their position by stating, "All things being equal, it's *just price.*"

> **Key Point:** • **Nothing is just a matter of price.**
> • **All things are *never equal*. You are different from the other guy.**
> • **You must see that what you sell is a part of a *process*, not a commodity to be consumed.**

I was a salesperson for the Trane Air Conditioning Company. Initially, I perceived my job as selling air conditioning equipment to dealers. I tried the features and benefits approach and was told by every dealer that my price was high. I almost gave up. I could not push harder and tell them again about our products' features. To many dealers, features didn't matter. To them, an air conditioner was an air conditioner.

I was challenged to put myself in the position of the ultimate consumer. I actually thought about buying an air conditioner for my own home and about my role as salesperson in the buying process for Mr. and Mrs. Jones. From that point of view I could see how I, as a consumer, would want the dealer to customize the heating, cooling, and energy experience in my home. I could easily understand that I, as a Trane salesperson, was the Mass and the dealer was the Customizer. It became very clear to me that the Trane Company and the dealers must be partners in the *process* of helping Mr. and Mrs. Jones get what they wanted.

From this view, I realized that my relationship with my dealers was not about equipment. Yes, I sold them products, but my role was to help them be good customizers. We developed a whole new way for our dealers to help Mr. and Mrs. Jones buy. I'll spare you the details, but my equipment sales increased exponentially when I transformed myself from salesperson to dealer consultant.

Think about it! You can get toilet paper almost any way you want it. If price is important, you can buy the one-ply offering. What if you own a hotel and you need to purchase toilet paper? To a hotel, toilet paper should not be about its features and benefits. It's about guest satisfaction.

Absurd as any example can be, every buying experience can be viewed as a part of a process.

Key Point: • **When your products and services are alike, your buying experience for the customer had better be different—*customized*!**

The first step in transforming the customer interface is to break the Mass Production view of thinking from the factory-out to the market. When you can see *"the business of the business"* from your customers' point of view, you will understand that the customer revolution is about speed, effortlessness, and trust —Mass Customization.

Chapter 4
Change

Change! How many times during a day do you use the word change? Change is generally used as a verb to imply the action of moving from one state of being to another. It is sometimes used as a noun or adjective: people resist change or the new change program. The word strikes fear in the hearts of some and is exciting to others. What an interesting process–change.

The process of change happens at three levels: behavioral, cultural, and structural.

Many books have been published about the nature of change itself. Therefore, it is not the purpose of this chapter to describe the three processes in detail. Instead, this chapter will help you understand that permanent change can only occur if all three levels are affected.

To help you understand this important concept, I will use a number of specific examples. With the examples, you will easily distinguish the three levels of change. The cultural and structural levels are often invisible, and people seldom think to address the issues contained at these levels. As a result, change at the behavioral level does not occur.

The following diagram illustrates the levels of change discussed in this book.

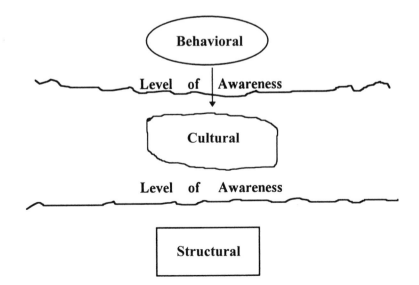

The Levels of Change

Behavioral Level

The behavioral level of change is very easy to understand. We see people, animals, and things behave. You behave in predictable ways based upon years of programming. You have a comfort zone of behavior. Observed behavior is categorized and explained in many ways. People are referred to as extroverts and introverts, analyticals and amiables.

There are thousands of words to describe behavior, and everyone has a desire to change the way they behave. Everyone has also been told by a parent, boss, or counselor that they must change some behavior to achieve success. Psychologists and authors have studied the attributes of highly effective people, and they constantly remind us of the behavioral patterns that lead to fame and fortune.

Things also behave. Traffic behaves on a freeway. It moves fast or slow, in and out. Cars stop at traffic lights and stop signs, and occasionally wrecks occur. Airplanes take off and land. Rockets fly through space, forklifts load trucks, and golf carts move around golf courses. All this behavior is visible and easily labeled with words that judge its appropriateness.

Animals, like humans, also behave. Horse races and dog shows are highly competitive events. People pay big money to watch animals behave. Dogs are trained to obey their owners and sheep obey the dogs. Geese fly in V patterns and many animals congregate in herds.

Behavior! It is easy to see and dominates the change agenda. Television advertising attempts to change your behavior. Companies want you to change your long distance carrier, your eating habits, and where you buy your next car. It is amazing when you think about how many stimuli you receive every day that intend to change your behavior.

What is it about behavior that causes people to want to change it? Behavior activates the judgmental self in every individual. A desire always exists for individual behavior to be more organized, efficient, effective, coordinated, cooperative, controlled, or safe.

Most organizational change initiatives attempt to change the behavior of a group. Group behavior needs to be synergistic and synchronized. Employees need to work as a team. People need to cooperate across functional boundaries. If employees are oppressed by management, they form a union that changes the behavior of the group. The entire labor force can coalesce for the collective benefit. This behavior is called collective bargaining versus individual negotiations.

The most prevalent behavior pattern that prompts a desire for behavior change is chaotic, random, individual action. We have all seen a large number of people assemble in one location without any organizing process. The behavior is chaos. Someone will *always* want the behavior to be organized or under control.

It is important to realize that behavior happens, but it is controlled or influenced by invisible factors. If you want to change behavior, you must impact what causes or controls the behavior.

Cultural Level

Behavioral scientists help us understand that the cause of most behavior is the culture of the person or group. We are all aware of the cultural differences between nationalities and religions. Change at the cultural level will produce change at the behavioral level. This is a well-known phenomenon and is the subject of thousands of books. The psychology section at the bookstore contains hundreds of books that suggest a change in attitude will change your behavior.

Culture is the combination of knowledge and beliefs that individuals hold to be true and that dictates how they behave. If you believe a snake will hurt you, you will behave accordingly when confronted with a snake. If a one-month-old baby is placed beside a snake, it will not react because it has no belief about snakes.

It is easy to understand the cultural level of change. People are told to get religion. Advertising is aimed at convincing people to vote Republican or Democrat. Courses that teach sensitivity, diversity, versatility, and empathy all stress understanding the cultural differences between people. People who have difficulty behaving within acceptable societal limits, generally have a cultural bias that needs to be corrected.

We all know how difficult, if not impossible, it is to change the cultural level of people. Wars are fought resisting a change in culture. "Convinced against my will is of the same opinion still." "Give me liberty or give me death."

We hear it said daily, "We must change the culture of our organization." My advice is *good luck*. It is almost impossible to do. It certainly takes a long time and is generally ineffective to attempt change at the cultural level.

Structural Level

Behavior does change, sometimes with amazing speed. People get religion or make dramatic changes in their cultural orientation. Companies often experience dramatic change with the introduction of new leadership. It is apparent at the behavioral level, and a new culture can form quickly. People are often easily inspired, motivated, empowered, enthusiastic, and involved. Change in behavior and culture can be dramatic and sudden if you change the structure.

Structural change? Seldom do change initiatives include a conscious change in structure. What does this mean? Think of a babbling brook. Why does the water babble? Most people say rocks. There are rocks in a lake and the water doesn't babble. The water babbles because of the structure of the land. The structure of the land is downhill. Combined with the force of gravity, water will babble. When the structure of the land changes, the water behaves as a river or a stream. If we put a dam in the river, we call the water a lake. A lake is a lake because of the structure of the land that confines the water. If we want the water in a lake to babble, we would need to change the structure. The behavior of the water would change instantly with a change in structure.

If cars on a highway are behaving chaotically, we can change the structure of the roadway to change their behavior. Traffic lights, stop signs, yellow lines, orange barrels, and concrete dividers are all structural elements that will instantly change their behavior. It does little good to try to change the behavior of cars at the cultural level. How many times have we tried to convince drivers to slowdown or be courteous? It helps, but effective change in car behavior results from structural change.

It is easy to see structural change when we relate it to water or cars. What about people and organizations? The rest of this book is about how to change the structure of a company to produce immediate and lasting change.

It is important at this point to understand that behavior, culture, and structure are all interrelated and often appear to be the same things. While they are interrelated, it is important to accurately differentiate between these three levels of change when formulating change initiatives. In the organizational context, it will do little good to try to change behavior or culture. Change must occur at the structural level first. If the structure isn't changed, the culture and behavior will not permanently change.

A common example of desired change that we are all familiar with is balancing the Federal budget. We all want the behavior of our lawmakers to change. Many attempts at cultural change have been made. Republicans and Democrats argue about the cultural agenda that would lead to a balanced budget. Elections change the culture as Republicans and Democrats trade places in the White House or the Congress, but cultural change doesn't balance the budget. Most people agree that it will never happen until there is a Balanced Budget Amendment to the Constitution. Why? The Constitution is the structure that dictates the culture that will cause lawmaker behavior to change.

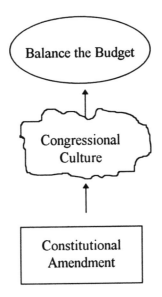

This example should help you understand how important it is to change the structure to change behavior. While behavior change often appears random and unexplainable, there is one irrefutable fact. All behavior change is the result of a change in structure, and we are seldom aware of how the structure changed.

Types Of Change

Just as there are three levels of change, there are three types of change: crisis, evolution, and transformation.

Crisis Change

A crisis occurs at the behavioral level. An explosion, car wreck, heart attack, fire, and hurricane are obvious examples of crisis behavior. There are always cultural and structural causes, but a crisis must be dealt with at the behavioral level. There isn't time to argue that a person should stop eating red meat and change their diet when a heart attack happens. When the Titanic is sinking, it is not the time to address the structural design deficiencies. The crisis demands action at the behavioral level. Emergency heart bypass surgery must be performed now!

Every crisis demands effective reactive service. Major businesses and industries specifically provide reactive service in response to a crisis. Fire departments, police, ambulances, hospitals, and 911 are obviously crisis change agents. In this context, it is easy to see that crisis-oriented change works from the behavior down to the culture and ultimately to the structure as illustrated in the following figure:

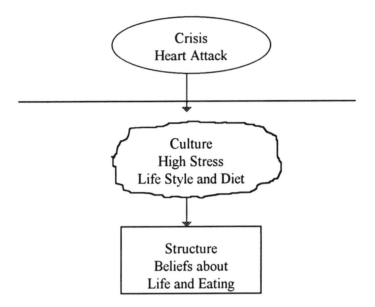

After the heart attack patient has bypass surgery, the behavioral eating patterns can be changed. After the surgery, the patient will be counseled to change the culture of their existence. They will learn to relax, be more sensitive, and reduce stress at the cultural level. The hardest change is at the structural level where they must change their beliefs about smoking, fatty foods, and differences in people. Some people refuse to change the structure even after the crisis.

From an organizational perspective, many companies experience a crisis. Competitors introduce a superior product or technology and the company faces bankruptcy. The company must change at the behavioral level. People are laid off, plants closed, and overhead is eliminated. The behavioral change is often sudden and unexpected. Impending bankruptcy, like the impending death from a heart attack, requires surgery.

Organizational change associated with the crisis, however, does not lead to permanent, positive change. After the crisis is relieved, change at both the cultural and structural levels must occur if the company is to survive long term.

An interesting phenomenon needs to be mentioned at this point. Many executives are excellent crisis managers. After the crisis is resolved, however, they are not able to shift to a different mode of change. They retain the crisis orientation and drive the company forward with one crisis after another. If a crisis doesn't exist, they will create one to feel useful, legitimate, and in control.

We have all experienced a crisis that has led to permanent change. We also know of a crisis that did not stimulate permanent change. It is important, therefore, to realize that the crisis neither identifies the fundamental cause of the problem nor will surviving the crisis guarantee effective, long-term change. You can win the battle and lose the war. The cause of the crisis is at the structural level, and many companies are unwilling to address the real structural issues that caused the crisis. There might be a temporary or even permanent change at the cultural level, but long term, the structural issues are seldom addressed.

Our Federal Government is a classic example. When interest rates hit 21% in 1980, the country was in an economic crisis. A change was made at the cultural level when Ronald Regan replaced Jimmy Carter as president. Changes were made by lowering taxes and addressing other life style issues. The crisis was alleviated, but the fundamental structural issue of a Balanced Budget Amendment (or other Constitutional adjustment) was not made. Certainly, laws were passed that implemented structural changes, and the crisis of high interest rates has not reoccurred.

The important point for our discussion is to recognize the need to change at all three levels when making a permanent change. The classic organizational agenda of solving the quarterly profit crisis is typically addressed at the behavioral level only. One of my clients has always attempted to keep their stock price up by shipping volume from next quarter, two months early. This avoids the crisis of a stock price decline, but long-term, permanent change does not occur as a result. The company has tried several cultural change initiatives, such as employee involvement and teamwork, but long-term, structural change has not yet been addressed. It's not a matter of whether a crisis will occur, but when and how severe.

Evolutionary Change

Evolutionary change is directed at changing the cultural level. Cultural dynamics represent all the societal aspects of people living and working together. In a macro sense, the culture of America is democracy while the culture of Cuba is communism. The culture of California is very different from that of New York.

The culture of most American businesses over the past 60 years originates from hierarchical models driven by the economics of Mass Production Thinking. The culture of most large, Mass Production companies is Thinkers think and Doers do what they are told. Managers were trained in MBA schools to plan, organize, and control the business. This structural context creates the culture associated with most American industrial giants.

Entrepreneurial companies reflect a different culture, at least initially. Everyone is involved with the founder in creating the business, and a culture of employee involvement and empowerment is common. Many entrepreneurs come from stifling hierarchical cultures. Consciously, or unconsciously, they create flatter, more team-based organizations. The past 15 years have seen a tremendous desire to change the culture to a team environment. Many hierarchical companies have created team-based plants in an attempt to improve the performance of their organizations. Many of these experiments have been successful, prompting other companies to want to change to a team-based culture.

Many executives tell me they are determined to change the culture of their organizations. They institute casual clothing, popcorn breaks, flexible working hours, and extend executive benefits throughout the ranks. Certainly, things change. At least *it feels better*, but often organizational performance does not improve. In fact, it often gets worse. Teamwork initiatives slow down decision making. Building a culture of consensus and trust takes time. Meanwhile, instantaneous improvement in profits does not occur. The command and control executive frequently blames the soft stuff, culture change initiative and often reverts to a hierarchical model.

Evolutionary change is generally about making the cultural dynamics more interdependent and the structural dynamics better. You will hear many "ER" words used in the case for change. "We need to do things bett*er*, fast*er*, slow*er*, cheap*er*, and smart*er*." The classic is working smarter, not harder.

The illusion of evolutionary change is illustrated below:

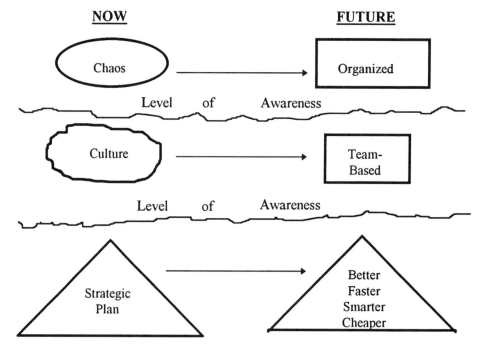

The executive level still does all the planning. The strategic plan at the structural level is about more of the same, done "ER." The assumption is that the chaos of the current behavioral level can become organized by changing the cultural dynamics. Many change initiatives of this type arrive at a sudden crisis because executives fail to recognize the need to couple cultural change with structural change.

Evolutionary change is about extending current reality forward in a comparative way. As the illustration shows, the intention of the change initiative is to do more or less of what already exists to arrive at a future state that is better than what exists now.

Listen to the evolutionary appeals of the politicians, "Are you better off today than when I took office four years ago?" They have typically raised or lowered taxes and passed legislation to make life style changes for various constituents. There will be those who have suffered, at the expense of others. At election time, the politicians will debate all three levels of change. They will talk about lowering taxes, changing the life style for all, and protecting the values of our American Constitution. They will promise to build a bridge to a prosperous future where everyone will be able to live the American dream. This is the illusion of evolutionary change.

One of my clients instituted a major employee empowerment cultural change initiative. As the empowerment culture expanded, the command and control factions began strategy debates. The word empowerment became the cynics resistance. Strategy is a structural issue and empowerment a cultural agenda. Finally, a new president put a stop to the evolutionary process by killing the empowerment culture and shifting the focus to the behavioral level by demanding attention to productivity. His efforts were intended to organize the chaos by instituting strict adherence to fiscal constraint and disciplined cultural considerations.

There are times that evolutionary change is important and effective. There is nothing right or wrong about any form of change. The key is to recognize what the organization requires and determine whether the dynamics of the selected change process will lead to the desired result.

From a personal perspective, evolutionary change, consciously practiced over a long period of time, will typically lead to the mid-life crisis. Likewise, in organizational life, evolutionary change perspectives, practiced over long periods of time, typically lead to a crisis of competitive market position. More of the same done "ER" seldom leads a company to sustainable success. The "ER" mentality is driven by an illusion that the company will eventually arrive at an organized behavioral level. The structural focus is only on strategy. How many strategic plans become obsolete before they are published? The era of strategic planning was based upon extending Mass Production structures forward to success. Now that Mass Production Thinking is being challenged at every level, the evolutionary models of change no longer work.

Transformational Change

Transformational Change is entirely different from crisis or evolutionary processes. Transformational Change accepts current reality as the way it is and seeks to *create* a *future* existence that is *different.*

Transformational Change cannot start when there is a crisis. As we have discussed, the patient must survive the crisis before a fundamental change in structure can begin. Transformational Change addresses all three levels of change, but the dominant agenda is to change the structural level.

The following diagram illustrates Transformational Change:

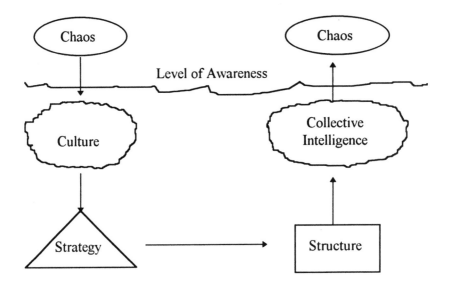

Transformational Leaders recognize and accept that chaos will always exist at the behavioral level. On a personal level, human behavior has always been complex and chaotic. Within the organizational context, market behavior is always chaotic. The most important premise of Transformational Change is that the behavioral level will always manifest chaos. Tom Peters wrote the book *Thriving on Chaos: Handbook for a Management Revolution* as a confirmation that it is an illusion to believe that you will arrive at a future time that is organized.

It is difficult for the Mass Production Thinker to accept chaos at the behavioral level. Military models prove that behavior can be organized. Thousands of meetings have been held to plan, organize, and control behavior. The Mass Production Thinker is compulsive about organizing the behavioral level and typically rejects the premise of Transformational Change as being too simplistic. If your company is driven by a Mass Production Thinker, you will feel the urgency to control behavior.

After accepting that the behavioral level of the future will be chaotic, the

Transformational Leader determines that the cultural level must manifest a collective intelligence to deal with the chaos. This is not a new concept. Centuries of experience prove that collective intelligence leads to success. The United States of America is a classic example. Our Congress is the collective intelligence, elected by the people to deal with the chaotic behavioral level. The pledge of allegiance starts with, "I pledge allegiance . . ." and ends with "liberty and justice for *all*."

If the future will be chaotic, the cultural level must be built on collective intelligence. No one person, acting alone, is capable of digesting the chaos for all the others involved. Every dictatorship has failed for this reason.

The most important step in the Transformational Change process is to *create* the underlying structure that creates the collective intelligence. Transformational Change initiatives *always* start by addressing the 10 structural elements provided below. Transformational Leaders recognize that a collective intelligence is derived from clear structural design. Underlying the Christian religion are 10 structural Commandments. The Commandments create collective intelligence and aligned behavior. The same is true with every religion. The cultural level is created from the structural design.

The structural level of any organization contains 10 structural elements. These elements, in turn, answer 10 questions that create the cultural dynamics.

Structural element	Question
1. Vision	What do we want to *be*?
2. Mission	Why do we exist?
3. Assumptions	What demands that we change?
4. Outcomes	What do we need to create?
5. Strategies	How will we deploy resources?
6. Competitive Advantage	What makes us different from the competition?
7. Customer Offering	What is the scope of our offering to the customer?
8. Philosophy	What guides development?
9. Core Values	How will we treat each other?
10. Measurement	How will we measure success?

These 10 structural elements are the antecedents for change. These elements must be created before change at the cultural or behavioral level will occur. Therefore, the cause of Transformational Change is the change in structure. The challenge of Transformational Leadership is to create the Structural Framework that will cause the collective intelligence to form and achieve the desired results in the chaotic business environment. I have written about this process in subsequent chapters of this book.

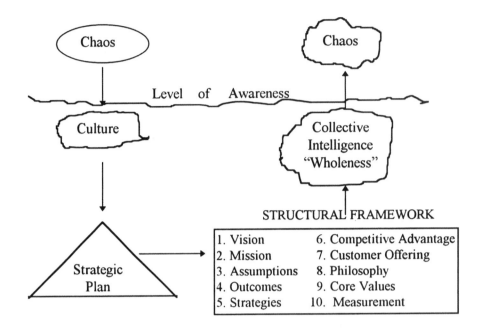

The structural level that supports the current reality of most organizations is merely a strategic plan. Seldom does the strategic plan identify or address all 10 structural elements. Because most evolutionary change processes are based upon more of the same done "ER," the vision of the future state of being that is different is typically missing.

Transformational Change, on the other hand, works backward from the future, using a vision of different to inspire people in the current culture to *create* a collective intelligence that will support the inevitable chaos of the future. Mr. Iacocca used the vision of being America's car company to inspire Chrysler employees to transform Chrysler. At that time, Chrysler was bankrupt and had 600,000 cars in stock that no one wanted to buy. Mr. Iacocca began his leadership of Chrysler by changing the structural elements to transform the company.

Many barriers confront Transformational Change initiatives. Many people cannot visualize the future defined by the vision. Current reality is so dominant that they will judge the vision as unrealistic. The judgmental mind of most people will not trust the motives and intent of the Transformational Change advocates. The journey to the future is perceived as risky, and it is safer to stay anchored to current reality.

Speculation is also a major barrier to Transformational Change initiatives. People mentally begin the change process and quickly arrive at a point where an insurmountable obstacle appears. "It's a good idea, *but* it will take a lot of money and . . ." The journey never starts.

Transformational Change, therefore, must start by creating a new Structural Framework for change. Creating the Structural Framework does not demand that behavior change.

Key Point: • **Structural level work can be done without a commitment to change either the cultural or behavioral levels.**

Because a crisis does not exist, there is no urgency to create the Structural Framework. Transformational Change, therefore, is driven by a desire to *be different* rather than a crisis of survival. The desire to *be* can incubate for a long time. Nothing demands action today. The evolutionary process can continue while the commitment to transformation builds.

The rate of Transformational Change depends on the commitment of participants in the change process. After the Structural Framework is complete, people can choose the time frame required for the transformation to occur. At times, the transformation will take years. It is difficult to transform the current reality of many Mass Production organizations. An imbedded investment has been made that is very difficult to change. Mass Production cultures are based on no trust. You cannot talk yourself out of no trust cultures. The culture will not change until the structural elements of Mass Production Thinking change. Therefore, the dynamics of Transformational Change must start at the structural level.

The important point is to understand that

Key Point: • **Transformational Change is a future-back approach, and it starts by changing the structure.**

It is important to involve all participants that must form the collective intelligence in creating the Structural Framework. The more they are involved in the process, the more they will be committed to bring the future into reality.

Chapter 5
Assumptions

"Why change?" "What demands that we change–everything is *fine!*" "We just had the best year ever." "Are they crazy?" "If it ain't broke, don't fix it!" "Here we go again, another change program." "Whatever happened to that empowerment stuff?" "Now they call it reengineering." "Wait until the quarterly results are bad, they'll abandon this one too." "If we all stick together, they can't force us to do it." "We'll change when they start walking the talk."

The list goes on and on and on. These are comments from employees about improperly structured change initiatives. If the simple question of "Why change?" is unanswered, *they* will be blamed for all the misery change will cause.

"Why change?" is a simple question, but it is not always accurately answered. When there is a crisis, the answer is, "...or we'll be out of business." Evolutionary change is driven by, "if we don't, we won't." "If we don't cut cost, we won't be competitive." "If we don't change the culture, we won't be here in five years."

Most change initiatives focus on the negative circumstances in current reality. Leaders project a negative vision of the future if the circumstances are not eliminated. The most common answer to "Why change?" is *survival!* "If we don't, we won't," is negative visioning. Psychologists call it *conflict manipulation*. If the leader can project current trends forward to the point where failure occurs, everyone can see how the company won't survive.

Conflict manipulators are experts in speculation and blame. *They* will also call for will power and exhort the organization to get organized; work smarter, not harder; and when the going gets tough, the tough get going. Will power strategies suggest that if you can't stand the heat, get out of the kitchen, and big boys don't cry. A whitewater-rafting trip will prepare everyone for the tough journey ahead. It will also be suggested that everyone dress informally because it's easier to work harder without the coat and tie.

The Muscle Memory

There are times when the question of "Why change?" is accurately answered and change still doesn't happen. Everyone knows they must change, but there is resistance. I hear it every day, "People resist change!" This is a very frustrating issue for many executives.

To help people understand resistance to change, I use the metaphor of golf.

Most golfers reach a level of ability and can't or don't improve beyond that level. Even with extensive lessons from a professional, something resists the change process. In golf, it's the muscle memory of the old swing. The same is true in every organization.

Key Point: • **Resistance to change is built into the muscle memory of the organization. It is *not the people*.**

Imbedded in every organization is a muscle memory. Years and years of programming have produced a set of rules that drive the organization. The rules have become policies, procedures, and traditions. This collective set of rules is called the *culture*.

Key Point: • **The culture is strong. It will resist change.**

From where does culture come? Does it just appear? Presto! There's a culture! A culture starts as *assumptions* about the way things are or the way things should be done. An assumption is a hypothesis that explains reoccurring behavior. If the same behavior happens repeatedly, the cause can be identified. It can then be assumed that the same cause will produce the same behavior in other people and locations. The hypothesis is tested over time, validating the assumption. Valid assumptions become rules. The same is true in physics, chemistry, or any physical science.

The assumption that the Sun revolved around the Earth was valid at one time. Then Copernicus challenged the assumption. Scientifically, he proved that the opposite was true and everything changed in the field of astronomy.

The rules of a Mass Production environment were assumptions at one time in history. The assumptions were made and validated long before you and I were in the business environment. We have learned to accept the rules and have been rewarded or punished for obeying or breaking them. In college, I received an "A" in Business Management because I learned the rules of Mass Production: plan, organize, and control. The assumptions and rules are the subject of hundreds of management books and seminars.

The imbedded muscle memory of Mass Production Thinking is very strong. There are rules how to *write rules*. There are guidelines for writing policy manuals, giving employees performance appraisals, and how to reward performance.

I have asked many people in hundreds of organizations, "Why do you do what you do?" The answer is often, "I don't know. That's the way it's always been done around here." When further asked, "Why don't you change it?" I hear something about the rules or the culture or they say, "*They* won't approve that." Who are *they*? "You know–management." Who in management? "I don't know, someone upstairs." The amorphous *they*!

Key Point:	• ***They are not people.*** **They are imbedded rules that are based upon old assumptions that are no longer valid.**

Rules! The important issue is to know that rules were at one time assumptions. Don't challenge the rules or try to change the rules directly; rather, extract the assumptions that are currently driving the business and retest them for validity. The validation process is open for debate without endangering the keeper of rules.

It would be tempting to list all the assumptions that became the rules of Mass Production Thinking. Many of these assumptions are no longer valid. Suffice it to say there are thousands of rules and again hundreds of books and articles on the subject. Read Chapter Seven of Michael Hammer and Steven Stanton's book, *The Reengineering Revolution: A Handbook*. The chapter title is "Assumption Busting for Fun and Profit." Assumption busting is a critical part of reengineering the corporation.

From Rules to Authority

It is difficult to separate truth from speculation when examining assumptions. Many assumptions speculate that if something is done, something will be the result. For example, "Long lot runs of standardized products lead to low cost products." This assumption is valid from a financial perspective. The assumption further assumes that customers want standardized products.

Some assumptions of Mass Production are still valid and accurately define the way it is in the business environment. Not all assumptions about the past are wrong and, therefore, some rules about the current organization are still useful.

Assumptions become rules and rules translate into *authority*. In a Mass Production model, authority resides with upper management. The assumption is that Thinkers should think and Doers should do for the system to be efficient and effective. Once rules become authority, no one dares examine the underlying assumptions behind the rules.

Key Point:	• **Living within the rules is called compliance. Compliance with authority is ingrained in our muscle memory at an early age.**

The interesting phenomenon is that compliance with authority generally produces only a neutral existence. Obeying the rules is expected! Failure to comply brings immediate punishment or pain. It's the choke chain on a dog. Heel! Many people have faithfully done what they are told for years, and they receive very little feedback or recognition for obeying the rules. If, however, they fail to do as they are told, they are written up or punished in some way. Many children learn, however, that the only way to get attention is to misbehave. The negative feedback system is quite common in Mass Production organizations.

Assume for a moment that a "do as you're told" culture still exists in corporate America. It sounds so cruel that some people bristle at that assumption. How did such a culture come to exist? Mass Production Thinkers *assumed* that the craftsperson could be split into hundreds of tiny tasks, each of which could be assigned to a workstation. The workstation could be operated by a pair of hands that required no talent or ability to think. Therefore, the assumption was that people are things. This assumption was translated into rules to *control things*. Have you ever punched a time clock? How many people still do?

We all know that people were treated like things in the early days of Mass Production. Henry Ford said, "Why did you give me people? All I need is hands." Industrial engineers used time and motion studies to make the assembly line go faster. It wasn't time and emotion. The feelings of things didn't matter.

In the 1970s, the assumption about people changed. "People are our most important asset" became the hypothesis. This assumption was a kind way of trying to change the rules of Mass Production. The Personnel Office was renamed Human Resources and the rules, which were based upon the asset assumption, were developed.

People are assets? This assumption still exists today in many places. The Mass Production Thinker tries to explain this assumption in a positive way, but in the *Context* of Mass Production, assets are depreciated, used up, and replaced over time.

This discussion is not intended to establish what is right or wrong about how people are viewed. The point is to help you understand how an assumption made by Henry Ford in the late 1920s became a rule that *still* manifests as muscle memory today. Mass Production Thinking contains hundreds of similar rules that still drive thinking in high places.

Transformational Change is very difficult when it arrives at the interface with the old rules. This is the point where the team initiative fails if senior leadership is trying to "fix the factory." Fixing or problem-solving initiatives are intended to *restore order within the old rules.* Team's have no authority to change the rules, yet they are asked to break them. Supervisors are now called coaches to encourage the assets to break the rules. Nothing will change, however, until the assumptions behind the rules are exposed and the new assumptions are validated.

Transformational Leadership is not about making new rules. It is about identifying new assumptions about the business environment that, if they are true, will lead to new *rules and authority.* Creating a clear vision is difficult, but no other process is more important than clarifying the *assumptions that will empower the collective intelligence to create new rules.*

The New Assumptions

The new *Context* of business is described in many ways. Mass Customization comes close to describing what's wanted from the customer's perspective. Partnering appears to describe the relationship dynamics between companies. Whatever it is, Mass is being removed from Production, and all the assumptions of Mass Production must be examined and revalidated.

What are some of the assumptions that must drive the new environment? From my experience with *The Organizational Transformation™ Simulation*, I have assembled a few of the more dominant assumptions that pose the biggest barriers to change. You will see the progression of thinking that is required to create the Mass Customization environment in the following list:

Vending	Supplying	Partnering
• We will decide what the customer can have. We will decide when to provide it.	• We will ask customers what they want, then decide whether we want to do it that way.	• We will work with the customer to create the future.
• People are things that do functions.	• People are our most important asset.	• People are people.
• The manager knows best and is in charge.	• The management will determine strategy.	• Managers are facilitators of the process.
• It isn't necessary for workers to know the end result of their effort.	• Workers should see their co-workers as customers.	• Workers should know the end customer very well.
• Blame and fear are effective motivators.	• Money and benefits are effective motivators.	• Contribution and involvement motivates.
• The sum of the parts equals the whole.	• The sum of the parts plus the interrelations of the parts equals the whole.	• The whole must be in every part.
• Practice time is about building inventory.	• Practice time is about perfecting functional skills.	• Practice time is about creating wholeness of process.

Vending	Supplying	Partnering
• Quality can be inspected into the product.	• Quality is a competitive advantage.	• Quality is a given.
• Rejects can be sold at a discount.	• Rejects can be reworked.	• There is no such thing as a reject.
• The customer will send us specifications.	• The customer is part of a market.	• The customer is a person.
• Quantity and quality are mutually exclusive.	• Quantity and quality are both important.	• Quantity and quality are givens.
• To lower cost, buy better.	• To lower cost, reduce the material and labor content.	• The cost of the product is less important than the economics of the process.
• To be successful, we must meet specifications.	• To be successful, we must control the specifications.	• To be successful, we must be innovative.
• Empowerment is about power. It is dangerous.	• Empowerment is about authority. We can delegate what is needed.	• Empowerment is about freedom to create and being creative, fulfilling the purpose.
• There are limited resources.	• There are finite resources.	• There is a world of abundance.
• Business is a contest against competition.	• Business is a game of chance.	• Business is about creating what you want.
• Nothing succeeds like success.	• Replication of success patterns will lead to utopia.	• Nothing fails like success.

When seeing a list of this type, it is common for a Mass Production Thinker to adopt the slogan "people are people" and try to use it to "fix" the Mass Production environment. Please, these are assumptions that must be used to *create* a new environment.

Key Point: • **The Context of Mass Production is obsolete because many of the assumptions that it is built upon are no longer valid.**

Consider the assumptions under the partnering column and envision what your organization would look like if it were *living* these assumptions. What would the culture be like? Who would have authority to decide? What would the customer interface be like? Would you have a channel of distribution?

If you consider the partnering assumptions, you will find that these assumptions have not yet been translated into rules. Maybe there are *no rules to establish*! Maybe the dynamics of the organization are such that rules are obsolete! This makes sense because rules establish control, and control has been replaced by alignment.[a]

---

[a] Refer to Chapter 15 for more information about how to create alignment.

Chapter 6
Structure

The bottom line of every organizational change initiative is to change how people behave and how work is performed. Teamwork, empowerment, partnering, and reengineering are all about changing the interaction dynamics between people–interactions that enable the work that they do to be done together rather than independently. Simply stated, most companies are trying to move from the time and motion processes of the Industrial Age to the interdependent network processes of the Information Age. This requires a huge shift in human behavior.

The first step in learning to change the way people work together is to understand what causes behavior. The field of behavioral science contains many theories on why people behave the way they do. Individual and group behavior has been studied for centuries, and some human behavior remains a mystery. The behavioral science approach starts by observing behavior and identifying repetitive, predictable patterns of behavior. Similar patterns are categorized into individual styles, such as introverts and extroverts. People are then taught to modify their behavior by modeling the behavior patterns of desired styles. Role models and idols become symbols for young people to emulate.

Just like individuals, organizations exhibit predictable patterns of behavior. Human behavior in the Industrial Age was controlled by time and motion engineers. Jobs were broken down into specific behaviors, and work was separated into efficient parts. Job descriptions were written to be certain people performed efficiently within the boundaries of their responsibilities. The integration of the parts to perform as a whole was the responsibility of managers and supervisors. The entire process was known only to those who engineered it.

Organizational patterns of behavior are classified as *cultures*. There is the work hard/play hard culture. The blue suit culture of IBM was a well-known model that many companies copied in an attempt to change their performance. Political behavior is classified as conservative or liberal, and politicians are labeled as Democrats or Republicans. Company images reflect the culture, and the patterns of behavior become rituals and traditions.

Classifying patterns of behavior is useful because it permits us to streamline communication and quickly extract meaning from observation. This, however, leads to judgmental evaluation of the culture and the style of people.

Judgmental evaluation of behavior is a common driving force for organizational change. "We need to work smarter, not harder" is a judgmental view of behavior. The cultural change that emanates from this thinking is often positive in intent, but frequently it punishes those who are judged "not smart." Changing behavior within a judgmental context also implies that one party is right and the other wrong. This approach leads to polarized debates and adversarial conditions surrounding the change.

There have been many attempts to change organizational behavior by trying to change the culture. This approach usually starts by encouraging people to be nice to one another. These approaches are perceived to be warm and fuzzy and seldom produce sustainable results. The fallacy of this approach is to believe that the people are the cause of the organizational dilemma. It is easy to see people's mistakes and believe that people are intentionally causing the organizational problems. Because something must be blamed for the problems, the culture is frequently judged the culprit.

One of the most important principles of Transformational Change is to understand that the problems of current reality are not caused by people. People are merely trying to work within a process, system, or structure that does not allow them to perform outside narrow limits of their job descriptions. The Mass Production systems of the Industrial Age still dominate most organizations today, and people have learned to live, work, and survive within those systems.

Thus, it is an illusion to believe that organizational behavior can be changed by teaching people behavioral modeling techniques. It is also not possible to change the organization by focusing on the culture. Both are merely symptoms that something else is going on. Permanent, sustainable change must begin by first identify the fundamental cause of behavior.

The Structural View

To effectively change organizational behavior it, therefore, is important to find an explanation of behavior that is both nonjudgmental and independent of culture. Is there something that explains behavior beyond the observable level? If we could find an explanation for predictable behavior patterns, organizational and personal behavior change would be greatly simplified.

There is a simple explanation. It is called *structure*. Structure, as we will refer to it in this chapter, is represented by the following matrix:

	HAVE	DON'T HAVE
WANT	1	3
DON'T WANT	2	4

There are four structures with predictable behavior patterns and emotional experiences. It is important to understand that these structures are independent of culture and free of judgmental evaluation. People in any country or of any nationality will behave the same way when they are in each structure. Therefore, the Laws of Structure that can be extracted from this structural view can be universally applied to guide any change initiative, regardless of cultural context.

Let's step back a moment and think about behavior in a nonhuman context. Think of a babbling brook. Why does the water babble? When I ask that question in seminars, people most often reply, "rocks." I suggest there are rocks in a lake and the water doesn't babble. The next answer is "gravity." Gravity also exists on a lake and the water doesn't babble. The answer is the structure of the land. The structure is downhill. Structure, combined with the force of gravity, causes the water to babble. As the structure that confines the water changes, the behavior of the water changes. We use many different words to describe the water, but the words really describe the structure of the land that contains or confines the water. The words stream, river, lake, pond, swamp, or ocean all describe the structure that contains the water. Water is water.

Likewise, people are people. There are hundreds of words to describe people: drivers, expressive, analytical, and amiable. Leader, manager, and supervisor are terms that describe the organizational role of people. Entrepreneur is a term that describes the behavior of someone who is creating a new business. All of these terms describe predictable patterns of behavior and place some value judgment upon the behavior. As we have said before, we can focus on the observable behavior and try to explain the pattern using judgmental terms or we can look below the behavior and understand what structure causes the behavior to occur.

Therefore, the first step in learning to change organizational behavior is to separate the people from the structure and understand what behavior is inherent to each structure.

The Have/Want Structure

People behave predictably within the structural framework of their existence. When people *have* what they *want*, they will exhibit the following behavior:

	HAVE	DON'T HAVE
WANT	*Keep it/enjoy it* *Use it* *Maintain it/love it* *Protect it* *Take it for granted*	
DON'T WANT		

If you *have* a car that you *want*, all these behaviors will occur. We typically *use it* everyday. Changing the oil is maintenance. Locking it is protecting it. We also take it for granted that it will start every morning and run smoothly when we push the accelerator. The same behavior exists with your home, clothes, money, electricity, water, or the freedom we have in this country.

Test these structural behaviors with anything you *have* and *want*. Change the "it" to "them" for personal relationships. Tangibles and intangibles alike all prompt these behaviors. If people of any culture *have* something and they *want* it, they will manifest these predictable forms of behavior.

It is important to develop a structural awareness and a nonjudgmental assessment of behavior. Why do people keep all their old college textbooks in the attic? It isn't because they are pack rats or lazy. It's because *they have them and want them.*

When people *have* what the *want,* they will also say predictable things about those items or relationships.

	HAVE	DON'T HAVE
WANT	*More of the same/ Improve/increase it Better, faster "er" words Everything is fine*	
DON'T WANT		

When people talk about something they *have* and *want*, they predictably say they want more of it. They will want to make it better, bigger, faster, or smaller–typically a word that ends in "ER." You can't have more of something unless you already have that something. Likewise, you can't improve or increase something unless you have that something. Thus, the language of the Have/Want structure is predictably about the sufficiency or insufficiency of what is contained in it.

People often say everything is fine. This simply means that what they *have* and *want* is sufficient. We all know the person who has everything. They are hard people for which to buy gifts. They are content and have earned a life style that is relaxed and comfortable. This structure is desirable, and if for only one day a year, we should give thanks for our blessings.

The Have/Don't Want Structure–The Problem Box

Life is not static. It is dynamic, and the law of entropy confirms that "nothing fails like success." When we have things and relationships, they often break, atrophy, deteriorate, or worse, disintegrate. If you have a car, it will break. All personal relationships experience conflict. It's not a matter of whether, but when. Welcome to the Problem Box.

Behavior in the Problem Box is again predictable.

	HAVE	DON'T HAVE
WANT		
DON'T WANT	*Problem Box* *Fix it* *Solve it* *Make it go away* *Resolve it* *Ignore it*	

When your golf swing doesn't work, you go to the practice range to get it fixed. When you accumulate trash, you put it on the curb to make it go away. When your car breaks, you *have* something you *don't want*. You take it in for repairs. When you cut your finger, bump your head, stub your toe, poke your eye, you *don't want* the pain and you will attempt to make the pain go away. Aspirin, bandages, and ice packs are effective remedies. The judgmental explanation for problems is you were careless. The real cause, however, is because you have a head, eye, toe, or finger. If you don't want to hurt them, don't have them in the first place.

The key is to recognize the *structural* explanation for a problem before assigning a judgmental cause. The structural definition of a *problem* is *having* something you *don't want*. This is very different from a judgmental or cultural explanation. The judgmental view is that stuff happens. This is not true. Problems happen because you *have* something that you *want*. If it is over used, not maintained, unprotected, or taken for granted, it will ultimately break. Simply stated, if you don't want problems with your golf swing, don't play golf. If you don't want brats, don't have children. If you don't want marital problems, don't get married. Reduced to its simplest terms, if you don't want problems, don't *have* anything. From a structural point of view, problems start by *having* what you *want* and allowing the law of entropy, over time, to cause the item to deteriorate or to become unwanted.

The Problem Box contains very specific language.

	HAVE	DON'T HAVE
WANT		
DON'T WANT	*Problem Box* *Not enough* *Just as soon as* *Oh ain't it awful how* *Poor me* *It's hopeless*	

The conversation in the Problem Box always starts with a reference to *enough*. People never have enough time, money, fun, or happiness. Sports fans are seldom happy unless their favorite team goes undefeated. Even when the team wins, the margin of victory wasn't *enough*. A golfer may shoot 75, but it still wasn't good *enough*. Companies never make *enough* money.

There are times when the conversation starts with *too much*. People often over shoot *enough*. They are overweight because they eat *too much*. There is *too much* crime in our cities and we pay *too much* in taxes. Both extremes of *enough* can open the Problem Box conversation.

Not having *enough* causes people to speculate when enough will exist. Thus, the next conversation is *just as soon as* (JASA). Everything will work itself out JASA we get a new coach, better players, a new congress, increased sales, cheaper products, etc. The JASA list is endless. Children will do their homework JASA the TV program has ended. The JASA game is addictive. When you adopt JASA as a life partner, you will always chase the carrot on the stick and exhort yourself to run faster, work smarter, and play harder. From an organizational perspective, results will always be better JASA sufficient effort is put forth by those responsible for performance.

The game in the Problem Box is exhausting. Nothing is ever *enough,* and there is always an excuse or someone to blame. The game is always the aftermath of *having* yesterday. Executives call meeting after meeting reacting to circumstances from yesterday.

A common scenario is the customer who calls with a problem from yesterday. The product or service that was promised by the salesperson didn't meet expectations. Managers are told to assemble a team to get things fixed! The fix-it mentality is everywhere. Fix-it becomes the culture of many organizations. The dynamics of the Problem Box are often oppressive and cruel.

The fix it process often doesn't work. The predictable conversation then moves beyond JASA to *Oh ain't it awful how* (OAIAH). We have all been in an organizational complaint session. Turn on the television and listen to any talk show. OAIAH is rampant. It often turns into violent action directed at those who should have provided *enough* and didn't. Listen to election campaigns. When it turns to mud slinging, you are listening to the *enough*, JASA, OAIAH game. The Problem Box hero promises to fix it if elected.

The Problem Box conversation doesn't end at OAIAH. The final chapters are *poor me* and *it's hopeless*. There is deep psychological despair in this structure. Some people are constrained to work and live in the Problem Box their entire lives. To them, "Life's a bitch, then you die."

Many businesses provide products and services exclusively for the Problem Box of life. Consider the work of hospitals, doctors, lawyers, auto mechanics, air condition repair firms, or trash disposal companies. They all exist to make *what you have and don't want, go away.*

The emotions in this structure are very negative, ranging from mild frustration to panic and desperation. The only way to survive the Problem Box is to blame someone for causing the problem. This appears to be true, but the structural view reveals another cause.

Key Point: • **Someone or something didn't cause your Problem Box. You have problems because you *have* things you *want*. If you don't want problems, don't *have*.**

This is not an inhuman or insensitive perspective. I appreciate the pain and suffering the Problem Box brings to many people and want desperately to help them solve their problems. The solutions, however, must accurately define the cause of the problem. The root cause of having an unwanted circumstance starts with *having* something you *want*. You are just unaware that the law of entropy will set in and create the unwanted circumstance.

Again, we must find the nonjudgmental level of thinking and analyses if we are to effectively change our behavior.

Want/Don't Have Structure

Is there relief from the Problem Box of life? Is there a *structure* where life is fun, where you can enjoy what you are doing? Is there a place where people can exist without conflict? There is, and it's the only structure with hope for dramatic organizational change. It's called the Outcome Box.

Behavior in the Want/Don't Have structure is again predictable.

	HAVE	DON'T HAVE
WANT		*Outcome Box* *Buy* *Create/invent* *Earn* *Build/design* *Borrow/steal*
DON'T WANT		

People love to *buy* and they love to *create*. These are two of the most enjoyable activities known to man. People create relationships that lead to marriage. In this structure, people are dynamic, alive, kind, loving, and behave in many dynamic and attractive ways. You and I were both created by our parents. The act of creating is the supreme expression of human love and affection. What a wonderful structure in which to be.

The operative word in this structure is *creating*. We must first realize that everything was somehow created. The explanations of how things were created contain many theories. Regardless of your belief about the process, the *act of creating* itself is one that motivates and inspires people.

Likewise, buying is a very popular behavior. People love to buy. The emotional energy that drives this structure is *powerful*.

Not all the behavior in this structure is positive. People often *want* things they *don't have* and steal or kill to get them. This behavior actually originates from an addictive Problem Box. Many people have not been taught how to create what they *want* and *don't have*, and they believe the only way to achieve that outcome is to take it from those who have it. The pure act of creating has nothing to do with relieving the pain of the Problem Box.

The Want/Don't Have structure always starts with a vision of the desired result. In Stephan Covey's famous book, *The 7 Habits of Highly Effective People: Powerful Lessons in Personal Change*, he lists "start with the end in mind" as the first habit. In the beginning, God created. Things that are created are always visualized in someone's mind before they are created in real terms.

A *creating orientation* must be the driving force for the organization that is seeking a new future. A Problem Box, fix-it orientation will not work. Something you *want* and *don't have* cannot be fixed into existence. You were not fixed on to this planet, and an organizational profit cannot be fixed.

Employees must be enrolled in *creating* toward *a vision*. When Mr. Iacocca took over Chrysler, he told the employees that the company must become America's car company. His vision was so strong that he told the American consumer, "If you can find a better car, buy it." This was at a time when Chrysler still had 600,000 cars in stock from the old game. This compelling vision was an inspiration for many, but for most of the old game managers, it was impossible to see.

Vision is a powerful motivator for those who want to *create*. For those who are invested in the Problem Box, a vision is generally perceived as unrealistic. The *enoughness* of current reality dominates their thinking.

The language of the outcome structure is again predictable. When someone is asked to identify something they *want* and *don't have,* they may identify something they would like to buy like a new house, car, or boat–something tangible. When asked, however, to identify something they *want* and *don't have* that they cannot buy, they typically want more of the same or to make something "ER." They start with the current reality of what they *have* and *want* and want more of it. Some people are so invested in resolving their Problem Box, they will tell you about relief from suffering Problem Box pain.

When challenged to identify something they truly *want* and *don't have* without starting from current reality, they will typically go silent, look up at the ceiling, and finally say, "I don't know." This predictable response indicates they lack vision of the desired outcome to be created. Many people are living to merely extend current reality forward.

Being visionless is a very common phenomenon. People, starting in childhood, are suppressed from thinking about the future because the Problem Box of their parents is so enormous. A child is told they cannot *be* something in the future because they "aren't enough yet." Worse yet, they are given negative visions of "if you don't, you won't." Many people graduate from college and have no vision of what they want to be. They earn a college degree, but they have not created a vision. Likewise, many people earn a living but are miserable in their existence. They lack vision that causes them to *create*.

As we will discuss in the Chapter 9, "Vision," it is very common for people to be working toward vague and meaningless visions. They work hard bringing into existence what they think management *wants* and *doesn't have*, only to find out that it wasn't the right thing.

For now, suffice it to say that *creating* is the right work. You must learn to *create a perfect* organization. The *perfection* is first created in the vision. It is *possible* to create a perfect vision that will inspire employees to perform perfectly. Realistic? It depends on your perception of perfect. In structural terms, we can define perfect. In behavioral terms, it is difficult to achieve.

Don't Have/Don't Want Structure

The final structure is driven by Don't Have/Don't Want thinking:

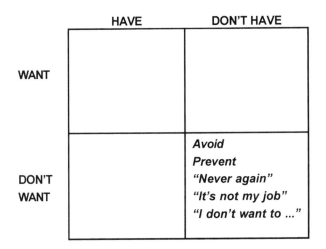

This structure is almost as addictive as the Problem Box. In this structure, people avoid and prevent unwanted circumstances from occurring. Many live in great fear that the unwanted will somehow happen to them. They will say "never again" and "it's not my job."

The positive behavior of this structure is to avoid getting sick or preventing disease by properly applying medication or good nutrition. Safety devices and guardrails prevent injuries and accidents. Fences and security systems are erected to prevent intrusion and vandalism. There are many useful activities associated with this structure, but all of them are driven by negative visions of unwanted circumstances. People who live and work in this structure become paranoid about the realism of creating what they want. They spend so much time preventing and avoiding, they seldom know the beauty of creating *wanted* experiences. They become cynical and guarded against everything. Parents become overly protective to shelter children from the *unwanted*.

In this structure, employees go to great lengths to avoid accepting responsibility for anything outside of their job description. When organizations announce employee involvement or team initiatives, employees band together to *prevent* the unwanted extra effort or responsibility from occurring.

Negative visioning often results from a negative past experience. If you previously owned a particular brand of car, for example, and had a bad experience, you would easily say, "I would *never* have a xxxxx car *again!*" Never again is a negative vision that is very difficult for organizations to overcome.

Transformational Change initiatives must recognize that many employees are heavily invested in negative visions from past experience. "We tried that once" or "that won't work." Many team-building retreats leave a bitter taste from executives who talk the talk but don't walk the walk. People have experienced downsizing and cost-cutting campaigns that were designed to get lean and mean. The meanness was often directed at those who made mistakes when workloads increased. Employees who have experienced the false promises of the past are very reluctant to begin new initiatives that promise to reengineer the organization to prosperity. They *don't have* and *don't want* the responsibility, pain, and extra work involved.

Structural Thinking Applied

Initiating change using a structural perspective helps people understand that change is not about *them*. It is *not about* personalities and egos. People can relate and enjoy the process of change, realizing that change is structural. Permanent and effective change can be made if the *creating orientation* can be activated and sustained.

The application of structural thinking is enormous. After we understand the behavior, emotions, and language within each structure, we can clearly identify where the desired behavior exists and learn how to focus the people to achieve the desired results. There is a clear difference between the creating and problem-solving orientations. Both are appropriate when properly applied.

If we look at the four structures, we can see these two applications:

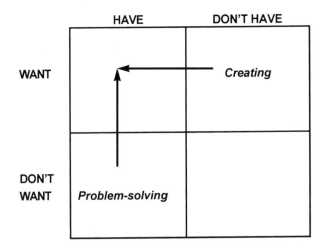

Creating is bringing into being something you *want* and *don't have*. Problem solving is restoring something you *have* and *don't want* to its original state or eliminating it all together. These two technologies are discussed and defined in Chapter 8, "Technology."

Moving the focus from one structure to another is a skill that can be learned and developed. It takes great questioning and listening skills and acute structural awareness. This skill is very helpful for salespeople in understanding their customers' expectations. Remember, people don't buy until they have a vision of the desired result. The product itself may be visible, but the people must see themselves owning the products. This purchase is illustrated as follows:

	HAVE	DON'T HAVE
WANT	*Existing car is adequate*	*Vision of owning a new car "Shopping"*
DON'T WANT	*Not enough money Can't afford a new car Existing car is getting older*	*Avoid payments*

Buying a car is a complex process when observed at the behavioral level. It is very simple if viewed from structural perspective. You must visualize owning the new car and the positive consequences of *having* what you *want*. The Problem Box will always warn you that you already *have* too many bills that you *don't want* and avoiding any new payments would be wise. The logical/emotional explanation for the purchase is "I got a good deal" and "I feel good driving it." The structural explanation is *I wanted* something *I didn't have.*

It is now possible to see why organizational and personal change is so difficult to accomplish. From the above example, it's obvious that all four structures exist simultaneously in the mind of a person buying a new car, yet the content of each structure is mutually exclusive. In other words, it is impossible to think about avoiding payments and envision owning a new car at the same instant in time. The mind can switch structures quickly, but the thoughts are mutually exclusive.

Key Point: • **All four structural influences exist simultaneously at every moment in time. The content of the structures remains mutually exclusive.**

In Transformational Change situations, the focus must be on the Outcome Structure. People must be able to visualize what they *want* and *don't have* and be enrolled in *creating it.* The vision must be clear, and the driving force of desire must be strong.

The most common error in initiating change is to start in the Problem Box. Problem Box thinking is driven by *not enough* and blame. The negative context of this structure generates the emotional force of compliance. While people sometimes perform miracles when driven by Problem Box thinking, they seldom create anything close to what is truly wanted or what was possible.

All behavior has an underlying structural explanation. It would be possible to explain everything you do within the structures. However, this would drive you crazy. Therefore, the application of structural thinking is best applied to design change initiatives.

The Laws of Structure

The many Laws of Structure are useful in designing major change initiatives. Some of these laws are as follows:

- You cannot arrive at what you *want* and *don't have* by eliminating what you *have* and *don't want*

- It is impossible to have a problem unless you *have* something you *want*

- *Wanting* what you *have* leads to complacency and decline

- Creating has nothing to do with the creativity of the creator

- Creativity is an attribute of people and is independent of structure

- *Not having* and *not wanting* is not a motivator for excellence

- It is difficult, if not impossible, to create toward a vague vision

- *Enough* is a powerful motivator to destruction and exhaustion

- *Just as soon as* perpetuates hope but ends up being an illusion

- Structural change is not about how you feel

- A group of people who are creating what they *want* and *don't have* will call themselves a team

- You cannot eliminate, solve, fix, or ignore yourself to prosperity

- Once a creation exists, we celebrate its arrival

- All creations bring potential problems into existence

- Creating starts with vision, not strategy

- Strategy debates without vision will merely extend current reality

- Imbedded assumptions and rules from past creating will prevent people from creating again

- *Knowing how* is a prerequisite for effective problem solving

- *Knowing how* is not a prerequisite for creating

- Avoiding responsibility is the biggest barrier to success

- Creativity is a by-product of creating

- Creativity applied while creating leads to innovation

- Creativity applied while problem solving leads to continuous improvement

- Current reality *is*

- Structural change is nonjudgmental

- *Having* what you *want* doesn't make you *be* what you *want* to *be*

- What you *have* does not define who you *are*

When the Laws of Structure start to make sense, they will reveal where organizational change strategies are flawed. The most common error is for executives to use problem-solving language when, in fact, they need to be creating. Knowing the difference is a critical leadership skill.

The structural view is at first strange. People have often justified or explained their existence using behavior terms and judgmental cause and effect relationships. The chaos of this approach is enormous and leads to the conclusion that the chaos must be organized or brought under control. This is an illusion. Chaos will always exist at the behavioral level. The structure underneath the chaos is invisible, but it is always predictable. If you want to change the behavior, change the structure. Awareness of this fact is a sign of wisdom.

Chapter 7
Leadership

Thousands of books and articles have been written about leaders and leadership. The attributes and skills of leaders are well documented. Many people believe that leadership, therefore, is about personalities and behavioral skills.

Key Point: • **Leadership is a process being applied by a person called a leader.**

It is very important to separate personalities of leaders from the process being applied. As I discuss in this chapter, the situation should dictate the process. Leaders will be effective if they apply the correct process within their own personality.

This chapter, therefore, is not about the attributes of leaders; rather, it is about the challenges that confront leaders and the various processes of leadership that can be applied. The following definitions are important in understanding this discussion of leadership.

Leader	A person who is responsible to lead
Leadership	The process of leading
Leadership challenge	The situation that creates the need for a leader and the process of leadership
Leadership responsibility	The boundaries that define the limits of the challenge

The word leadership can be used as a noun or an adjective. It is important to think of leadership as a process independent of the leader as a person.

The Leadership Challenge

Let me first suggest that the leadership challenge in the current business environment is very different from that of the past 60 years. Both the *Context* and Content of the business environment are changing simultaneously. The *Context* is changing from Mass Production to Mass Customization and the Content is changing from hierarchical functionalism to collaborative networking. The relationship dynamics of this new environment are *different*. The pace is dramatically different. Technological obsolescence makes it imperative for organizations to be designed for responsiveness. Quantity and quality are still essential ingredients, but words such as speed, nimbleness, flexibility, virtual, and seamless have become the design criteria for new organizations. People must be integrated to create process wholeness. The competitive advantage has switched from competencies to capabilities. Mass Production models no longer contain the answers to meet this challenge.

The leadership responsibilities of this new environment are beyond the experience of many people in leadership positions today. The challenge, therefore, is to establish leadership based upon the ability to create a collective intelligence that can "learn as it goes." This ability is not described in many leadership books because it is not an attribute in the *Context* of Mass Production. Peter Senge's book, *The Fifth Discipline, The Art & Practice of The Learning Organization*, describes this ability as creating "the learning organization." Mr. Senge suggests that the competitive advantage today is the capability to learn. The important issue is not whether learning is the key; instead, something has changed that requires totally new thinking concerning competitive advantage.

In the past five years, I have witnessed many leader-driven corporate change initiatives. The intent is to improve the competitive advantage of the company. Many have been announced with great fanfare. New visions proclaim the intense determination to be the industry leader or "world class." Nationally famous consulting firms are hired to guide reengineering processes. Major cuts in overhead displace lifetime employees. The tough choice between operational excellence or customer intimacy is made. In most cases, operational excellence wins. Advertising campaigns are created to assure customers the company is still committed to red carpet service. Information systems departments explode trying to keep up with the need for new technology. The information systems budget is staggering. One year after the announcement, the leader reports the outlook is optimistic, but the momentum of the Queen Mary is difficult to change.

After the change initiative is announced, many leaders go into lengthy, often secret meetings to figure out the strategies that lead to world class status. Benchmark studies begin. In the interim, business continues as usual. The people wait for the leaders to explain the strategies. The determination surrounding the announced change makes people afraid to make mistakes. Action toward the new vision is slow or doesn't occur. The leaders see waiting as lack of commitment to the journey. A revised vision adds clarity to the meaning of world class and increases the determination to succeed. At this point, several senior executives leave or are fired. Their departure is explained by, "They couldn't stand the heat." Employees become afraid that more cuts are coming and that they will not survive the next round.

Key Point: • **Living and working in fear does not inspire people to use their creative talents.**

The psychological experience surrounding many change initiatives is very tense. The leaders don't experience the emotional aftermath of the announced change initiative in the same way as the people who must implement the change. Everything remains very logical at the leader level. The vision is translated into a plan of attack by consultants and senior executives. The new strategies reflect the need to "do more with less," "work smarter, not harder," and "work together in teams." Team-building retreats produce transient bursts of cross-functional cooperation, but the reality of doing more with less is truly an oppressive experience for the people who must execute day to day.

I have seen this scenario play itself out in many places. While it appears to be the failure of a leader, it is a classic example of misapplying the *leadership process*.

Never has the challenge to lead been this way. Why doesn't a new vision produce results? Why are re-visions required? Why can't people understand word class? Why do people wait? Why are people afraid? The answer to these questions is simply the leader has selected the wrong process of leadership. Leaders must understand how to make the correct choice.

The Leadership Processes

Recall Chapter 4, which discusses change. There are three types of change (crisis, evolution, and transformation) and three levels of change (behavioral, cultural, and structural).

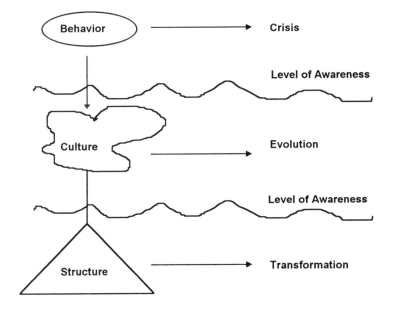

The leadership process is very different depending upon the *Context* of the circumstances. Many mistakes are made linking the process to the *Context*. The most common connections are links between crisis and behavior, evolution and culture, and transformation and structure. These are familiar processes of leadership. Let's examine them one at a time.

Crisis Leadership

The Crisis Leader is easy to recognize and widely acclaimed for heroic feats. The Lone Ranger saves the town from a crisis by eliminating the oppressors and restoring the peace. Likewise, many companies are confronted by an oppressive marketplace and seek the help of a Crisis Leader. Lee Iacocca quickly comes to mind. Losing sports teams search for new coaches. In almost every case, the initial focus is on changing *behavior*.

The Crisis Leader is a single person. Crisis Leaders must possess experience that exceeds their responsibility. This experience permits them to act immediately.

Crisis Leaders must know how to solve the problem with current reality. They must know how to quickly modify people's behavior. Quick action is generally required. People must be mobilized to meet the crisis at hand. Costs must be cut. Nonperformers must be immediately dispatched and new big hitters found. There is no time to worry about culture changes or changing "the Business of the BUSINESS." Action at the behavior level is needed *now*!

An organization in crisis is headed toward failure. Whether it is sports or business, the organization is losing more than it wins. The competitors appear invincible and the leader must have experience with similar situations. This is not a time for nice guys or wannabes. *Experience must exceed responsibility.*

The Crisis Leader arrives only after the existing leader is fired. The previous leader was blamed by the Board of Directors and stakeholders for the crisis. The deposed leader promised a turnaround a year ago and did not produce results. The enthusiasm from the whitewater rafting retreat is gone. Morale is low across the entire organization. The most recent quarterly results continued to decline. Something must be blamed, so it is the behavior of the ex-leader.

Crisis Leaders are unique people. They must have experience saving sinking ships. They must have charisma to immediately inspire and motivate people. Their own behavioral presence is critical to success. They must talk the talk of tough-minded discipline and be determined to purge the system of the problem. Everything that needs to change appears to be at the behavioral level. The promise of restoring the winning tradition is very appealing to the oppressed stakeholders.

There is nothing wrong with Crisis Leadership. Eighty percent of all leader-driven change initiatives start with a crisis. Mr. Iacocca was a no-nonsense person. He knew what needed to be done. The patient was terminally ill and drastic action was needed. The Crisis Leadership process works, and it requires a strong person to make it work. Without this form of leadership, many companies would fail and global peace would be in constant turmoil.

The Crisis Leader receives a lot of publicity. The crisis is often newsworthy and the leader is a hero. We all know how Franklin Roosevelt personally saved our country from the Great Depression. Winston Churchill saved Great Britain from the ravages of World War II. American history is full of heroes, and many leadership principles have been extracted and published from their performance. "When the going gets tough, the tough get going."

The downside of Crisis Leadership is that many Crisis Leaders continue to use the Crisis Leadership process long after the crisis is alleviated. They are masters at problem solving and don't know how to shift to a *creating* orientation.

Evolutionary Leadership

There are times when the only thing that occupies the leadership agenda is a midcourse correction. Numbers predict an impending crisis if the current operating environment is extended endlessly into the future. The trend lines are conclusive proof that a midcourse correction is necessary. There is no need to panic, but there is a need for change. The old management is often near retirement or at the end of their term. It's time for those who are being groomed to take over. Smooth transitions are planned, and the next Evolutionary Leader assumes control.

To be effective, the Evolutionary Leader must possess experience with most, if not all, of the areas of responsibility.

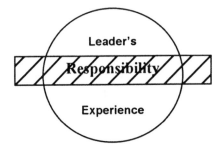

To execute the responsibility that remains outside of their experience, they can count on the past leader's advice, the management team for support, or "fake it until they make it." It's a sign of weakness for many people to admit that they aren't ready for the assignment. They, therefore, pretend to know or conduct lengthy fact-finding interviews to formulate the desired course corrections.

The domain of responsibility that lies outside the leader's experience is often known by consultants. New Evolutionary Leaders often employ large consulting firms to study the problems of the evolving organization and recommend new strategies to the leader. Anointed with the consultant's advice, the leader is now able to expand experience beyond responsibility and make effective evolutionary decisions.

The Evolutionary Leader promises to value the past and begins to change the culture to reflect more harmony, cooperation, and teamwork between divided factions. During the 1996 presidential election, Mr. Clinton persuaded the electorate to "stay the course" and "build a bridge to the future," and he insisted on a new spirit of "bipartisan cooperation"–evolutionary leadership.

Evolutionary Leaders do not go down in history as part of the elite. Evolutionary Leaders are not heroes. They have the benefit of time to think things through, study the trend lines, and plot a new course. The key to Evolutionary Leadership is *strategy*. Redeploying resources from the haves to the have-nots is a popular approach. In the corporate arena, I frequently see renewed commitment to training and developing people. There is always a conscious attempt to impact culture to affect change.

Evolutionary Leaders are often boring. They lack the charisma of Crisis Leaders. They calculate how new strategies lead to success as defined by "commonly accepted accounting practices." No one disagrees with balancing the budget. It's only a matter of who must suffer the loss to reestablish balance.

Evolutionary Leaders are masters of polarity management. Many mutually exclusive operating extremes can be used to arrive at success, and the

Evolutionary Leader is good at reversing the polarity of the existing culture. The current shift to empowerment is a classic Evolutionary Leadership strategy.

The illusion of Evolutionary Leadership is often in the intent of the process. While change initiatives are advertised to change the culture, the actual emphasis is on improving economics. Some Evolutionary Leaders communicate everything as in the spirit of teamwork. An Evolutionary Leader often has a strong back-to-basics mentality and the basics are typically grounded in Mass Production economics.

Evolutionary Leadership, practiced over long periods of time, leads to predictable intervals of leadership change. Most organizations, associations, and clubs have regularly scheduled leadership transitions. The outgoing president is recognized for outstanding progress during their term of office and the new leader promises to continue the tradition while rethinking strategies for continued success.

We all know the Evolutionary Leadership process. Many people avoid the process. Who wants to lead next year's membership campaign? Evolutionary Leadership is often burdensome, boring, and eventually arrives at the upper limit of achievement. The linear extension of growth eventually ends. The process will fail during someone's watch.

I worked with a company that had arrived at the fourth generation of Evolutionary Leadership. The pictures of the distinguished great-grandfather, grandfather, and father hung in the hallowed walls. The son had just assumed Evolutionary Leadership and he was terrified by the challenge of evolving the culture one more time. He was determined, however, that the company would not fail on his watch.

Evolutionary Leadership fails to recognize the need for Transformational Change. If dramatic changes are proposed, the changes are almost exclusively cultural. The evolutionary son promised to be friendlier to the union and started a reengineering project to change the culture.

Evolutionary Leaders frequently initiate new strategies toward customers. The trend lines of the company always reflect some customer dissatisfaction and neglect. The culture change is often justified to restore customer satisfaction. The new strategic plan typically contains a renewed commitment to exceeding customer expectations. The cultural emphasis is reinforced by a new slogan that promises customers service beyond their wildest dreams and to value people, "our most important asset." You know the drill, Evolutionary Leadership.

The New Leadership Mentality

We are all familiar with the Crisis and Evolutionary Leadership approaches. To use the currently popular phrase, "been there–done that." The challenge for leaders today is to properly diagnosis the situation and apply the correct leadership process.

When an organization realizes that something must change and new leadership is required, it is usually a result of *deteriorating conditions of current reality.* The vital signs of the organization reveal problems with the way it *is.* It is very important to understand that the typical activating mechanism for new leadership is a problem with current reality. Hopefully, it has not yet arrived at the crisis stage.

A new leader will typically arrive on the scene when the symptoms of the problem have been identified and are beyond the capability of the existing management to handle. The symptoms manifest as declining economic trends, customer dissatisfaction, and low employee morale. The new leader is expected to find the cause and eliminate it. Think for a moment about Chrysler, General Motors, Sears, IBM, your favorite sports team, your city, our Federal Government, or any entity that has experienced a need for new leadership. The circumstance that activates the need for leadership is *a problem.*

Our experience with leadership, therefore, is crisis-evolution-crisis-evolution-crisis-evolution. Most MBA courses teach students how to handle crisis times and how to manage, not lead, in evolutionary times–plan, organize, and control.

In the *Context* of Mass Production there doesn't appear to be a need for leadership when current reality is fine. If the organization is performing well, the talk is about how well the organization is being managed. Very few organizations perceive that the leader's role is vital until there are problems with current reality. As a result, many leaders invent problems and keep them alive and unsolved to establish the importance of their role. The bigger the problem, the greater the hero.

On the other hand, what if there is a need for leadership not because of a problem in current reality, but simply because there is a desire to be different in the future? (*Please reread the previous sentence. It is very important to grasp the significance of this question.*) The amazing characteristic of our current business environment is that both the *Context* and Content are changing. You can see this as a crisis to be reacted against, but the truth is this signals a desire to be different. When the *Context* changes, a Transformational Leadership process must be implemented.

By now, everyone is familiar with the mentality of the entrepreneur. Initially, they are perceived to be founders or creators rather than leaders. After their company is successful, they are referred to as leaders. Many, like Bill Gates of Microsoft, have replaced the icons of the industrial age as the leaders of our modern era. The leaders, founders, and creators of these companies don't start by trying to solve a problem with an existing organization. They *create* a different business from scratch. They don't wait for a crisis to occur, nor are they interested in the role of Evolutionary Leadership.

Thousands of interviews have been conducted with these modern-day entrepreneurs, and the driving force is always a vision of what's possible rather than eliminating unwanted circumstances in current reality or restoring the winning tradition. The new leadership mentality is a desire to be different.

The challenge, therefore, is for leaders *within an existing organization* to recognize the difference between fixing the current organization and creating a new "Business of the BUSINESS." This is the Transformational Leadership challenge.

On Being Different

One of the major leadership mistakes is in deciding *what* must be different. There are fundamentally two choices: the organization or the business.

An organization supports a business. The organization functions to execute "the Business of the BUSINESS." On the other hand, the business is defined by the activity performed with and for the customer. An automobile business and a pharmaceutical business are obviously very different businesses. Both, however, can have similar organizations.

The leadership challenge is whether to change the organization or change "the Business of the BUSINESS." The choice will be embodied in the vision.

Crisis Leaders usually change the organization. The behavioral orientation typically eliminates the cancer from the organization that is causing the crisis. However, the truth is the business, not the organization, is often failing.

Evolutionary Leaders always change the organization. The focus is on the cultural dynamics of how the organization functions. Organizational changes, such as centralization and decentralization, are typical Evolutionary Leader initiatives. "The Business of the BUSINESS" remains unchanged. Many Evolutionary Leaders reorganize the organization to establish complete control in the executive suite.

Key Point: • **The organization that exists to execute the organization is a bureaucracy.**

The leadership challenge is to recognize that the business of a Mass Customization business is *not* the same as the business of a Mass Production business. "The Business of the BUSINESS" is different. The business may still make automobiles, but the business *is different*. It is also true that the way the business is organized is different. Both the *Context* and Content are different.

Key Point: • **A business must be created before the organization of the business can occur. Changing the existing organization and expecting a different business to emerge is an illusion.**

Leaders, therefore, must begin by defining their business. They must then determine whether they need to change "the Business of the BUSINESS" or merely reorganize the organization. Both are legitimate leadership priorities. This is the single most important decision for leaders. The change initiatives will take two totally different directions depending on this defining moment.

The most recent reengineering revolution is a classic example of how this leadership mistake is made. Michael Hammer and James Champy, in their book *Reengineering the Corporation: A Manifesto for Business Revolution,*" are very clear that reengineering is about changing "the Business of the BUSINESS," not reengineering the organization of the corporation. Many reengineering efforts have been started to reengineer the organization that supports the business. This is a major mistake made by managers who misinterpreted Hammer and Champy's principle.

Transformational Leadership

Transformational Leaders are first and foremost *aware* that "the Business of the BUSINESS" must be changed and that all three levels of the existing organization (behavioral, cultural, and structural) must be transformed. They can see "below the water" of behavior and understand the powerful influences of culture. They understand that cultures are created by structural elements. The real *challenge of leadership* is not to solve the problems of current reality. Instead, the challenge is to create the structural framework that will cause a collective intelligence to form and produce the desired behavior of a new business.

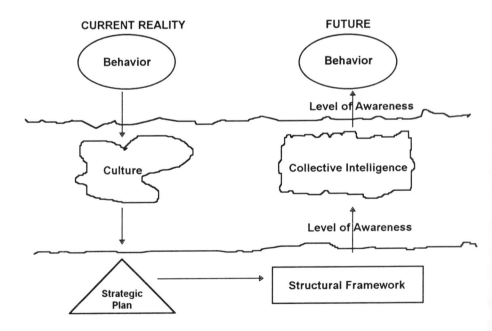

Transformational Leaders accept the chaos and ambiguity of current reality as the way it *is*. They know that over-analysis of the way it *is* can be interpreted as an organizational crisis which in turn activates the crisis mentality of those who want the behavior and culture changed. The crisis mentality will camouflage the need to change "the Business of the BUSINESS."

Transformational Leaders know that they must first create *structure* for the future to be built on a firm foundation. Consider our Founding Fathers. They did not see that uniting the states was a problem to be solved; rather, they created the Constitution as the structure on which the states could unite. When the future is properly structured, a collective intelligence will form to create the desired end result. The structure provides guidance to the people who must implement the change.

Transformational Leadership, therefore, is not about effort. It is not about being heroic. The Transformational Leader's role is to provide the structure that will cause the collective intelligence to form to create the future with confidence and commitment. The realism of the journey is far less important than the possibility of fulfilling the vision.

Transformational Leaders are very clear that their experience is often less than the responsibility entrusted to them. Their responsibility is to create a business and supporting organization that is different from what exists today. The responsibility is beyond the experience of any one person.

We can now see the major differences between Transformational and Crisis Leaders. Crisis Leaders constrain the organization to fit their own past experience. Transformational Leaders are able to let go of knowing it all and challenge everyone to experience a new reality. The Transformational Leader sees *people as people* to be enrolled in a journey. The Crisis Leader sees *people as assets* to be used to resist the forces of evil.

The primary skill of the Transformational Leader is to enroll the collective intelligence in the vision of the new business and encourage them to grow their experience to exceed the responsibility.

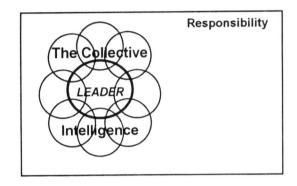

When President Kennedy announced the vision of landing a man on the moon, the experience of the collective intelligence was far less than the responsibility of the challenge.

Key Point: • **During times of Transformational Change, responsibility always exceeds experience. Not knowing how to perform is not a sign of weakness. You must learn to take action without knowing how.**

If the needed knowledge and skills are beyond the awareness of the collective intelligence, the entire group must be open to new experiences. As I suggest in Chapter 9, "Vision," a leader can use benchmarking and simulations to expand the awareness of the group to know what's possible. People must learn to take action toward the vision without knowing whether their actions will work. The environment is trial and error and the ability to learn is a critical skill.

We could draw many experience/responsibility models to illustrate what is currently happening in our business environment. The following figure provides one example.

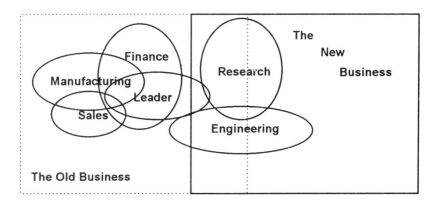

In this example, the leader's experience overlaps the experience of all the functional groups. The leader must somehow pull the finance, manufacturing, and sales groups into the reality of the new business. Research and engineering are already aware, but the operating divisions are often unaware of the possibilities of being different.

Try to draw an experience/responsibility map for your organization. It doesn't have to be right. It is an interesting step in creating awareness and alignment between functional groups. The process is fun to watch, and it is a great Transformational Leadership exercise.

Simple – Not Easy

Many executives feel that creating structure isn't tough enough. "Leadership should be hard work." "The Board Room agenda is about war and how to defeat the enemy." Again, Transformational Leadership is not about solving a problem with current reality. It is not about eliminating the oppressor and saving the oppressed. Transformational Leadership is about creating new ways of doing business and new organizations to support those businesses.

The Transformational Leadership process is *simple*! It is not, however, *easy* to do. Frankly, it is the toughest assignment any leader can undertake. As I have said before, very few people have any experience with the process. Think how hard it would be to play professional golf if you have no experience with golf. It's absurd! The muscle memory of the Transformational Leadership process does not exist within the Mass Production models of the past. The existing muscle memory knows only how to deal with crisis and evolutionary change. Very few leaders have the muscle memory that is needed in the new business environment.

The most difficult aspect of Transformational Leadership is tolerating *delayed consequences of immediate action*. The problem-solving mind expects immediate relief from pain. When we act to solve a problem, we want immediate results. The *now-now* expectation between action and results is very addictive.

The transformation process contains a *now-later* mechanism. Creating structure does not produce immediate results at the behavioral level. It takes time for the collective intelligence to form and create mechanisms that enable new behavior. It took nine years to land a man on the moon. The old adage "Rome wasn't built in a day" is a constant reminder of working and living with delayed consequences from today's actions. What you do today, however, will determine what you will be 10 years from now.

It is important to realize that Transformational Leadership is a critical agenda. Our Federal Government must be transformed. Mr. Clinton himself declared, "The era of big government is over." Yet, we continue to see the Evolutionary Leadership process being applied. "A bridge to the future?" What's the vision for the future? If our leaders were transformational, would they create new structure? Does that include a Constitutional Amendment to balance the budget? Can you hear the debate about using a Transformational or Evolutionary Leadership process? It is an awesome responsibility to create new structure. It's easier to raise or lower taxes, save Social Security, change the culture of those on welfare, defend our traditional values, and survive for four more years.

The argument is always that leadership is leadership and we are talking semantics. The strategy battles of either/or thinking will always result in the death of either *or* or. One is wrong, the other right. Turn on your television tonight, watch Crossfire, and listen to the left and the right.

Key Point: • **Transformational Leadership is not about right *or* wrong. It's about *and!***

The world appears flat *and* it is round. There is a market for both round *and* flat world boats. The leaders of Aztec boats need to decide what business they are in *and* create "the Business of the BUSINESS." It is possible for Aztec to make *both* types of boats, but they cannot make round world boats if they only see a flat world.

Our business environment needs Transformational Leaders. Main frames *and* laptops, big cars *and* small cars, insurance *and* financial planning, banking *and* investments, quantity *and* quality, individual *and* team, mass *and* customized, low cost *and* high value, local *and* global. How many change initiatives could we list where the *Context* has changed and either/or thinking still dominates the leader's mind? That's the way problem solving, Mass Production Thinkers think. They aren't wrong. They are technologically obsolete.

The Context Has Changed

Wake up leaders! The era of Mass Customization has arrived. Technological obsolescence is everywhere. The organizationless business is a reality. The Internet is making traditional selling obsolete. The *Context* shift is dramatic and permanent. It is not a passing fad.

Regardless of how you perceive the new realities, *they are not problems to be solved*. It is not possible to evolve the culture of the existing organization to achieve these new realities. The challenge is to create a different business and organize the business to be a seamless, responsive partner with customers. To create the future you will need to become a Transformational Leader.

I am not suggesting that the future will not require Crisis Leaders. There will be crises and a need for heroes. Our Federal Government will continue to evolve. Leaders will appear to deal with these situations as they occur. The existing challenge, however, is to learn the process of Transformational Leadership to *create the future* because you want it *to be different*.

Chapter 8
Technology

As companies approach the future, leaders must be consciously aware of the technology their employees will use to produce the desired future state. The technology? Yes, there are two choices: the Technology of Problem-solving or the Technology of Creating.[a] Both are useful and important in organizational life, but seldom do organizations distinguish between the two.

The Technology of Problem-solving[a]

Problem-solving technology is focused on current reality. The current reality of any organization contains many problems. A problem by definition is *an undesirable condition that exists in current reality.* Problems activate negative emotions that are the result of judgment and polarized thinking. Polarization confirms that something is right or wrong with the way it is in current reality. Judgment quickly establishes the cause as a person or the people closest to the problem.

Many problems exist because of *enoughness* addiction. "We don't have enough sales, profits, output, customers, or people." Because enough is seldom accurately defined, most organizations arrive at the state of *too much.* Costs are too high, customer expectations are beyond reasonable, or there are too many people and there is a need to downsize. There are thousands of examples of problems that exist in the current reality of any organization.

Key Point: • **Problems are the *aftermath of yesterday.***

A problem cannot exist unless yesterday occurred. When an organization is focused on problems, it is inherently reactive. In any Fortune 500 company, hundreds of meetings are held each day to address problems. Some problems are severe. Chrysler had 600,000 autos in stock that customers would not buy.

---

[a] Organizational Technologies for Creating is a registered trade mark of Robert Fritz, Technologies for Creating, Inc. For additional reading on the subject of creating versus problem solving, see Robert Fritz's books *The Path of Least Resistance: Learning to Become the Creative Force in Your Own Life* and *Creating.*

Inventory is the result of yesterday, and *not enough* and *too much* are the agendas for every problem-solving meeting.

Problem-solving technology, therefore, starts with current reality and looks backward to yesterday for the cause of the problem. Problem-solving technology is *cause and effect* oriented. If the cause can be located and fixed or eliminated, the problem won't reoccur.

Problem-solving often requires great analytical skills. Experts examine the problems of current reality and categorize and document cause and effect relationships. Many problem situations can be reduced to mathematical formulas, diagnostic procedures, and prescriptive solutions. We all seek the advice of cause and effect experts. When our body is sick, we go to the doctor. When our car doesn't run, we are relieved to find the mechanic that can diagnose the cause of the problem.

Libraries are full of books on the Technology of Problem-solving. Physics, engineering, and science courses teach the predictability of cause and effect relationships. Problem-solving technology is an integral part of the customer offering of every business.

We have all been trained in problem-solving techniques. MBA students have been given case studies from past organizational experiences and asked to determine a course of action to solve the problem. In most cases, there is a "correct" answer because the experience from the past is known and some level of right and wrong can be used for comparison. We, therefore, see the sophisticated application of problem-solving technology as the driving force for most educational experiences.

When problems remain unsolved for long periods, people activate three predictable strategies to make the problem go away: determination, willpower, and conflict manipulation. We have all experienced the application of these three approaches. Determination is when the going gets tough, the tough get going. Willpower is a form of determination, but it is polarized toward deprivation. Conflict manipulation intensifies the conflict of the problem to stimulate action from those who should be solving it. Conflict manipulators use negative visions, "if you don't, you won't" or "if we don't, we'll fail." Problem-solving organizations always have fires to fight and lack enough time to learn new skills.

There are those who are calm and collected when confronted with problems. They attempt to resolve problems in an orderly manner using logical, methodical, rational approaches. Time, however, always creates urgency for action and often defeats the orderly approach.

Key Point: • **Constant problem-solving produces a dominating, negative emotion in employees.**

We have learned to attach blame to those who cause problems. Attitude surveys conducted in problem-solving organizations generally reveal low morale and poor customer relationships. Celebrating success is deferred until the problems are solved, and solutions seldom coincide with programmed celebrations. The national sales meeting is a time to celebrate, *but* sales results are still not good enough!

We have all lived and worked in a problem-solving environment. Further descriptions of the conditions and scenarios that exist will only increase your tension about the reality. The key is to recognize that the problem-solving environment is not a function of personalities; instead, it is the result of the acute application of problem-solving technology.

Key Point: • **Problem-solving resolves the problems of yesterday, but it does not necessarily create anything.**

Problem-solving is the wrong approach if the future requires that the organization be totally different from current reality. It is important to understand that problem-solving, as a technology, is linear at best. In most cases, it is merely restorative. The problem-solving mind is always thinking *back to basics*, restoring a time from the past when things worked.

The problem-solving orientation seeks to identify the cause of the problem and attempts to eliminate it. The cause of most problems, however, is seldom in close proximity to the effect in space or time. A person's poverty is not caused by the environment in which they live. It is caused by their conditioned consciousness and the resulting choices that the person integrated years before the poverty appeared.

The cause of our current organizational dilemma is not the work ethic of the people or information technology. These are merely symptoms. The cause is the *Context* of Mass Production Thinking, the conditioned consciousness of the organization that dominates the assumptions, beliefs, policies, procedures, and strategies of the organization. People frequently identify performance problems in organizations and explain the problem as "this is the way we've always done it." Old assumptions become rules, cultural norms, and ultimately lead to problems.

Key Point: • **The cause of most organizational problems is not in close proximity to the effect in space or time.**

Because the cause of the modern business problem is far removed from the effects we experience, Transformational Change cannot be accomplished using problem-solving technology. We know the cause is the Mass Production *Context* that has dominated our thinking for years. It isn't wrong, and it cannot be eliminated. The fact is Mass Production Thinking will not go away. We, therefore, must learn new thinking and program new beliefs to transform the organization. New learning is not problem-solving. It is *creating*.

The Technology of Creating[a]

Creating is the process of bringing into being something that doesn't exist in current reality. Creating is a verb and is frequently confused with the adjective *creative* or the noun *creativity*. The process of creating starts with a vague notion of a desired end result. The notion incubates until desire translates into action. The action of bringing the desired end result into being is called *creating*.

In the organizational *Context*, the desired end result may initially manifest as an idea how to solve a problem associated with current reality. The idea, however, is about doing things differently. This is the first stage of the creating process. If the idea survives the "yeah but" cynics, it is translated into a vision or a goal statement. Accurately formulated, it answers the question, "What do we want to *be* in the future?"

Many creations are the result of problems with current reality. People realize that current reality is insufficient and that problem-solving doesn't lead to the desired results. They, therefore, choose to create something new or different rather than fix current reality. If, for example, the employees of an organization have outgrown their office space, they can choose to create a new corporate office building. Some will say they solved the problem by building a new office. The truth is they created what they wanted that didn't exist in current reality. In the process, the old building was not eliminated or destroyed. If it was, demolition was a step in the process of creating the new building.

The desire to create does not need to be linked to a problem with current reality. You are a creation of your parents, and you were created because they wanted you.

Key Point: • Many people create because they want to create.

The thought process of creating does not concern itself with cause and effect relationships. The thinking of creators is focused on taking action toward the desired future state rather than eliminating unwanted circumstances.

The creating process is simple to understand. It is not easy to do. Creating takes time. It requires commitment to accurately picture the desired result. The picture is referred to as a vision. Many visions are initially vague–be world class, the industry leader, or operationally excellent. It is very difficult to take action toward creating an end result that is vague or idealistic.

Creating often requires that people take action without knowing how to do something. Inventors are creating. They are not necessarily creative. They employ trial and error over long periods of time. If they create often enough, a level of creativity develops. When the inventor combines creativity while creating, innovation results.

It is important to distinguish between creating and creativity. Creating is the antecedent, and creativity is the consequence. Children begin by creating. They scribble with crayons. Parents typically judge the creativity of the drawing and challenge the child to color within the lines. The child creates another drawing and this time tries to be a little more creative (or stay within the lines). As the process continues, the child learns to create within the rules of the lines. A child who creates only to receive approval from the parent, will be restricted from creating what is possible.

The same scenario plays itself out in many organizations. People learn to apply their creativity within the lines. The rules of Mass Production Thinking are well established. The rules, however, define current reality and restrict creativity to problem-solving within current reality. The rules from the past will extinguish the creating process.

Many creating initiatives start with enthusiasm and ceremony. Bands play and motivational speakers exhort people to reengineer. Creating can be quickly killed, however, by speculation or realistic thinking. The paradox of either/or thinking generally dominates the initial mind-set of most participants in the creating process. People judge the probability of success and quickly conclude that it's not realistic for conditions in current reality to ever change.

Key Point: • **Creating is a deterministic process.**

People must be willing to take action toward the desired end result and then *determine* what to do next. This trial and error approach does not lead to instant results. This is very different from the planning regime of most organizations. Planners attempt to determine the orderly process of arriving at the future in advance. Creators take action toward the desired vision and determine what to do next after each step. Planning is important; however, in the creating process planning is often a useless activity.

In the creating orientation, people must be willing to take action without fear of failure or reprisal from management. Creating organizations are driven by positive emotions and commitment. This type of environment is frequently present in entrepreneurial organizations. When people are creating, they are inspired by the process. The culture is typically collective and holistic. They have little fear of failure, and the leader rewards people for ideas and learning.

Key Point: • **Creating is not a linear extension of current reality.**

Some of the elements of a new creation may appear similar to what exists in current reality, but everything will likely be different. A computer is not a typewriter. Computers are different even though the keyboard and printed documents are similar. To create a computer it is helpful, but not necessary, to start with the typewriter.

In our lives, we naturally and instinctively create and solve problems. Both technologies are useful. The key is to consciously select the technology that will produce the desired end result. If the future of your organization must be different from what it is today, you must employ the Technology of Creating.

Transformational Change

The future you are about to experience cannot be solved into existence. Your problem-solving skills are useless in creating a web site. The new *Context* is about creating a Mass Customization business. It is about creating wholeness of process within the minds of your employees. The interaction dynamic that is required is teamwork.

Key Point: •   **Teamwork is a very natural process when people are creating together.**

The new *Context* is about possibilities and awareness. You must take action toward the desired vision of Mass Customization, irrespective of the realism of that vision. From the perspective of current reality, the existing organization has many problems. Many people judge that it is not realistic for the business to be all things to all people. This perception is based upon the reality of Mass Production Thinking. The tension around this reality is very frustrating for the problem solver. On the other hand, the creator is willing to undertake the possibility of creating the desired end result and easily enters into a new mode of learning.

The new *Context* of business is about the possibility of creating a Mass Customization business. Nothing suggests that Mass Customization is a solution to the problems of your current reality. Mass Production isn't wrong. It works and will continue to serve the needs of many organizations. You can continually improve the Mass Production organization. However, if you want to create a team-based, cross-functional, seamless, empowered, partnering organization, you must understand that this reality is not a linear extension of Mass Production Thinking. This future state must be created. One thing is certain–fixing the old organization to participate in the new business environment is the wrong work.

Chapter 9
Vision

Leadership and Vision somehow go together like apple pie and ice cream. At least every time I ask participants in leadership classes to describe the attributes of a leader, the first answer is visionary.

It is easy to talk about Vision, but it is the most difficult thing for many executives to create. This chapter, therefore, is about the process of creating a Vision and helping you understand the importance of the process.

What Is "It"?

Vision is a picture of a *future state of being*. A Vision can exist in the mind of a person long before the actual process of creating the Vision begins. Children are asked what they want to be at early ages. Their dream often incubates for years. After the Vision is translated into a *desire*, the process of achieving the Vision begins. Some people can see themselves achieving a level of existence way beyond their current reality. They can see the entire environment in vivid detail.

Technically, Vision is the dominant antecedent for the *process of creating*. An antecedent is something that must precede or exist before action is taken to create. The process of creating brings into being *the state of being* that is visualized.

A Vision is not required to solve a problem. Problem solving is reactive and restorative. If you break a window and cold air is filling your home, you do not need a Vision to begin the process of fixing the window.

However, you do need a Vision to land a man on the moon, be America's car company, or be an integrated society. President John F. Kennedy, Lee Iacocca, and Martin Luther King were visionary leaders because they created Visions to activate the process of creating.

A Vision is the picture on the box of a jigsaw puzzle. Consider the laborious task of putting together a puzzle without benefit of the box top. Worse yet, picture a jigsaw puzzle where all the pieces are white and the title on the box top is Snow Storm.

Creating or crafting a Vision appears to be the domain or responsibility of a leader. It seems like such lofty work. Vision, however, is an inherent part of everyone's daily activity. How many times have you said, "I need to figure it out"? You need to figure out what you want to do in life. You need to figure out where you want to live. All people have worked at figuring it out thousands of times in their life. When people say, "We need to figure it out," I immediately ask them, "what is *it*?" This always draws an immediate stare as if I have insulted their intelligence, but it is an important question. What is *it*? They are looking for a Vision of *it* to start the creating process. Without a Vision of *it*, people wait.

A leader of a very high profile business confided in me that he was frustrated trying to figure out what *it* was the organization need to do in the future. I asked him to consider what the organization needed *to be* rather than *to do*. He was confused by my statement. Vision is a picture about *being* not *doing*. Recall the puzzle box top. The picture on the box shows what will be when you are finished doing. People who try to figure out what they want to do seldom consider what they want to be.

What is *it*? *It is a state of being. It* must be expressed in the form of being. You must do "to be," not do "to do." Vision must, therefore, be expressed in a being form. The leader mentioned earlier had never considered the difference. Being must precede doing. Vision is an antecedent. Without the Vision of being, the doing may be misguided and take the organization in the wrong direction.

Finally, a Vision must be specific. In the initial phase of Vision development, all Visions manifest as vague notions of possible states of being. We often hear executives say they want to be "world class," successful, the industry leader, or profitable. These are great desires, but they are vague. What does world class mean in specific terms?

One leader I was working with told his people the company needed to be world class. For 14 months, his employees worked diligently trying to create what they thought he meant by world class. It wasn't happening. He was frustrated, and the people were frustrated by the constant pressure of creating without the box top. Finally, I suggested the leader draw a picture of world class for everyone. Using a marker, he drew the following crude picture on a flip chart:

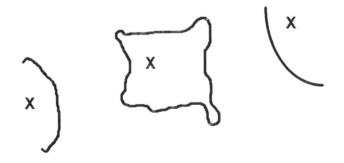

The Xs represented fully autonomous divisions in Asia, the United States, and Europe. "That's world class!" His employees responded, "Why didn't you tell us that 14 months ago?" Armed with a specific Vision, they immediately begin to figure out how to create *it*.

What's Possible

A Vision is a picture of a *future state of being*. Two questions confront leaders as they begin formulating a Vision: what's possible and what's realistic?

Possibility emanates from *desire*, and realism emanates from *past experience*. Many people are not aware of what's possible. They are very aware that current reality does not contain sufficient resources. Therefore, it isn't realistic to want things that are currently unaffordable. Possibilities are not dependent upon the sufficiency of current reality. Creating what's possible never starts with money. It always starts with desire.

Key Point: • **Vision must be translated into a desire. People must want to be what the Vision defines.**

When leaders communicate a Vision, they must transcend the judgmental, skeptical, cynical realism of current reality and seek to identify the possibilities of the future. This is such a simple thought. Yet, during most organizational changes, the realists are typically in charge of the organization and are determined to keep the problems of current reality alive and unsolved. This is called job security.

Key Point: • **Those who apply realism in pursuit of Visions seldom succeed.**

Two years ago, the president of a large company announced a new Vision. It was, admittedly, a little vague, but it contained some excellent descriptions of a future state of being. There was sufficient detail to help all the executives craft a Vision for their own division in alignment with the big picture. One division was dominated by realistic thinkers. While they openly embraced the new Vision, the Vision that they crafted for their division was merely a new plan of how to solve the problems of the marketplace faster, cheaper, and better. The plan was a more determined strategy to lower cost and achieve operational excellence. The realism of current reality prevented them from seeing the *possibilities of being different in the future*.

Key Point: • **Being realistic is a debilitating disease.**

Think about how many people must have told Christopher Columbus, "It's not realistic." Leaders themselves even doubt the realism of their own Visions. Thousands of athletes never achieve their potential in life because someone reminded them everyday, "It's not realistic to be an Olympic champion."

What's possible? What a great question. It is very refreshing to work with executives who are interested in possibility thinking. Again, there are many books on the subject. Many psychologists have accurately documented the positive emotional engagement of people who are in this mode of thinking.

To be a possibility thinker, you must perceive that there is a world of abundance. The realist in you is driven by a world of scarcity mentality. We all are capable of *both* ways of thinking. Neither way is right or wrong. Both have valid applications.

The world of abundance mind-set suggests that the genesis for all creations already exists. All the buildings, cars, roads, and possessions that we have in this country were not brought to America by the Pilgrims. Neither were they stored in the homes of Native Americans. However, all the resources for their creation were already here when the Pilgrims arrived. Things are created as the awareness of people grows, enabling them to create cars, boats, planes, and buildings. The process is obviously called inventing, and inventors are clear there is a world of abundance. Sculptors can see the statue within the block of granite.

The world of abundance mind-set is an absolute prerequisite for Transformational Leadership. The leader must be able to see possibilities and express those possibilities in the Vision for the company or organization.

It is, however, a common dilemma that leaders are not aware of what's possible, or their views do not extend far enough to reflect the possibilities 10 years in the future. This dilemma creates the opportunity for futurists to practice their trade and help people perceive the possibilities of someday living on Mars.

In running today's modern business organization, it is often frustrating to be too futuristic. While it would be nice to be able to see 20 years in the future, it is often frustrating to think that far ahead. The people who are responsible for day-to-day operations must have a shorter term view in which to operate. Technological obsolescence is rampant and very few futurists can accurately access what they don't know.

With the world of abundance and the positive emotions of possibility thinking, the leader or leadership of any organization can begin the process of crafting a Vision. However, the key is *it does not have to be realistic, and it does not have to be created by next week*. It will take time. It may take a year. If there isn't a crisis to be solved, there is plenty of time.

Using Benchmarks, Metaphors, and Simulations

Crafting a Vision from nothing is almost impossible. Therefore, it is important to use other reference points to help establish what's possible. There are two very effective ways of crafting a Vision: benchmarking and simulation.

The benchmarking process examines other companies, organizations, or processes that are similar to the way you would like to *be*. The benchmark does not have to be in a similar industry or field as long as you look at it from a structural point of view. You could benchmark how our Founding Fathers created the United States of America. Your findings would reveal the Constitution as the bedrock of the process. You could then ask your executive group to spend time creating a constitution for your company.

Many companies have performed benchmark studies in the past 10 years *looking for solutions to problems*. Again, this is the wrong approach. You must examine the structure of the organization being benchmarked to find what they have that you must create. Do not be deceived by observing behavior and culture alone. The answers are in the *structure*.

One of my clients initiated a massive benchmark study. Observers were sent to 15 world class companies in seven different industries. Thousands of pages were boiled down to an executive summary that in essence said, "We must be a kinder, gentler company." In other words, "We must change our culture." The study totally missed the mark and the company is still in search of excellence.

If you benchmark, know how to listen for and observe structure. Document the structural redesign that occurred as the benchmark company achieved world class status. The structural elements will always be the same.

Another effective way of benchmarking is to use metaphors. Metaphorical benchmarking is intentionally comparing your company to a dissimilar organization or entity to extract similarities and differences to expand awareness. I use professional golf as a metaphor of a perfect world against which every company can compare hundreds of behavioral, cultural, and structural issues. Is professional golf perfect? Of course not, but it is certainly based upon a *Context* of win-win-win-win that would benefit every company.

The metaphor of nature is also a good one. Companies that compare their process to nature will quickly learn the law of entropy. In nature, it is called survival of the fittest and effortless effectiveness. Teamwork and partnering are processes intended to create effortlessness.

Metaphorical benchmark results do not always apply to the *Context* of business. There is nothing in the process that suggests there is a perfect metaphor. The process merely challenges executives to think outside the realism of the past and be aware of what's possible in a universe where apparent perfection exists. The process is always effective in revealing *possibilities*.

Another effective way of examining possibilities is to use a simulation. With the advent of computers, researchers have been able to set up simulated models of nuclear explosions and budget balancing scenarios. The simulation does not have to be right or accurate. The simulation must reveal possibilities. From the possibilities, leaders can make choices in directing current reality toward or away from projected end results.

Simulators are widely used in teaching airline pilots to fly new airplanes. Within the simulator, the pilot can *experience the possibilities* and be prepared to handle the real-life situations in a calm, collected way. The Apollo astronauts were put through simulated space flight to prepare for going to the moon. As we all know, even the most brilliant scientist cannot anticipate or be aware of what they don't know.

Launching the Journey–Commitment to Begin

Crafting a Vision, therefore, must be a dynamic process. The leader must begin with the vague notion of what's possible and launch the journey forward irrespective of realism and clarity. The only thing that is certain is the *desire to be different*.

Transformational Change should be undertaken when things are fine. One of my clients had just completed the best year in their history. When the leaders assembled for a strategic planning session, they were all of the mind-set, "it's not broke, don't fix it." I assured them that this was an accurate perspective, but I suggested that when it isn't broke is the time to begin to transform it. This was strange to their problem-solving minds until we examined their assumption that nothing succeeds like success and found the truth that nothings fails like success. Again, the metaphorical benchmarks of nature and golf revealed this reality.

Transformational Change must begin. This is a very important concept. You must *begin* the journey. You cannot wait until the crisis occurs.

Beginning is very different in the Crisis, Evolutionary, and Transformational Change approaches. Crisis Leaders begin by eliminating something. Evolutionary Leaders begin by reviewing the past and challenging people to make it better. Transformational Leaders begin by creating the structural framework that will inspire collective intelligence to create toward a new Vision.

Transformational Leaders have control of the speed of the transformational process. They can proceed at whatever rate they desire. Because there isn't a crisis to be solved, there isn't anything to react against. Remember that everything is fine. From the perspective of realistic thinking, there is a sense of urgency. The Transformational Leader is aware that the competitive advantage of the company will be easily matched if the organization doesn't move forward in the process. Transformational Change, therefore, can happen very quickly if people are properly enrolled in the process.

The Transformational Leader knows that the muscle memory of the old culture is strong. From the metaphor of golf, the muscle memory of the old swing will not be easily replaced. It takes time to create new muscle memory and it comes from *practice* (not only practice, but perfect practice). Therefore, the new beginning for the Transformational Leader is to institutionalized practice. I have suggested that people commit to practice together for one hour a week to create the envisioned state of being. One hour a week? That's not enough time! Enough is not the agenda. The agenda is *commitment to begin*.

Several examples will help you understand that commitment to begin is critical to Transformational Change. This activates the law of exponential results.

If you commit to save one cent today and double the amount every day for 30 days, you will have approximately $10,737,417. If you commit to do one sit-up and double the number every day for 30 days, you will be doing the same number of sit-ups. The key is commit to begin.

I was working with a manufacturing plant that had struggled with union problems for 30 years. The plant was in terrible shape both physically and economically. The parent corporation had threatened to close the plant if the labor problems couldn't be resolved. You know the drill. I suggested that the situation required a transformational approach. Four Crisis Leaders had failed to solve the problem.

We assembled the plant management team and the union bargaining committee and used a simulation to help them visualize what was *possible*. From the possibility perspective everyone agreed that a world class plant would provide everyone what they wanted–win-win-win-win. The simulation was a struggle for the realistic minds. Thirty years of adversarial relationships was deeply imbedded in muscle memory.

We identified a list of critical success factors of a world class plant. We prioritized the list to reveal "the low-hanging fruit." The problem solvers always look for easy things to eliminate. While the real opportunity was to create trust in intentions, I realized the transformational process must begin with something as simple as saving one penny.

The plant was filthy. There were papers and trash everywhere outside the building. Everyone agreed, a world class plant would not look that way. Everyone disagreed on who should clean up the mess. Because the mess was outside the building, it wasn't a part of the union contract. The clean up should be contracted with an outside landscape maintenance organization.

The filthy habits had spilled over to the plant. There were cigarette butts on the production floors, paper left on tables in the cafeteria, and many other apparent housekeeping issues. The housekeeping issues had spilled over to neglect of safety rules. People refused to wear steel-toed shoes or safety glasses and the list went on. The Crisis Leaders had fired those who neglected published safety rules, leading to 27 pending union grievances on safety matters alone.

To make a long story short, I suggested that a world class plant was possible if they were willing to begin. The beginning I defined was to clean the plant and create a safe environment. Everyone agreed to the need. Very few, however, were willing to begin. Beginning to them appeared to be more of the same old confrontational process. I told them the one-cent story and asked if they would take action toward world class even though the process appeared to be too small in scope. Everyone agreed.

I asked them all, union and management together, to go outside the building and pick up one piece, not two pieces, of paper and bring it in and put it in the wastebasket. Reluctantly, they did it. I suggested that no one should be fired or file a grievance as a result of picking up one piece of paper. It was common courtesy. I also asked them to *commit* to continue the process and double the amount of paper picked up everyday for 30 days. In other words, pick up two pieces of paper tomorrow, four the next, eight the next, and so on. I also suggested they *enroll* one additional person per day in the process of creating a world class plant by asking them to join in the clean-up process.

I hope you see the process. *Commitment to begin.* The end of the story was predictable. The plant manager called me and said the three magic words, "you can't believe." The plant was clean in seven days. I can believe. I've seen it happen many times. People linking behavior to structure will create a collective intelligence to create what they want. In this case, everyone wanted the security of a world class plant and were willing to take action to *create it.*

Live no illusion, the low-hanging fruit is easy to pick. The Transformational journey gets tougher and will always test the will to continue.

Translating Possibility Into Realism

In his book *Paradigms: The Business of Discovering the Future*, Joel Arthur Barker said it best. "Vision without action is but a dream. Action without Vision is passing time. Vision with action can change the world."

The Vision is the antecedent. It gets the journey started. People will begin with vague notions of an idealistic state of being. The journey starts with possibility and becomes realistic as people take action. This is a critical role of the Transformational Leader. Everything must be linked to the initial Vision. The Vision will remain a dream if action toward the Vision is not taken.

Therefore, the next step in the *beginning* process is to enroll people in creating the structural framework. Creating the structural elements requires that people take action. They must work together to define all elements of a successful journey. The process inspires people to see the journey as realistic. The possibility thinking turns into realistic strategies for change. The entire process accelerates quickly as collective intelligence builds.

Vision is the first structural element. It liberates people, if only for a moment, from the paralyzing grip of current reality. The Transformational Leader realizes the enormous power in the words "just suppose." These two words coupled with "you could be that" have inspired thousands of people to achieve great things. It all starts with a Vision of *what's possible.*

Chapter 10
Competitive Advantage

The strategic imperative of organizational change is competitive advantage. Businesses must compete. Change is needed to improve or transform the competitive advantage of the company.

Key Point: • **If you accurately define how the competitive advantage must change, everyone will understand the strategic imperative for change and be committed to fulfill their role in the process.**

There is massive confusion as to what constitutes the competitive advantage of any organization. I have asked executive groups of all kinds, "What is the competitive advantage of your organization?" The answers typically include
- Our people
- Quality products
- Service
- Fifty years of experience
- Our branch locations
- Our sales people are all college graduates
- Price
- Convenience
- Innovative technology.

This list contains most of the elements that companies have recognized as important for years.

The answer to the next question, however, focuses on the problem. "Does this competitive advantage still set you apart from competition today?" The answer is always *no*! In almost every case the competitive advantage has been matched or eclipsed by competition. Even innovative technology has been copied. What was protected with a patent for years, has been modified, reverse engineered, and changed.

The stimulus for organizational change, therefore, is caused by the erosion of the competitive position of the company. Sales begin to slump and customer satisfaction declines. The challenge to the competitiveness of the organization creates urgency for action. The answer is a change initiative.

Most change initiatives aimed at improving the competitive advantage further assume that the solution is to lower cost or improve quality. However, cost and quality are merely parts of a much larger issue. The advantage today goes to those companies with which it is easy to do business. Cost and quality are expected. Today, more than ever, words such as seamless, responsive, and flexible define the relationships that customers want. The exhaustion and frustration around the issue of business relationships is at the core of the need for change.

The "at War" Approach

Books have been published about the marketing strategy wars between Coke and Pepsi, Ford and General Motors, and IBM and the rest of the computer giants. The challenge of foreign competition to our manufacturing might is a war that continues to this day.

The "at war" approach sets up a negative *Context* in the organization. Survival is at stake. The focus is on defeating the enemy. This mentality creates a reactive orientation that cannot be alleviated until the war is won.

Key Point: • **The dominant thought in winning the competitive advantage war is reflected in "ER" words.**

When a company is "at war," something must be bigg*er*, bett*er*, fast*er*, small*er*, cheap*er*, strong*er*, saf*er*, high*er*, deep*er*, wid*er*, low*er*, or tall*er*. To achieve the desired "ER" result everyone needs to work smarter, not harder.

Key Point: • **"ER" thinking is comparative.**

Thinking "ER" will only cause the company to seek comparative increases or decreases in the existing competitive *Context*. "We must fight fire with fire." "Where's the beef?" "Our burger is bigger and juicer." The comparative battles are fun to watch and at times do create significant consumer appeal.

Another strategy of the "at war" approach is to outflank the competition. This approach seeks to differentiate your offering from the competitions'. The intent is to be different. "Tastes great–less filling."

Most attempts at differentiation begin within the realm of products or services. Highly differentiated products are unique in quality, technology, or functionality. Service differentiation typically focuses on speed, amenities, and convenience. In most cases, the differences can be observed and easily matched by your "ER" competitors.

This phenomenon has led many executives to refer to the Board Room as the War Room. The exhaustive strategic planning processes of the last decade are testimony to the importance placed on finding the competitive edge.

Shifting from Product to Process

Starting in the mid- to late-1980s, the search for competitive advantage shifted from visible to invisible factors. The quality revolution raised the level of quality to unprecedented heights. Product improvement opportunities appeared to be exhausted. Many companies finally realized that the leverage point was in *relationships.*

Key Point: • **The emphasis shifted from products to processes. Building integrated relationships to create competitive advantage was the beginning of the end of Mass Production dominance.**

The Japanese appeared to achieve differentiation using quality circles. The relationship revolution was on. The focus shifted to process improvement through teamwork, reengineering, and partnerships. The simultaneous development of local-area network systems enabled people to communicate in much different ways.

Key Point: • **Within the Mass Production *Context*, the focus of the relationship revolution was to eliminate waste, improve performance, reduce cost, and solve problems.**

It is important to understand that the *Context* of the relationship and process improvement revolution is still Mass Production (see Chapter 2 for more information about the concept of *Context*). Thousands of Total Quality Management (TQM) initiatives tried to change the "Thinkers think and Doers do" model of Mass Production. As TQM approached the executive suites, the message was often, "senior leaders must walk the talk." This was an enormous threat to Mass Production Thinkers with years of invested experience in autocratic command and control approaches.

Key Point: • **Many TQM initiatives brought the executive suites unwanted problems. The fix the factory mentality backfired into fix the Thinkers.**

The Mass Production *Context* masked the purpose of many TQM initiatives. The competitive advantage was eroding or had been totally eclipsed and the company was now embroiled in relationship blame. We've seen it and it still exists today. The partnering revolution is being played within a highly adversarial *Context.* "Lower your cost 10% or we'll find another vendor." The implication was that the vendors were the cause of all the problems. "Oh, by the way, improve the quality while you're at it!" No attempt was made to understand the impact of lower cost on the supplier. "Just do it."

The need to lower cost and improve quality further exacerbates the need to eliminate people and do more with less. This vicious circle drives the search for competitive advantage within the Mass Production *Context*.

There are as many prescriptions to this dilemma as there are War Room meetings. Hundreds of ideas have been volunteered by employees. Cost reduction and waste elimination techniques have reached highly sophisticated levels. Just in Time inventory systems reduced the cost of carrying inventory. We have all experienced the "ER" revolution.

Key Point: • **The "ER" revolution appears to be over and it's now time to grow again.**

Many companies are emerging from the "ER" phase. Costs are down, quality is up, and computer systems have streamlined the processing of information. Many companies feel they are now ready to establish large, bodacious growth goals and attack!

The employees that must execute the new plans are psychologically relieved. At least the downsizing is over.

Key Point: • **A new barrier to growth exists. The people lack the necessary skills to play the new game.**

Through all the downsizing and waste reduction, very few companies prepared their people to play the new game. The focus was on problem solving. Teams were taught to problem solve, reduce costs, and eliminate waste. No one considered the assignment for the teams after the waste was gone.

The challenge to grow rekindles the need to compete and the competitive advantage appears to be worse than before all the downsizing started.

Returning to the list of competitive elements at the beginning of this chapter, when I ask growth-oriented strategists to identify their new competitive advantage, they reply with the same list. What has changed? In many cases, *nothing*. The customer offering has been modernized and the quality is much improved, but all competitors have done the same thing. Free agency in sports has occurred in business as well. Look around most reengineered organizations and you will find a conglomerate of new managers from broadly different companies. The average tenure of executive experience within some companies is often less than three years. The old gang is gone and in their place are the new big hitters. At least the attitude and enthusiasm of newness is a positive.

Through it all, the changes have been dramatic, *but* the challenge to competitive advantage remains. Within the *Context* of Mass Production, the bar has been raised and the pace has accelerated. To be a player you must now master time. The vision of a 30-hour workweek has evaporated. People now work longer hours than ever before. It takes hours to answer all the e-mail messages that are now a part of the relationship revolution.

Key Point: • **There is no time to compete. Everyone is to busy fulfilling the obligations of internal communication.**

Try to call a company today to buy something. If you can master the voice mail greeting and weave your way through the maze of instructions, you will hear a recorded message. "The person you want to talk to is either out of the office or away from their phone. If you leave a message, they'll get back to you" at their convenience–*not* yours.

Key Point: • **The relationship revolution changed the internal dynamics of Mass Production. People are far more insulated from the customer than ever before.**

With the vast improvements in product quality and service amenities, an impersonal relationship revolution was born. People were eliminated, and in their place are technological wonders that communicate with the customer. If you can't master the ATM, voice mail, or the Internet, you are in trouble.

The competitive advantage arena has changed. It now requires high tech and high touch. User friendly is the term used by computer systems engineers.

Key Point: • **You cannot win the war. You can, however, change the game and choose to create different relationships with customers that preclude war.**

The "at war" mentality in and of itself is the wrong approach to creating competitive advantage. The factory out Mass Production model is exhausting. It won't go away and it is doubtful if you can win anything other than the immediate battle. Sustaining the "at war" mentality will not lead to growth.

Key Point: • **The most important growth agenda today is in creating the collective intelligence of the organization.**

The traditional competitive advantages of Mass Production have been matched. The new game requires a shift in thinking from winning the war to creating peace with customers.

Key Point: • **After peace is declared, growth can occur.**

Ending the war is a critical step to growth. The internal war of blame must end before the company can create the capability to compete at a different level.

The Structural View

Below the visible maze of behavior and emotions is the *structural* answer to the competitive advantage dilemma. To help you visualize how to create sustainable competitive advantage, I offer the following formula:

$$\textbf{Competitive Advantage} = \textbf{K}_e(\textbf{C}_1 \textbf{ x } \textbf{C}_2)$$

It is important to find simple answers to the enormous chaos and complexity at the behavioral level. The factors in the formula are defined as follows:

$K_e =$ **Constant**
Trust
Ethics
Image
Reputation
Financial stability

$C_1 =$ **Competency factors**
Products/services/people
Technology/knowledge
Location/proximity
Functional expertise

$C_2 =$ **Capability factors**
A process–seamless delivery
Invisible forces
Integration of competencies
Cross-functional teamwork
Collective intelligence applied.

The following sections define each of these factors in detail. It is very important for executive leaders to separate their thinking into these three factors. The dominant illusion of Mass Production is to believe that competing on *competency factors* is the answer. The competency arena is "hyper" as Dr. Richard D'Aveni explains in his book, "*Hyper-Competition, Managing the Dynamics of Strategic Maneuvering.*" The real leverage point lies with *capability* factors.

The integration of all three factors, however, produces true leverage. Note that the factors in the formula are all multiplied together–there are no addition signs. This dispels the myth of either/or thinking.

Key Point: • **People must know their role in the formula.**

The most important issue is to translate competitive advantage to those who must execute "the Business of the BUSINESS" so they understand their role in the formula.

I was working with a company recently that had made the decision to grow. The annual sales conference proclaimed, "It's now time to attack." The conference introduced four new and modernized products and the technology link between all the players was complete. Everyone was asked to stretch their quota expectations. Many of the old sales managers were gone. A new cast was in place.

Everyone agreed to stretch. Yet, in side conversations, everyone was perplexed as to how they would fulfill their commitment. I asked them to identify the new *core competency* and *core capability* that would enable the growth to occur. The universal answer was, "We don't know." No one knew the term core competency. Very few knew more than their quota had been arbitrarily increased.

Leaders must *create structure*. Structure includes defining the core competency and core capability. If, in the above case, everyone had been aware of the elements of competitive advantage, they would have spent time at the conference translating the new competitive advantage into language at the customer interface. They would be confident that the entire company was committed to fulfill new promises, and everyone would know their role in the process of serving customers.

The conference ended with a rah-rah video showing high performance teams at work and a declaration that the old game was over. The tragedy of it all was the CEO thought that everyone was committed to achieve growth. The truth is everyone was still in compliance, trying to achieve a vague and idealistic vision. They were equipped with new products and technology that merely matched that of their competition. The need to customize the products and integrate the offering dominated every presentation. Yet, the language of Mass Production remained and the core capability was left undefined.

It can be done differently. When a company accurately defines competitive advantage in terms of $K_e(C_1 \times C_2)$, it is amazing to watch teamwork and commitment appear. People who know their role feel strategically important at last.

Key Point: • **The customer promise goes beyond price and quality. The company must be committed to sustained performance.**

A conscious comparison of your $K_e(C_1 \times C_2)$ factors verses your competitions' reveals true differentiation and the language at the customer interface instantly changes. Sales people exude confidence in your organization's capability to fulfill the promise.

Sales people who know that the competitive advantage is based upon a core capability can easily defuse the price objection. The vendor mentality is instantly relieved. *Capability-based* relationships are sustainable and the "at war" mentality vanishes.

By looking at each element of the formula in detail, you can realize the enormous leverage this approach provides.

The Center of Gravity–K_e

The first element of competitive advantage is K_e. K_e is a *constant* much like π in the formula πr^2. K_e represents trust, ethics, image, reputation, and financial stability of a company. It is easy to neglect the transformation of these factors as the company approaches the future.

Many companies take K_e for granted because they have been around for years. In the new *Context* of the global business environment, tenure and physical size do not mean anything. Having 100,000 employees worldwide is a meaningless statistic.

In the old Mass Production *Context*, trust and ethics were defined in terms of honesty, sincerity, integrity, and a host of other *personal attributes* of senior executives. Vast sums of money were and continue to be spent entertaining customers to create the intangible bond of trust and personal relationships. It is an effective way of building K_e in the Mass Production orientation. Many companies continue to believe that business is done on the golf course.

There are as many books and articles about business ethics as there are authors and consultants. Everyone recognizes and acknowledges the need for trust and ethics. Advertising agencies create campaigns to enhance the image of companies in the mind of the consumer. Slogans are developed to create K_e impressions. "Babies are our only business," "A lot is riding on your tires," "We bring good things to life," "Nationwide is on your side," and "We do what ever it takes" are just a few examples of slogans intended to build K_e.

K_e is a serious agenda for every organization. People don't buy from companies they don't trust. Maintaining the integrity of K_e is called "walking the talk." Slogans are easy to say, but it is not always easy to translate the intention of the slogan into organizational behavior. Spill a little oil in Alaska or have a contaminated gel cap in Chicago, then watch how the organization responds to preserve K_e. It takes years to create K_e. It often takes moments to destroy it.

The New Way of Thinking about K_e

The old Mass Production model of K_e was focused on personal attributes of people. Many companies developed K_e around the philosophy or personality of the founder. The fallacy of this approach is that people change. New management brings a change in personal attributes and philosophies. Many companies have been bought and sold and the personal commitments from the golf course are lost.

Many Mass Production companies build trust in a brand name. As the core competency section in this chapter indicates, generic brands can easily match or negate the competency advantage. What, therefore, is the *new* way to create K_e?

K_e must be perceived as the *center of gravity* of the organization. The center of gravity of anything is the point around which balance exists. For stationary objects, the center of gravity is the point around which *static balance* exists. For objects that are in motion, the center of gravity is the point around which *dynamic balance* exists. The center of gravity of a physical object is easy to locate. When designing products, it is critical that the center of gravity be properly located.

If the center of gravity of an object is outside of its physical boundaries, the object is incapable of rotating around an internal axis of rotation. The physics of rotation and location of center of gravity are competencies for mechanical engineers.

Two questions must be answered to *design* the organization of the future: "What is the center of gravity?" and "What is the axis of rotation of the organization?" This is a strange concept for executives to consider. The physics metaphor doesn't seem to apply.

The center of gravity of any organization is the answer to the question, "Why do we exist?" This is the mission or the purpose of the organization. The axis of rotation is the alignment of the organization on that purpose. If all the employees of your organization have the same answer to why and they are committed to fulfill their role in that purpose, the organization will have dynamic balance. A balanced organization will be perceived as seamless, effortless, and integrated in serving the customer.

What is the *purpose* of any organization? Most people quickly say, "To make a profit." This myth exists in the mind of almost every Mass Production Thinker. Larry Wilson, founder and creator of *Counselor Selling* and author of *Changing the Game, a New Way to Sell,* has written for years that the purpose of any business or organization is to help customers (people) get what they want. In most cases, the purpose is to help customers solve a problem that exists in current reality.

This statement prompts a knee-jerk reaction from most people. "What about making money? If you don't make a profit, you'll go out of business." This is true. The *objective* of any business is to make a profit (or pay the bills in a nonprofit organization). This thinking immediately sets up an issue of semantics. Purpose and objective–they mean the same thing to most people. Worse yet, people see helping customers *and* making a profit as paradoxical. In other words, they put an "or" between the two processes.

The acid test is to put yourself in the buyer mode and ask yourself, "What do I want from every company or business?" The answer is simple, help solving a problem or assistance in creating the future. If you are wearing glasses while reading this, ask yourself, "Why did I buy glasses?" The answer, to help you see. Therefore, the *purpose* of LensCrafters is to help customers see. Their *objective* is to make a profit.

Every company subscribes to the philosophy of win-win. For years, executives have said "win-win," but seldom do people know what creates win-win relationship. *Purpose* defines winning for the customer and *objective* defines winning for the company. If you see no difference between the words purpose and objective and you define them both as "to make a profit," your organization will lack dynamic balance and frequently practice win-lose with customers.

If you define the center of gravity as "to make a profit" and your company seeks to align its organization on that objective, your organization will suffer severe imbalance. Have you ever seen a washing machine when the clothes are not evenly distributed during the spin cycle? Severe vibration and ultimate shut down results.

Think about how a company makes a profit. The sales department has responsibility for top line revenue. Manufacturing is responsible for cost of goods sold. Other groups add overhead costs and account for who is operating beyond the limits of the budget. A company aligned on the objective of making a profit will experience severe *imbalance* in the form of conflict and blame. Those with *not enough* will criticize those with *too much,* and conflict will drive the organizational dynamics. The organization will constantly be out of balance. This will manifest as customer indifference and neglect. It is as irritating to a customer as the imbalance of the washing machine is to you.

Every Mass Production company has experienced this imbalance. The typical solution to the problem is to seek alignment around *strategy.* The era of strategic planning produced some degree of dynamic stability, but the imbalance was not permanently resolved. Strategic plans produce static balance; they do not guarantee dynamic balance.

Creating Dynamic Balance

Dynamic balance can only be created if *everyone* is committed to the *purpose of helping customers get what they want.* Every organization exists for that purpose. When this purpose is the center of gravity of the organization, the customer experience is guaranteed and K_e (trust, ethics, image, reputation, and financial stability) is assured. Everyone walks the talk. The company slogan has true meaning and it can be translated into real-time behavior by everyone.

Purpose as K_e transcends the attributes of individuals or the personal ethics of a specific manager or leaders. It is permanent and never changes. Purpose brings tremendous discipline to the organization. In a purpose-driven company, people are hired to fulfill an important role in the process of helping customers and they can be fired for failure to fulfill that role. The organization that is aligned on purpose has dynamic balance. The customer experience is always win-win. It isn't optional.

The purpose-driven company always defines winning from the customer's point of view and consciously defines the process to fulfill that purpose.

Key Point: • **The company that is aligned on purpose is known for the constant of trust–K_e.**

How a company creates this alignment is the subject of the "Alignment" chapter in this book. The key is to change the awareness of what creates dynamic balance in the chaotic, ever changing global business environment. If you believe it comes from profit-making strategies, you are living an illusion. The Transformation in thinking is to understand that it comes from commitment to helping customers get what they want. Competencies change. Capability changes. K_e–alignment of purpose is a critical agenda for every organization.

Key Point: • **In a business environment that is fueled by technological obsolescence, the dynamic balance provided by purpose is the only constant that can be found.**

Core Competency Factors

C_1 in the formula of competitive advantage is *competency*. There are four main competency factors: products/services, technology/knowledge, location/proximity, and functional expertise. Companies must have *knowledge* that is desired by the customer. Knowledge is translated into products, people, services, locations, or technologies.

It is easy to see the *core competency* of many companies. The core competency of a law firm is knowledge of the law. Accountants know accounting. A barber knows how to style hair. The core competency of most retailers was (and is) where to locate stores and how to display merchandise. Someone knows the demographics of the market being served and decides where to locate the business. Marketing 401, at one time, taught location, location, location, when the subject was retailing.

The core competency of an insurance company is actuary. The knowledge of how to calculate risk and subsequently price policies to reflect the statistical probability of insuring the correct market segment is the core of any insurance company.

Many companies have been built around a patent that protected a core technology. Thousands of products became household brands because of the core technology they contained. Protected for 17 years, many companies built dynasties on the technology of an invention.

It is true that companies have multiple competencies. There are many knowledgeable people in every company and they are *all* critical elements for success. Ask CEOs what is their core competency and they will often list many areas of expertise that make up the core of their businesses. However, there is *one* core competency. At Honda, it's engines. They put engines in cars, motorcycles, lawnmowers, and many other products. The core competency of an air conditioning company is compressors. For Xerox, it is the technology of xerography.

It is often difficult to identify the core competency of large conglomerate companies. Different divisions may have different core competencies.

Core competencies experience two rather startling dilemmas. In many companies, the core becomes routine to the point that everyone is bored providing it to customers. The second dilemma is that, overtime, the core competency is taken for granted. In many companies, the core competency has existed and been successful for so long that everyone assumes it will always exist and always serve to sustain the business.

When the core competency was unique, everyone was excited about its development or creation. The leverage it provided to a new company was often exponential. Think of the early days of television, computers, digital electronics, pharmaceuticals, fast food restaurants, and shopping centers. Consumers flock to buy new products and experience the service. The core competency is initially, innovative. "I wonder who thought of it?" Overtime, however, the competency is quickly matched by competitors and it becomes routine and boring.

Key Point: • **In today's technologically advanced business environment, it is possible to quickly and easily match or neutralize the competency factors of your competitor.**

If the knowledge resides in people, competitors can hire your people. Products can be reverse-engineered and improvements can be made that negate patents, copyrights, or trademarks. Generic brands have neutralized the advantage of many powerful brand names.

Location as a competitive advantage has been neutralized. Witness the rise of catalog and Internet sales. You can buy anything from home. There is a fast food restaurant or a gas station on every corner. Banks are everywhere. ATM machines permit you to bank anytime and anywhere.

In professional athletics, teams easily acquire the super star players through the free agency system. Sustaining a competitive advantage by having the best players is almost impossible. Likewise, in business today, people are very mobile. The era of long careers with one company is over. Competency, in the form of people's expertise, is easily acquired.

Matching a *competency-based* competitive advantage is easy. This has led to the "at war" mentality. The pace of change is fast and furious within the realm of competency-based competitors. Many products have been reduced to commodities and the only question appears to be "What's the price?" Seeking differentiation through product features and benefits is almost impossible.

This phenomenon alone has made many sales processes obsolete. For years, sales people were trained to sell features and benefits. They were taught to close on the benefits that were important to the customer. Today, everyone has the same features and benefits. No one is better than the other. Products are alike. A fax machine is a fax machine. A copier is a copier. True, one will collate faster than another, but the differences are small and seldom justify large differences in price.

We have gone through several revolutions to improve competency-based competitive models. The most obvious are the quality and customer service initiatives. Foreign competition exceeded the quality competency of many U.S. products. The auto industry dilemma is a classic example. The U.S. manufacturers had to improve quality. It wasn't optional, but it has been done. U.S. cars and trucks have now matched the quality of most global competitors.

The customer service revolution initially brought smile training for many service-based companies. Telephones were answered within three rings and courtesy was emphasized. Of course, this approach could be easily matched. Service representatives were then trained to *exceed* customer expectations. Companies began to stress value-added service. Amenities were added that the customer did not expect. McDonalds added playgrounds. Frequent flyer programs became the rage in the airline industry. Grocery stores offered green stamps redeemable for merchandise. Thousands of novel value-added services multiplied the number of customer service strategies, *and* they were quickly matched by competition.

Competency-based approaches have increased consumer expectations of quality products, value-added service, responsive behavior, and convenient locations. Customers have become pampered to the point that they are spoiled. Anything less than value-added is met with contempt. The increase in value-added services costs money, and the costs are buried in the price of the service.

To counter the spiraling value-added mania, many companies created budget approaches. Economy car rentals, budget hotels, and discount stores appealed to those who weren't interested in the value-added approaches. Southwest Airline flourished as did K-Mart, Budget Car Rental, Red Roof Inns, and many budget approaches.

Many manufacturers were confronted with the need to have good, better, best models. Sears invented sell-up as an effective competency selling approach. Proliferation of product models and sizes was common. All these approaches were easily matched.

Within competency-based companies, marketing became a science. With the arrival of computers came database marketing. You are a statistic in a number of databases, all capable of predicting your buying patterns and statistical habits of consumption. Competitive advantage was gained through target marketing. Companies could target market segments by zip code and street addresses and telemarket only those select consumers that had the highest probability of buying. Telephone solicitation became an effective tool to reach the consumer using competency-based approaches. Today, everyone uses telemarketing and it has become the number one nuisance to consumers at dinnertime.

If we continue to chronicle the competency-based approach to competitive advantage, you would feel the pace of the treadmill accelerate. It is exhausting. Many employees are told, "If you can't stand the heat, get out of the kitchen." "This is war." MBA students are prepared for the combat. Case studies of success and failure prepare them to withstand the pressure. Go to Park Avenue in downtown Manhattan and watch the game. This masochistic approach to life is justified as necessary to win the competency game.

Articles about vision and mission propose relief from the exhausting ritual. Occasionally, executives reaffirm company values to the troops. However, the competency game is one of *strategy*. It's war! In war, values are often compromised. When there is a battle to fight, there is very little need for vision or a new mission statement that promises further enhancements to already inflated customer expectations.

For many companies, customer offerings have reached outrageous levels. The average fast food menu board contains more items than can be delivered fast. The issue is how to streamline operations and become the low cost producer. Operational efficiency replaces customer service as the new strategic agenda. "You can't be customer intimate and operationally excellent." "Take your pick because you can't do both." Books on the subject reinforce the selective strategy doctrine and the competency-based *illusions* continue to dominate the War Rooms of many American companies.

Meanwhile, on the shop floor, people are being asked to work in teams to reduce product costs and save the company to prosperity. After all these years, employees must have some ideas of how to win the competency game. "If the MBAs can't figure it out, maybe the employees can." "Let's get them involved." "Let's empower them to make decisions." All the worthy initiatives, linked to a competency-based competitive advantage, just spread the exhaustion throughout the organization.

Core Capability Factors

The Transformation of the global business environment is almost exclusively about *creating capability*. For years, Mass Production Thinking has dominated corporate strategy. The focus is on building the core competencies of the business. Strategists believe that success is the result of a unique product or service, proximity to markets (location), talented people, or a patented technology. The formula for success resided in the core competency and companies have gone to great lengths to protect it.

All companies have competencies. They have intelligent people, quality products, good locations, and innovative technologies. The focus of a competency-based company is how to become smarter, faster, better, and more effective in improving competency factors.

The challenge is not how to improve competencies; rather, the challenge is how to integrate the competency factors effortlessly, timely, synergistically, or responsively. Capability is the *process* of integrating organizational competencies. Capability is the interrelationship of people, locations, or things. It is intangible. It can't be wrapped or shipped in a box. When capability exists, it is called teamwork, seamless, empowerment, commitment, synergy, coordinated, integrated, or a partnership. All of these terms refer to interrelationships. Capability on a personal level is called hand-eye coordination, and people who have it are called athletic, coordinated, artistic, and talented.

Key Point: • **Capability must be created.**

Capability does not exist in a newborn baby, nor does it exist in an entrepreneurial startup company. The process of creating capability is often perceived as risky. The baby might fall. The new company might fail. Many companies today are encouraging people to take risks. For what? To create capability or for some other undefined purpose?

We celebrate the development of capability when a child begins to walk. The new business celebrates the capability of satisfying their first customer. We have all been to awards banquets where individuals were acknowledged for their performance. The universal acceptance speech always gives credit to the overall capability of the organization that enabled individual achievement. Why is it then that organizations only focus on and celebrate bottom-line results when organizational capability is the key ingredient for success?

Key Point: • **Capability is the most over-promised under-delivered component of every sales transaction.**

Capability is referred to as customer service, quick turnaround, overnight delivery, on-time departure, and thousands of other marketing-oriented slogans.

Customers get very angry when it's missing, slow in responding, or intentionally neglected.

Sales people promise capability, but many companies have erected barriers to its fulfillment. Voice mail systems make it impossible to reach companies with ease. Policy manuals define how quickly capability can be applied. It's very common that functional entities that must fulfill the promised capability are "at war." Engineering, manufacturing, and sales executives are often at teambuilding retreats because customer satisfaction surveys indicate the company is not fulfilling capability promises. Blame, mistrust, anger, fear, and intimidation are used to explain capability deficiencies.

Organizational capability is very hard to create. It is not tangible and impossible to define on paper. It is the interrelationship of the functional departments. People create capability within departments, but there are enormous barriers to creating it between departments. Companies, therefore, determine what the company can reasonably deliver rather than create the capability to meet actual expectations of customers. Delivery cycles and service levels are set to match the capability of the company, not the expectations of the customer. Special requests by customers may take forever or the company may ignore the customer altogether. Order a special hamburger at McDonalds and "please step aside." Order a car with something special and wait 12 to 14 weeks for delivery.

There are many sophisticated methods for improving and creating capability within the *Context* of Mass Production. Industrial engineers know how to streamline manufacturing processes. Products are built and stored in warehouses to fulfill the capability of quick delivery. Robotics and integrated logistic systems move mass-produced goods to customers with amazing capability. Most of these improvements, however, are within a functional competency. Cross-functional capability may still be missing. In addition, most of these improvements are intended to control or eliminate people. It is very difficult for people to engage in teambuilding when the intent is to eliminate their jobs.

Creating organizational capability is, therefore, very dependent upon the perceived *intention* of the process. The role of leadership is to align intention so people will be motivated to integrate and cooperate across functional boundaries. If the alignment is not correct, people will retard or restrict capability. We have all experienced the indifferent attitude of customer service representatives who can't or won't activate the capability of the organization to perform. Organizations that depend on human intention to deliver capability experience frequent power failures.

Key Point: •   The alignment of intention is very difficult to create.

The Mass Production Barrier

Why are so many companies deficient in capability? Why don't functional departments behave seamlessly? It sounds so logical and strategically important. The fundamental purpose of any organization is to have the ability to do more collectively than one person acting alone. Isn't synergy between individuals the driving force for forming any organization? Of course! Then, why must capability be created? Why doesn't it naturally exist?

When a company lacks capability, the problem always appears to be the attitude of people. The real problem, however, is Mass Production technology. Mass Production Thinking is based upon the intentional separation of Thinkers and Doers. The interrelationship of the parts is not considered important. The dominant management philosophy is plan, organize, and control. The fundamental *Context* of Mass Production is independence of parts, controlled by financial measurement of efficiency and effectiveness. The role of management is to integrate the parts by telling the parts (people) what to do.

This sounds cold and harsh, and in some way, it is. The intention of Mass Production Thinking is not about creating cross-functional capability. It focuses on competencies. It's about winning the war against competition.

We have reached the point when there is very little economic leverage in Mass Production Thinking. We have perfected the systems of Mass Production. We have reached the low-cost producer position. We cannot eliminate additional costs. Some companies believe they can reduce labor costs by locating factories off shore. This is true. This approach, however, is a competency-based strategy that will always strain the capability of the organization. The gain in lowering cost will typically be offset by increased cost in logistics. Improvement is linear at best and focused on reducing or eliminating people.

It is very difficult for people to be inspired while working in a culture focused on eliminating them. Workers, consciously or subconsciously, live in fear that they are next. We have all lived through the lean and mean approaches that attempt to motivate people to perform miracles while working smarter, not harder. It's the illusion of Mass Production Thinking.

Mass Production Thinking is based upon the model that Thinkers must tell the Doers what to do. Doers are capable of cross-functional cooperation, but they have been stripped of the *authority* to do *it* unless they are told. In most Mass Production systems, capability does not exist. The missing ingredient is the willingness and authority to exercise *it*.

To solve this problem, the Thinkers often decide to empower the Doers to do things without being told. The empowerment movement was and is an attempt to activate the inherent capability of the organization. Other processes of activation are employee involvement, quality circles, and many of the current teamwork initiatives. All of these processes are well intended, but the *Context* of Mass

Production remains. In addition, the measurement and reward systems that drive Mass Production organizations are seldom changed as a part of the empowerment process.

Bursts of capability appear, typically focused on solving tough problems, but once the problem is solved, cross-functional cooperation disappears. Capability in a Mass Production system must always be activated by the Thinkers. Activation and deactivation are constant management challenges in the Mass Production *Context*.

Key Point: • **The customer promise goes beyond price and quality. The company must be committed to sustained performance.**

To fulfill the promises of the customer-focused organization, we must learn to create a different form of capability. The Mass Customization *Context* is totally dependent upon capability as the competitive advantage. Without *it*, the organization will remain in a Mass Production model.

Creating Capability

The transformation occurring in the global business environment is about creating organizations where the whole equals the sum of the parts plus the interrelationship of the parts. The parts are the competencies and the interrelationships the capability. Many organizations have a clearly identified core competency. They must now identify and create core capability. This sounds simple, but capability is not easy to create.

As we have discussed, the biggest trap is to begin to define capability from the Mass Production mind-set. If you begin with the factory and work out to the market, you will be seeking improvement of the existing Mass Production process. This will *not* create the capability of Mass Customization. Therefore, we must start with the customer and work backward to the factory.

Capability is experienced by the customer as a seamless, effortless interaction with the company. These are customer perceptions. Put yourself in the customer role and think about how you interact with businesses. Recall the restaurants, banks, insurance companies, dry cleaners, auto companies, and suppliers that you perceive as seamless. Capability is something the customer feels and experiences.

The process of creating capability, therefore, starts with the customer (not the market) and makes two fundamental assumptions. The customer wants the *entire process to feel customized, and* they want it to perform within *their time expectations*. These assumptions will not be perceived as realistic by the Mass Production Thinker. We have, however, arrived at a time when it is possible for people to get what they want and feel like it has been delivered in a customized way. It may be an illusion, but perception is reality. The facts are that information technology is enabling this transformation to occur and *Mass Customization is a reality*.

The key to creating this reality is capability. We must change the interrelationships of the parts to change the process of serving the customer. This requires a total shift in thinking about why the organization exists.

Key Point: • **A process designed to serve a customer is not the same as a customer service process.**

It is important to emphasize that the capability to serve a customer is not the same as customer service. Customer service in the Mass Production *Context* is a competency. Many Mass Production organizations have developed very sophisticated customer service departments. Customer service is a reactive function. Capability, on the other hand, is a *process designed to serve the customer* that transcends all the functional departments. Capability is the *proactive ability* of the entire company to serve the customer.

Institutionalized Practice

Core capability is a process. It is the interrelationship of the competencies. It is how things and people work together. It doesn't just happen. Capability is created during practice time. An orchestra practices. All sports teams practice. We have all gone to practice for something. Therefore, to create capability, organizations must institutionalize practice. Capability cannot be created while fighting the daily fires or at a once-a-year teambuilding event.

It sounds so obvious that people should practice to create capability. Mass Production Thinking, however, has a negative *Context* for practice time. It's called unapplied labor and training. Both reduce gross margin or increase overhead. Mass Production measurement systems have found ways to reduce practice time to a minimum.

The major shift in thinking of the Mass Customization organization is to see capability as the competitive advantage and the leverage point for superior performance. Perfect practice inspires people to want to perform. Do you recall the last time you had a good practice session at the driving range? Most people can't wait to go play. People develop confidence and trust in each other from practice.

Key Point: • **Practice time must be institutionalized and legitimate within the context of financial performance.**

Effective practice often includes the customer as a partner in the process. If the customer is not physically involved, practice needs to begin with the expectations of the customer. The expectations of customizing the customer's experience with speed must be practiced.

Initially, practice is not perfect. To create capability takes time. The assumption that customers can be served as they expect will be tested many times. The barriers are enormous, especially if there is an existing Mass Production organization to be run. Time for practice is limited. The reality of the battle will easily discourage everyone from embracing the possibilities of Mass Customization. Everyone is easily reminded of the Mass Production assumptions that "we can't be all things to all people" or "we should stick to our knitting."

The Pace of Capability

Mass customization capability is about speed and responsiveness. The pace of a capability-based organization is fundamentally different. People must be in shape physically and emotionally to meet the expectations of a capability-based business.

The pace of Mass Production is often brisk. The pace of Mass Production, however, is maintained by compliance to the Thinkers orders and the programmed speed of the assembly lines. The pace of many Mass Production organizations is driven by one crisis after another. "It's a constant fire fighting drill." The crisis orientation creates exhaustion in people and the relief is "Thank God, it's Friday."

Pace in a Mass Customization organization comes from *commitment to the customer*, not compliance to orders. When the organization commits to help customers get what they want, that commitment creates pace. It is totally different to be driven by commitment versus compliance.

The pace of commitment inspires people to take risks, be empowered, and take action without authority. The adage of "ask forgiveness" rather than "ask permission" applies. When the organization is committed to a purpose of customer responsiveness, it is alive with positive energy. The energy is inherent to creating what you want.

In a capability-based organization, people are free to perform. The rules of Mass Production Thinking are gone. There are principles to live by, but there are not rules that prevent people from fulfilling the capability promise. Many people ask, "How can this be true?" "People will take advantage of the freedom."

Key Point: • **People who have practiced together are committed to fulfill their role in the process.**

Because they have simulated the actual experience during practice, commitment replaces the need for rules.

The commitment to practice is ongoing. If there are situations that pose risk, the people can change the process of handling these situations during the next practice session. More importantly, institutionalized practice provides the opportunity to improve the process beyond the initial customer expectations. A capability-based organization can truly exceed customers' expectations.

Many people are unable to work in a capability-based environment. Many Mass Production managers have become plow horses. The race today requires a thoroughbred. They are not only the wrong kind of animal; they are out of shape. Frankly, the pace of a Mass Customization organization would kill them. The manager that must be in control and figure everything out is too slow for the capability game.

The business environment is changing rapidly. The ticket to the game is to compete on capability.

Key Point: • **The toughest challenge is for the whole to manifest in every part.**

When viewed from the customer's perspective, the flight attendant *is* the airline, the waitress *is* the restaurant, the teller *is* the bank. Every employee must manifest wholeness. They don't have to "do" wholeness, but they must accept responsibility for the whole. Coming from an era of Mass Production Thinking where employees were neither supposed to think nor privileged to know anything other than their job, the challenge for Mass Production Thinkers is a mighty one. The transformational journey ahead must be driven by creating a core capability that manifests as wholeness to the customer.

The New Approach

Executives who approach the competency dilemma as a problem to be solved, look for the cause of the problem and often conclude that the solution is to improve competency factors. This is a circular trap. Problem-solving approaches oscillate between mutually exclusive poles: operational excellence or customer intimacy, quantity or quality, value-added or low cost. The problem-solving approach will always move between too much and not enough.

In one sense, the problem-solving approach is useful in that it identifies the paradox that keeps the company from seeing new possibilities. The paradoxical barrier is always driven by either/or thinking. Many companies struggle, trying to embrace customer service or make a profit. It is obvious that companies must do both, but many are constantly oscillating between these two mutually exclusive extremes.

The new approach to the competency dilemma is not to confront the business environment as a problem to be solved, but rather to seek to create a competitive advantage that is totally different. The answer lies in changing the interrelationship of the competencies while continuously improving the competencies themselves. This shift is called a capability-based competitive advantage, and it seeks to compete by changing the economics of relationships. Teamwork and partnering are two examples of the new approach that seeks to change the dynamics of both internal and external relationships.

Collective Intelligence

The new approach not only creates new capability, but it also creates a *collective intelligence* that leads to innovation in new competency development.

Mass Production Thinking does not promote the development of collective intelligence. The Thinkers create the strategy, managers execute the plan, workers perform the work, and vendors provide the materials to support production. An independent culture forms that may be friendly, but seldom does a Mass Production organization realize the power of collective intelligence.

In the Mass Production *Context*, product innovation is the domain of research and development. Huge sums of moneys are allocated to research centers that are dedicated to creating new competencies.

The new approach is to recognize the possibility of collective intelligence. Ask 10 people to write down one idea how to change the competitive position of the company. The 10 ideas constitute the collective intelligence of the group. The old approach would evaluate each idea and discard them one at a time. Each would be judged for realism. It is easy to discount most ideas using the criteria of too much or not enough. "That's a good idea, *but* we don't have enough money in the budget to pursue it," or "Top management would never agree to it."

The new approach looks for the process that all the ideas collectively describe. Collective intelligence always describes a process of working together to do things differently. Capability-based organizations have a process advantage over competition. Hertz and Avis both rent cars. The Gold Club process at Hertz differentiates Hertz from Avis. Avis may try harder, but Hertz has made the process of renting a car effortless.

Collective intelligence not only leads to seamless, effortless processes; it allows people to be creative in creating new competencies. Innovative product ideas often come from people who are involved in the process. The leverage of this new approach is startling. People who are closest to the customer often see ways to serve customers or modify existing products that research and development would never perceive.

New competencies will continue to emerge. Technology will accelerate at alarming rates. New customer service concepts will be developed and the Internet will become the location for almost anything. The core competency of many companies will become obsolete as new competencies are created. Nothing suggests the competency strategies shouldn't be of major concern to every executive suite. The point is to balance competency with capability and trust that the collective intelligence will produce answers that one mind, acting alone cannot possibly conceive. The era of the autocratic control is over. Mass Customization demands quantity, quality, and responsiveness. The paradox of effortless effectiveness must be understood.

Chapter 11
Outcomes, Strategies, and Measurement

"To achieve the vision, what do we need to *create*?"
"How will we deploy resources?" *and* **"How will we measure success?"**

Let's suppose it's 1497 and news has reached Portugal that Christopher Columbus was successful in reaching a new land. It has now been confirmed that the world is round. You are the president of Aztec Flat World Boats. How would you respond?

There are many choices. On one extreme, "Who cares!" "We dominate the flat world market!" On the other hand, you may decide to become a global boat builder. Sound familiar? The vision of how you see the world begins the process of change.

Vision is a critical structural element. A new *Context* for seeing the world generates many questions concerning *the Business of the BUSINESS* and how to deploy resources.

Creating Outcomes

The question becomes "What do we need to *create* to achieve the vision?" The answer at Aztec Boats might be big boats. However, what supports the production of big boats?

In 1972, the energy crisis hit American industrial giants like a sledgehammer. Many executives accepted the challenge and began to transform *the Business of the BUSINESS*. The energy consumption of appliances, heating and cooling equipment, automobiles, and airplanes was transformed. The changes were more than linear improvements of existing designs. New engines, compressors, and combustion processes were created.

Consider how many companies were confronted with the question, "What must we create to achieve the vision of being energy efficient?" This question is very different from "What is our goal?" or "How will we deploy resources?"

Key Point: • An outcome defines what we need to create.

The word *outcome* is a non-Mass Production term and defines something that doesn't exist in current reality. It is very important to realize that the new environment is not a linear extension of current reality. The Content to support a round world boat building company did not exist in the flat world factories. Therefore, many things must be created during the process of Transformational Change. It is very important to use new terminology to facilitate the shift from Mass Production to the new business environment.

Mass Production Thinkers have used the terms goals, objectives, strategies, and critical success factors to describe the factors of organizational success. Everyone knows "you gotta have goals" if you have heard Zig Ziglar speak. No one can argue with the methodology of goal setting and strategic planning. Look at your goals and see how many of them contain words such as more, better, improve, increase, or eliminate. Goals define action that must be applied to *things* that currently exist. Within the *Context* of Mass Production, goal setting is linear, predictive, prescriptive, and logical. Extending current reality forward at a predictable rate is an effective growth strategy if you want to do more of the same faster.

However, what if current reality is obsolete? What if "made in Japan" no longer means cheap? What if people will no longer buy the gas-guzzler that is planned to fail in 50,000 miles?

What if you must *create* a *new Business of the BUSINESS*? What if your people don't have the skill sets necessary to compete in the new environment?

The vision defines what we must *become* and outcomes put meat on the bones. Outcomes add depth to the vision. Outcomes define the processes, systems, products, infrastructure, and relationships that will exist after the vision is achieved. Collectively, outcomes describe the organization and interrelationships within the new business.

Key Point: • Outcomes can be difficult to define.

If the new environment, defined by the vision, is dramatically different from current reality, people will find it difficult to define outcomes. Who could have defined the laptop computer in 1972? Computers were housed in large rooms. Who could describe a titanium metal driver when Arnold Palmer first won the Masters? The difficulty of envisioning product creations is easy to understand because the processes and technologies to create them do not exist.

The Transformation to Mass Customization is almost impossible for Mass Production Thinkers to envision. The technology to dismantle the high volume, large lot run factories from the 1970s does not exist in many industries. To many manufacturing executives, "It will never happen." "We have 37% of the market!" "Who cares about the niche player?"

Creating Outcome Statements

Outcome statements specify an end result that must be created.

Key Point: • **Every outcome statement contains a *Context* change from current reality.**

While working with many Mass Production Thinkers, the first cut at writing outcome statements reflects a strong problem-solving orientation. They use improve, enhance, increase, decrease, eliminate, preserve, protect, maintain, back to basics, solve, fix, and restore as operative words. All these words confirm that they are extending current reality forward. Using these words to describe outcomes will only lead to incremental change.

A vision is an antecedent for creating something *different*. The outcomes that support the vision must likewise reflect something different. Outcome statements serve as the generative force to activate the creating process.

The following is a list of outcomes that are common in transforming the traditional Mass Production organization.

1. Create a *transformational leadership process*

2. Create a *seamless distribution process* that can deliver the new offering to the market

3. Create a *proactive customer interface*

4. Create a *collective intelligence* that digests complexity and change

5. Create a *learning environment* that supports our growth

6. Create an *integrated information system*

7. Create a *financial infrastructure* that accurately identifies how revenue, expenses, and profits flow through the organization

8. Create a *performance management* process

9. Create *strategic partnerships* with supplier organizations

10. Create an *electronic business capability.*

Note the operative word *create*. This suggests that the new environment is *not* a linear extension of the past. The process of creating the outcomes will require collaborative, cross-functional effort. Teams must be formed to create the outcomes. Team-creating skills become a critical ingredient to successful Transformational Change.

In comparison to goal statements, outcome statements are neither quantitative nor specific in size, time, or magnitude. Goal statements typically contain specific size and quantity levels because they are in comparison to existing levels of performance. Outcome statements are similar to visions. They are a succinct statement of what needs to be created, irrespective of time lines or measurement criteria.

Creating Strategies

After outcomes are defined, then it is possible to identify the specific action steps that must be taken to create the outcomes.

Key Point: • **A strategy defines action to be taken to begin creating the desired outcome. The first step is to define the current reality of an outcome.**

The first step in defining strategies is to accurately define the *current reality* of the situation. This is an important step because it establishes the gap between *what is* and what needs to be created.

Outcome #1:   Create a *transformational leadership* process
Action strategies:
       1. Confirm that the *Context* has changed.
       2.
       3.
       4.
Current reality: We have a traditional Mass Production management process.

The current reality statement should be nonjudgmental and free of blame. No one is to blame for the way it is; *current reality just is!* It is very important to accept current reality as the way it *is*. The problem solvers in your group will have difficulty accepting this advice. They constantly see current reality as a problem to be solved and want to identify the cause of the problem.

After current reality is defined, you should be able to see a distinct gap between *what is* and the desired outcome. It is now possible to define what action needs to be taken to begin creating the outcome.

At this point, most Mass Production Thinkers want to develop an elaborate plan. They want to attack the problem and make the outcome appear.

Key Point: • **The process of creating is deterministic.**

I suggest to my clients that they initially need only two or three strategies under each outcome. Because creating an outcome is a dynamic process, you must act on a small number of strategies then determine what to do next based upon the results revealed by the strategy work. The action strategies can be discussed at practice sessions, and the next steps can be decided. This work builds collective intelligence and creates Alignment on Purpose.

To the Mass Production Thinker, this approach does not feel "in control." Mass Production Thinkers want a well mapped-out set of action items, with delegated responsibilities and time lines. This gives them control over the process. Creating an outcome is a very different approach.

The outcomes can be assigned to specific teams for initial exploration. Again, this is not the same as a task force or committee. The team is empowered to *create,* not just investigate and report to management.

Each outcome becomes a living microcosm of activity that spreads across functional boundaries. If you look at the previous list, you won't see any outcomes that are specifically the domain of sales, manufacturing, engineering, or finance. All outcomes and corresponding strategies are cross-functional.

The strategies define the hard work of transforming the organization. People will be caught between doing their old job and creating the outcomes of the new environment. This is not easy for people to do. Don't make it an exhausting process. Set aside one hour a week to work on the new strategies. To many people this doesn't sound like enough time. Remember *enough* isn't the issue! Commitment is the issue.

Measurement

After work on creating an outcome begins, it will become glaringly obvious that the organization likely doesn't measure anything other than financial results. How would you measure progress toward creating a Transformational Leadership process? How would you measure proactive activity with customers?

Within each outcome, there must be measurement criteria. I wish I could tell you these criteria are quantitative, objective, and based in specific time frames.

Key Point: • **Measurement of Transformational Change is subjective. It must feel right.**

Recall the illustration from chapter four, page 56, a part of the Structural Framework is a section entitled *measurement.* In that section, you should establish measures for

- Financial performance
- Customer satisfaction
- Cultural comfort
- Learning

There is nothing more difficult for the Mass Production Thinker than to deal with subjective "touchy-feely stuff." I have seen more change initiatives killed because the Mass Production Thinker can't "get his hands around it."

I worked with a local bank on an empowerment initiative for almost two years. There were 60 people in the process and 80 more scheduled for the next year. The results were truly astounding in terms of emotional fulfillment and empowerment. In the middle of the process, a new president arrived on the scene. While reviewing the budget for the next year, he saw the budget for empowerment training. He quickly did a line item veto and said, "We aren't going to do that California stuff!" We're going to do "productivity." The empowerment program ended and *no one* was able to say the "E" word ever again.

No one was able to show the new president, in bottom line form, what the "empowerment stuff" had produced. The measurement issue is enormous. It is a massive barrier to Transformational Change. It would be easy for me to tell you to kill all your accountants before you begin a Transformational Change initiative. The accounting mind-set struggles with the concepts of transformation. I have conducted the *Organizational Transformation™ Simulation* for accountants, and they readily admit that they don't know how to measure Mass Customization. The financial logic of a lot run of one just doesn't make sense.

It is not my purpose to resolve this issue for you. Know that it exists and here is the key:

Key Point: • **Don't start any journey by asking how you will measure success.**

You won't know how to measure success until you start to experience it. The paradox of this issue is huge. You must assume that you will find a way for everyone to win. If the vision defines a state of being that you want to achieve, the measurement criteria will appear after you begin creating the outcomes.

Measurement is the tragedy of many peoples lives. Many parents raise their children with deployment strategies and objective measurements rather than a vision of becoming. There are millions of children who are measured by the grade on their report card rather than what they are learning. Children learn to cheat to get the grade rather than learn to learn to *become*.

The same is true in many Mass Production organizations. Customers are routinely over-promised and under-delivered to enhance the bottom line.

Obviously, you must measure results. What would any game be if you didn't keep score?

Key Point: • **Convert subjective experience into objective measurement.**

Measurement is very simple after the Transformational Change initiative is perceived as legitimate and sustainable. You will begin to hear the phrase,

"You cannot believe what happened."

When you hear this phrase, ask the question, "How did we measure that?" In most instances the measurement will be based in subjective evaluations and "touchy-feely stuff." Try to capture the meaning of the statements and turn them into some objective measures within the four categories listed earlier in this section. You will develop, over time, a very good list of objective measures of what is seamless, effortless, organic, and fun.

Chapter 12
Forces

Organizational change is obviously a very complex process. Transformational Change, specifically, is very difficult because people are caught between two *Contexts* of existence. They must simultaneously run the old organization while creating the new business. This is very confusing for many people. Why can't the new exist now? As we have discussed in other chapters, *creating* takes time, and the consequences of our actions today will not produce results for weeks, months, or even years. We must stay the course.

This brings us to the very important issue of *forces* that drive change. I am reminded of the line from Star Wars, "May the force be with you." As you begin to change your organization, you must be aware of the forces at your command and know how they should be applied to support a Transformational Change initiative.

Let's recall the discussion about *structure*. Water behaves based upon the structure of the land and the invisible force of gravity. In the case of water, a structural engineer has two forces with which to be concerned: gravity and hydrostatic pressure. Without an in-depth understanding of these powerful forces, many engineering mistakes would be made.

People behave based upon structure plus the invisible forces that influence them. As with water, we must understand the forces or psychological damage can be done.

We can see the visual manifestation of forces being applied. We can observe people who are excited, enthusiastic, passionate, bored, obedient, angry, or apathetic. The emotional result of forces being applied is called *attitude*. We have all been told to change our attitude to change our behavior. Attitude appears to be a force that produces change. Manipulating our attitude, such as using affirmations and mantras, at times produces results. Attitude is not, however, a force. It is the result of a force being applied.

What are the forces that drive attitudes and create the predictable behavior we see in the four structures? Four dominant forces exist within every organization and are applied by every person:

1. Power
2. Authority
3. Influence
4. Desire.

There are obviously hundreds of books written about these forces. It is, therefore, not the purpose of this chapter to describe the forces in detail. Instead, this chapter will help you understand how they impact people who are trying to implement change.

The forces like gravity create both dynamic and static behavior. The forces drive the structures that produce the behavior and cultures we describe as organizational life. To totally understand the forces, we must look at them from a structural perspective. If we understand what creates the forces, we can easily activate the forces that will produce desired results.

Definitions

Let's first define the forces. I like the definitions of power, authority, and influence offered by Dr. Ichak Adizes in his book *Corporate Lifecycles: How and Why Corporations Grow and Die and What to Do About It.* I would highly recommend Dr. Adizes work for those who want to examine another view of organizational change.

While there are many definitions for these terms, the following definitions simplify the discussion about the affect of force on organizational change.

Power:	**The capability to reward or punish**
Authority:	**The right to decide "yes" and "no"**
Influence:	**The ability to persuade without using power or authority**
Desire:	**The internal need to resolve tension**

It is important to realize that all four forces have positive and negative polarity. The opposite poles of power and authority are obvious. Influence can be used to benefit or deceive. Desire is both constructive and addictive. It is easy to see how reversing the polarity of a force can change a person's behavior. The switch from rewards to punishment is a popular use of power. Reversing polarity causes predictable oscillation between mutually exclusive extremes. The oscillation process seldom produces sustainable change. Worse yet, constant reinforcement using one extreme alone will cause over indulgence, addiction, and severe imbalance in the organization.

Key Point:	• **Change can occur by reversing the polarity of the force being applied.**
	• **Reversing the polarity leads to oscillating behavior.**
	• **Transformational Change requires a change in both the force itself and the origin of the force.**

One of the most important concepts in Transformational Leadership is to avoid polarity management and learn to change the force being applied and the source or origin of the force itself.

Let's look at an example of all the forces being applied. When my daughter Pam was six years old, she would not spinach. She had no desire to eat it. Spinach did not create any tension that would cause her to put it in her mouth. My desire was for her to eat it. I, therefore, tried to apply the three *external* forces available to me as a parent. I tried influence, "Eat your spinach and you'll grow up to be big and strong like Popeye." No results! I then tried authority, "Eat your spinach, I'm your father!" In other words, my position as father gave me authority to decide on her behalf. No results! I then tried power, "Eat your spinach and you can have dessert. Don't eat your spinach and you'll go to bed early." This is the reward and punish approach. Still, no results!

Where was the spinach from a structural perspective for Pam?

	HAVE	DON'T HAVE
WANT		*OUTCOME BOX* *Dessert*
DON'T WANT	*PROBLEM BOX* *Spinach on her plate* *Angry father* *Threat of early to bed*	*Taste of Spinach* *Muscles like Popeye*

There is nothing about spinach that appears as a positive outcome for Pam. In other words, she *doesn't want* it and *doesn't have* it. No force I tried to apply produced any desire for her to *have* and *want* spinach in her stomach.

This example clearly illustrates how I tried to manage the polarity of the forces available to me to get Pam to change her behavior. Polarity management did produce a result. Pam refused to eat the spinach and we sent her to bed early. When everything fails, the negative pole of power will produce action, even if it isn't the desired result. As all good managers know, you must follow through on your threats to retain power.

Where was the spinach from a structural perspective for me?

	HAVE	DON'T HAVE
WANT	*Power* *Authority* *Influence*	*OUTCOME BOX* *Pam to be healthy by* *eating vegetables*
DON'T WANT	*PROBLEM BOX* *Pam is defiant* *Pam testing my* *resolve* *Pam doesn't listen*	

The spinach activated my desire for Pam to create a healthy body by eating vegetables. I quickly lost my focus on the desired result and turned my attention to my desire to have Pam be an obedient child. Pam would not listen to influence, defied my authority, and tested my resolve to exercise power. Basically, Pam ignited my Problem Box and I showed her who was the boss.

It is interesting to note that eating, as a behavior, starts with the force of desire. Hunger causes tension, and it is typically resolved by consuming something we *want* and *don't have* called food.

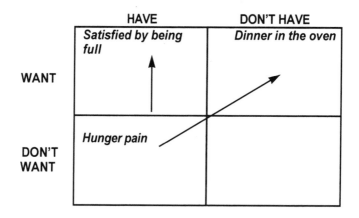

Proper eating is a process of creating a healthy body. For many, eating is merely problem solving–making the hunger pain go away and restoring the feeling of being full. It's the difference between eating to live and living to eat. In our "eat you spinach" example, my desire was for Pam to create a healthy body, but I turned it into a problem-solving session by sending her to bed hungry. I failed as a parent to create alignment of desire with Pam. All I proved was that I was a powerful father.

Key Point: • **The external forces of power, authority, and influence produce desire in other people.**
              • **The alignment of desire produces desired results.**

As change leaders, we must be very aware that external forces create the personal desire to perform at work. Desire has both positive and negative polarity in organizational life.

Key Point: • **People who work with negative desire are in compliance. They will achieve mediocre results.**
              • **People who have positive desire are committed.**
              • **Teamwork is the alignment of positive desire.**

Whenever a corporate change initiative fails or produces less than the intended results, the misapplication of force is the underlying cause.

Let's examine the forces one at a time and determine how each force works and how to produce alignment of desire.

Applying Power

Power is the ability to reward or punish. The positive pole is reward and the negative pole is punishment. We have all seen movies where the conflict between two groups is all about power! A war is typically about who should have authority to decide, but the resolution of the conflict is generally determined by who has the most power. In the United States, we had one Civil War to determine who should have authority. The issue was decided by proving who had the most power.

Power is a very emotional issue. A robbery is the naked use of power. Innocent lives are ruined by bullies who just want to hurt someone. On the other pole, winning a million-dollar lottery is a powerful emotional experience.

In the organizational *Context* all people have power.

Key Point: • **Assuming freedom of choice, power is the willingness to cooperate with authority.**

The negative application of power is illustrated by a labor strike. During a strike, people withhold cooperation with authority and attempt to punish the company by not working. The strike is a blatant form of negative power. Negative power is often applied very subtly. Functional departments often don't cooperate. The constant battle between the actuary, claims, underwriting, and sales functions within an insurance company is the negative pole of power being applied.

Power is also applied in positive ways every day. Many people perform outside their job descriptions doing things they are "not authorized to do" to enhance the image, performance, or results of the company. This behavior is called value added if applied to a customer and generally referred to as above and beyond the call of duty. Positive power is *cooperation* with the wishes of those who have authority. People cooperate every day to receive the reward of a paycheck.

Power is most often applied in combination with the other two external forces of authority and influence. Power combined with authority becomes authorized power.

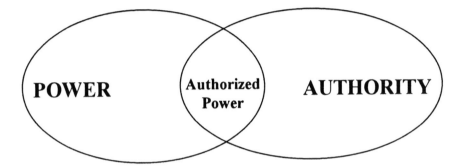

Management has authorized power and decides what rewards and punishments employees will receive. People who perform are given bonuses. People who don't perform are fired. Managers are authorized to decide who, when, where, and how much.

Power combined with influence uses potential rewards and punishments as persuasion tools.

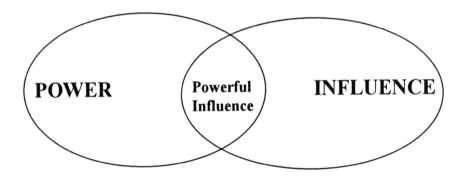

People are powerfully influenced by advertising. The bigger the reward, the stronger the influence. In large-scale negotiations, the larger the potential to punish, the more influential the negotiator can be.

Empowerment is a recent buzzword of many organizational change initiatives. Assuming that freedom of choice exists, empowerment is about getting people to take action without first seeking authority for their action. The fallacy of this word is that all people already have power. They can choose to cooperate or not cooperate. They make choices based upon the perception of rewards and punishments. They don't need more power. Empowerment, therefore, is about authority. It is about combining authority with power to eliminate the fear associated with making an incorrect decision.

Applying Authority

Authority is the ability to decide "yes" and "no." Once again, authority has two poles. The most effective application of authority is to have the ability to decide both "yes" and "no." The poles are frequently split, and it is quite common that no one can say "yes" in many organizations.

Authority is appointed, elected, assumed, and vested. It is legal and informal. It is a heavy burden for some and a compulsive desire for others.

Key Point: • **Authority gives people the ability to decide, but it does not guarantee the ability to implement the decision.**

Authority alone does not implement anything. We have all made a decision to go on a diet. New Year's resolutions are typically good decisions. Seldom are they implemented. Therefore, the application of the force of authority is an *antecedent* only. Someone with authority must decide what to do before those with power can cooperate to make it happen. Authority alone is almost useless. The King without the power of an army cannot collect taxes. The authority of the law does not cause people to obey.

Many properly authorized change initiatives fail. Managers write memos pronouncing new policies, procedures, strategies, missions, or visions. The strategic planning retreat was a great success, and management decided again to be the industry leader. It is true; management has authority to decide.

When implementation fails, managers frequently blame the delegation of authority. Middle managers, therefore, are given authority to decide. Budgets are created that give financial limits to "yes" decisions. Policy manuals give managers and supervisors authority to decide. Over time, authority is carefully distributed throughout the organization and decisions can be made at many levels.

Distributing authority to say "yes" always *has a limit*. Authority to say "no" *has no limit*. Deciding "yes" has risk. Deciding "no" has no risk. Therefore, delegating authority is a well-intended process, but applying the force of authority becomes very imbalanced. Many organizations arrive at the point where the limits for saying "yes" are so narrow that no one will risk deciding "yes." "Yes" is reserved for someone high up in the organization. Many "yes" decisions are the domain of the Board of Directors. An organization where no one can say "yes" is called a bureaucracy!

When authority resides in only one person, the person is called a dictator. The dictator is perceived to be a very powerful person. The dictator is typically a very desperate person who survives by rewarding and punishing people rather than making effective "yes" and "no" decisions. Recall my attempt to have Pam eat her spinach? Twenty years later, she hates spinach because she was sent to bed early by her dictatorial father.

> **Key Point:**   • **Organizational change initiatives frequently confuse power and authority. Believing that power makes decisions and authority implements is an illusion.**

Applying the force of authority, deciding "yes" and "no," seems so simple, yet effective decision making is the most difficult process facing leaders today. Deciding "yes" is a terrifying process for many people. The risk associated with a "yes" decision carries enormous consequences. Committing to spend millions of dollars to change the way a company does business is an incredible leadership challenge. While the force of authority is almost useless without the power to implement, the effective application of the force of authority is a talent of enormous proportions.

Applying Influence

Influence is the ability to persuade people without using authority or power. We all know very influential people. Advertising is influence being applied. An image advertisement does not ask you to make a buying decision or suggest any rewards or punishments for your actions. Image advertisements are designed to persuade you to feel positive about the company in the future.

Influence has both positive and negative polarity. We all know people who have been a positive influence in our lives. The reverse is also true. Some advertisements try to motivate you. Others try to scare you. Recall the last election campaign. Mud slinging is negative influence. Positive campaigns intend to prove that the candidate is influential in a positive way.

A salesperson has only influence with customers. Salespeople are told to sell themselves. If the customer "buys you," they perceive you as being a positive influence. Selling is a difficult skill because the customer has the authority to decide and the power to reject the salesperson.

> **Key Point:**   • **The only force an organization has with customers is the effective application of influence.**

Influence is the external force most clearly intended to create desire. Influence creates desire *to be, to do,* and *to have. Being* influence is the most sustainable. People can be influenced to "be like Mike." They can be influenced *to do* in order *to be–*"eat spinach to be like Popeye." People want *to be* Olympic champions, and they are influenced by the picture of their idol hanging on the wall.

People are influenced *to do*–to take action without changing their state of being. "Try it, you'll like it" is a common advertising slogan. Influence *to do* is not linked to becoming anything different. It merely maintains the current state of being.

Likewise, there are many attempts to influence people *to have.* Impulse advertising is a have it now influence strategy. When people are influenced to have, the outcome is instant gratification.

The force of influence within an organization is often ineffective. Attempts by the sales department to influence engineering seldom work. "We're busy. I'd love to help you out, but unless management changes (authorizes) our priorities, we can't get to your request until next year." As a result, many organizational cultures are completely void of influence. The official memo must authorize anything to happen. Yet, the only way the organization can attract customers is with influence.

Key Point: • **You can't give away what you don't own. An organization that lacks influence internally will seldom apply it well externally.**

The organization that lacks influence internally will appear cold, apathetic, pushy, arrogant, or unethical externally. Advertising campaigns will be perceived as insincere or manipulative. Worse yet, the advertised promise will seldom be fulfilled or delivered by the company's products or services. The company that lacks influence will always over-promise and under-deliver to customers.

The force of influence applied in a positive way is dynamic. Entrepreneurial companies possess a strong influence orientation. The force of influence properly applied creates desire and willingness. When two people positively interact with influence, as the only force between them, they both want the same thing that neither acting alone can create. Neither has authority to decide for the other person. Neither person can reward or punish the other person. The reciprocal force of influence creates alignment of desire *to be, to do,* and *to have* together. A marriage partnership is the alignment of desire resulting from the positive application of the force of influence.

Influence skills are generally missing in many hierarchical organizations. If you work there long enough, you'll learn to apply power and authority to get what you want. Influence skills are perceived as being weak or soft when the alternative of hard core power or authority is available. Yet, the tough guys turn nice guys when they are around customers. Customers often believe that the organization behind the nice guy can deliver. Without internal influence, the over-promise and under-deliver scenario will play itself out. "You can't give away what you don't own."

Applying Desire

Desire is a personal force. It is very different from power, authority, and influence. It can be positive, negative, or neutral. Power, authority, and influence reside in the policies, procedures, and traditions of the organization, independent of people.

Key Point: • **Desire is not an organizational force.**
  • **Organizations do not have desire—people do.**

Desire is the internal, personal need to resolve tension. Tension is created in each of the four structures.

	HAVE	DON'T HAVE
WANT	Tension *"Static"*	*OUTCOME BOX* Tension *"Dynamic"*
DON'T WANT	*PROBLEM BOX* Tension *"Dynamic"*	Tension *"Static"*

The resolution of tension in the form of desire is both dynamic and static. Dynamic tension leads to very visible forms of desire. It is often explosive. Static tension, in the form of stress, is invisible and creates desire that will implode.

The static tension of the *have/want* structure is typically very neutral. We all know someone who has everything. They are very content. They take many things for granted. The tension in this structure does not create desire that will cause change.

The desire to resolve the tension caused by the Problem Box is immediate relief from pain. When your bladder is full, the tension is relieved by going to the restroom. When you have a headache, you take aspirin to relieve the pain. When you are bored, television provides relief. Thousands of problem resolution situations create desire in us everyday.

Problem-solving desire is typically negative and reactive. The tension is associated with something we *don't want!* The tension occurs and we react to it. The desire to restore comfort, safety, love, and control are well known reactive strategies.

Problem Box tension is often explosive. As we discussed in the "Structure" chapter of this book, the Problem Box is full of blame. Blame will cause immediate and often instantaneous reversal of the polarity of power. Children are spanked for spilling milk and employees are criticized for making mistakes.

Living and working in the Problem Box of life will always oscillate between mutually exclusive rewards and punishments. The desire created by this structure is based in negative pain relief.

It is interesting to note that people who can easily and effectively resolve Problem Box tension are in high demand. The Crisis Leader is such a person. They are often perceived as being heroes.

The tension and resulting desire produced by the outcome structure is very different. The tension is to *want* something that you *don't have* and to bring it into being. Desire driven by this form of tension causes us to buy things. People love to buy to resolve the tension of *wanting* and *not having*.

Wanting and *not having* causes people to *create*. The desire to have children results in the act of love between two married people. The force of desire is driven by tension to achieve a future vision.

The creative application of desire is also very dynamic. People pulsate with desire to learn and the tension is not resolved until the desired outcome is a reality. A college degree is the outcome of sustained desire to create. The desire to create can be sustained over long periods. Creating takes time, and sustaining the tension of the creating process within an organization is a critical leader skill. The desire is activated by a vision of what is *wanted*. If the desire to create the vision is strong, the tension to sustain desire will build exponentially.

In the organizational *Context*, desire has both reactive and proactive polarity. The dominant tension for most people in organizations is reactive problem solving. The desire to get finished or produce immediate results is very strong. Both activities are aimed at making the tension associated with the problem go away.

Transformational Change initiatives must be driven by proactive desire. Proactive desire is created by a vision of a *desire future state of being*. Recall the examples of earning a college degree or being an Olympic champion. Both situations must be preceded by proactive desire that often begins years before the outcome is achieved.

Key Point: •   **Proactivity is the ability to sustain the desire of**
**   *wanting to be*.**

"Many people have the will to win, but only a very few have the will to *prepare to win*." This famous quote is about proactivity. Proactive people are driven by the desire to be prepared when it matters. They also, as we will discuss later, define winning in very different ways than those with reactive desire.

In most Industrial Age, Mass Production organizations, proactive desire is missing. People have learned to work with the forces of power and authority, and those who are promoted are those who have the desire to tackle tough problem situations. Creating takes too much time, and many people have no desire to wait for results.

The tension associated with the *don't have–don't want* structure is very negative. People don't have responsibility and they don't want it. Asking someone to volunteer for an assignment creates tension that they want to avoid. "I'm too busy" or "it's not my job" are expressions of negative desire. Many organizational change initiatives are stymied by "we tried that once, it won't work." The tension of a negative vision does not create positive desire.

When the force of desire is positive and in full bloom, people will be perceived as committed.

Key Point:
- **Commitment is the positive application of the force of desire.**
- **Organizational commitment is the alignment of desire within a group of people.**
- **People committed to the same desire will call themselves a team.**

Every executive wants people to be committed to change. Commitment is not about power, authority, or influence. It is about desire. People must *want* what they *don't have* for the positive force of desire to be present.

Key Point:
- **Desire is an internal personal agenda for people. It is activated to relieve structural tensions.**
- **Personal desire to create organizational outcomes does not naturally exist.**

It is very difficult to activate the positive force of desire to create organizational outcomes. True personal desire to create organizational outcomes seldom exists. For example, very few people are committed to produce a profit for the company. Not many people know how a company makes a profit. When the company does make a profit, management says, "it wasn't good enough" or "we need to work smarter next year." It is always implied that the performance of the people had a negative impact on profits. Being blamed does not produce positive desire to perform differently. To have true personal desire to create a profit is rare.

Tremendous confusion exists about applying the force of desire. It isn't an issue of what should be rather what is. Many people don't have positive personal desire within the organization. They remain neutral to negative. They cooperate with authority and trade time for dollars, but they remain cynical and pessimistic about organizational performance. Cooperation, the positive exercise of power, is perceived as desire, but positive desire is very difficult to create at work.

The Self-Directed Team Revolution

A specific misapplication of all the forces is the self-directed team revolution. Many self-directed team initiatives are started to downsize the organization by eliminating middle managers. Middle managers have authority and power that must now be transferred to the team. The term self-directed implies that the people will fulfill the role of manager by making decisions and rewarding and punishing themselves.

Personally, many people *don't want* authority to decide within the *Context* of the organization. The *Context* of Mass Production intentionally separates Thinkers from Doers. To suddenly ask Doers to Think and make management decisions is a contradiction to years of programming. In many situations, the negative component of desire is very strong. Labor and management disputes have established a strong compliance orientation.

Self-directed team initiatives are often announced as empowering workers to be more involved in decisions that affect their work and work environment. The intent is worthy, but the force of desire is not created. It's also common that management holds on to authority hoping that the self-directed workers will merely cooperate more. The workers begin the self-directed journey and quickly realize that their ability to decide still has very narrow limits.

The average worker has very little desire for extra responsibility without increased rewards. If rewards are not increased, the intent of the self-directed initiative will be perceived to reduce cost and reward the shareholders.

Any self-directed team initiative requires a *very clear* understanding of forces. It will backfire if the forces aren't understood. The source of the force must be changed, and the forces being applied must create the positive force of desire.

Organizational Transformation of Force

Organizational transformation is about changing how people behave and how work is performed. It is about effectively applying the external forces of power, authority, and influence and creating the positive, personal force of desire. Countless attempts have been made to transform the forces that drive organizations. Reorganizations of the authority structure are the most common. The new organization chart tells everyone who can now decide "yes" and "no." Thousands of promises have been made to change the power structure. New benefits are provided and the employee of the month plaque appears. All these initiatives merely reverse the polarity of the forces of authority and power.

Attempts to reverse the polarity of influence are started with "close to the customer" campaigns. Customers are promised "red carpet service," "We try harder," "Doing whatever it takes," and "One investment at a time." There are thousands of slogans designed to reverse the polarity of the force of influence.

Key Point: • **Permanent change cannot be accomplished by reversing the polarity of the forces.**

Reversing polarity is a popular management strategy. There are some excellent books about polarity management. These books suggest that both poles are important, but merely managing the polarity is not sufficient to sustain Transformational Change. People must be able to decide "yes" and "no." Rewards must be both positive and negative. Influence must motivate and warn you. Problems must be solved and outcomes created. Organizational life is not an either/or game. *It is both.*

We, therefore, come to the dominant leadership issue of managing forces.

Key Point: • **Effective managers know how to effectively apply both poles of all forces. Reversing polarity, as appropriate for the situation, is called management.**
• **Leadership is about changing the force being applied to produce a totally different result.**
• **Leadership is also about changing the origin of the force.**

These are three key concepts in Transformational Leadership. Leaders must understand that the forces, like gravity, have predictable consequences on people. In the hierarchical organization, top management is the ultimate authority. In the transformed organization, the ultimate authority is the mission statement, not a transient person or constantly changing budgets.

Key Point: • **The mission statement gives continuity to the decision making process, authorizes people to serve customers and influences customers to buy.**

The power to implement decisions already exists. The mission defines the need for effective cross-functional processes to serve customers. The authority of the mission changes cooperation from functional to cross-functional. Teamwork changes the implementation process. Everything goes faster because no one needs to wait for management approval. In this *Context*, people appear empowered.

Influence in the transformed organization is a function of *process wholeness*.

When everyone knows their role in the whole process, employees are partners in process. The force between them is influence, which creates personal desire. The alignment of desire appears as commitment to the customer.

This change in thinking about applying forces appears too simple. It is strange to Mass Production Thinkers. The risk factors of this approach appear enormous. Transferring authority from the executive suite to a mission statement is terrifying. This is a major shift in origin of force. Remember, however, that authority alone cannot implement a decision.

The true need is to transform desire. People must personally *want* something they *don't have* at work. It isn't money, parking spots, benefits, or other tangible rewards. It isn't authority or to be empowered. The issue is fulfillment. People truly have a desire to apply their creative talent at work. It's that simple. Live no illusion, desire is not easy to create in the Mass Production organization.

Let's go back to Pam eating spinach. For years, I tried to manage the polarity of forces with my children. You do it as well, *and* it isn't wrong to do so. Effective parents know how to manage polarity. However, if I want Pam to eat vegetables, I must help her *create* desire for them. The focus must switch from vegetables to what would make them desirable. Pam loved chicken and noodles. We learned to mix vegetables in the gravy along with the chicken and she ate them without any external force.

Transformational Leadership is the same process. Mix a little fulfillment in with work, and they will eat it up. When leaders help people find fulfillment in their work, profit possibilities abound. If people are challenged to work from the authority of the customer backward to the factory, they will create a process to serve the customer. Everyone will be empowered to execute their role in the process. The success of the process in serving customers will create fulfillment, and individual desire will manifest as commitment to perform.

May the forces be with you.

Chapter 13
Psychological Experience

We have talked in other chapters about the impact of change on companies, customers, and employees. We have talked about the logic behind the changes. Information technology has enabled companies to dramatically improve the functional competencies of the organization. However, increases in functional efficiency alone, seldom translates into effective customer service.

The process that serves a customer is horizontal across the organization. The need for cross-functional effectiveness spawned the reengineering revolution. Modern information networks now enable companies to achieve cross-functional capabilities never before dreamed possible. The enabling technology is available, but it must be properly applied.

The logic of change is irrefutable. The logic of automation leads to eliminating the hired hands of the Mass Production assembly lines and validates that it's possible to do more with less—more production with fewer people. The more with less orientation brings temporary relief for organizations that are struggling to survive. The logic of financial analysis reveals leverage points where more investment in technology can justify further reductions in numbers of people. The logic that justifies change always leads to the same conclusion, which is eliminating people.

The logic of more with less, applied within the *Context* of Mass Production, activates a management style called *determined compliance*. When it becomes apparent that change must happen, the call for action is often communicated with determination to be the industry leader. "We will be in relentless pursuit." "We will settle for nothing less than . . ." "When the going gets tough, the tough get going." The company must overcome the challenge to its survival with intelligence, not extra effort. The logic of more with less brings out the work smarter, not harder challenge and everyone tries a little harder to be smart.

Mass Production logic has become very sophisticated. Within the *Context* of Mass Production, it is possible to project a level of performance called the low cost producer. This is the ultimate state of financial existence where all economic factors have been optimized, and the cost of delivered goods or services has reached a level that precludes competition and assures acceptable bottom line results. Everything is standardized—one size fits all. These projections further assume maximum efficiency from the companies *most important asset—people*.

The low cost producer level has enormous appeal to senior executives. It is logical that it can be achieved assuming people are committed to company success. This logical level of projected success leads to the determination reflected in the industry leader speech delivered by the CEO at the annual stockholders' meeting. That speech also contained the announcement that a reorganization would be coming soon.

The low cost producer mentality is based on the belief that winning in the marketplace is just a matter of price. Mass Production Thinkers argue that low prices lead to high volumes, which spread fixed costs over a broader base and reduce product cost to the lowest possible level. All this thinking emanates from logical analyses by the financial *Content* experts of Mass Production.

It is logical to reduce overhead to achieve low cost producer status. Overhead is *people*. People must be eliminated, but aren't they our most important asset? The assumption that people are assets sets up a paradox that many managers struggle to resolve. How can the company grow without the most important assets? If assets are important, why are people being eliminated? Maybe people really are things?"

> **Key Point:**   •   **Logic cannot resolve the paradox of either/or thinking. Are people assets or things?**

I distinctly remember the day my boss called and told me the company was reducing overhead and I needed to fire a person. I had just hired two people to support growth. It didn't matter, "Fire one!" Whether people are assets or things, they certainly are overhead.

The question is not whether to eliminate people; instead, it is who must go? The obvious answer in the past 10 years has been middle managers. If the producer level can be empowered, committed, and self-directed, there is no need for middle managers. The paradox is resolved by choosing to keep the assets of production and eliminate the overhead of managers. Logical!

We have seen hundreds of companies reorganize the organization to be lean and mean. Tom Peters, in his famous book *In Search of Excellence*, justified the logic. Thousands of organizations went on a diet and eliminated the heart of the Mass Production control system from their companies. Middle managers with years of experience were given severance pay and outplacement counseling.

The logic of Mass Production Thinking serves as the basis for change in most instances. It creates, however, a *psychological experience* that is based in *fear of being eliminated*. Even the senior executives who are driving the process are often terrified. Behind closed doors, they will admit they don't know how to do what needs to be done. Insecurity at the management level creates insecurity throughout the organization. Talented people begin to leave. Departures are justified saying, "They can't stand the heat." The more with less problem-solving approach extracts a very heavy emotional toll.

Key Point:	• **Logic translated into action doesn't appear logical.**
	• **What starts as logic arrives at emotions.**
	• **Past experiences form a formidable barrier to change.**
	• **The psychological experience surrounding the change initiative will determine its success.**
	• **The paradox of either/or cannot be resolved.**

Recall the saying, "The best laid plans of mice and men often go astray." Said another way, the logic of the plan seldom accounts for the emotional trauma of those who must implement the plan. Translating logic into action suffers from psychological interpretation. The imbedded muscle memory of past experience is strong. Organizational change initiatives, therefore, must include a deep-rooted concern for the psychological experience of the process.

Importance of Emotions

Emotions cannot be changed with logic. *Emotions are based in experience.* You fear heights because your past experience with height created fear. All the logic about the safety of an airplane will not make someone relax if they fear flying. People who are ready to make their first bungee jump will experience fear that immobilizes their body. Logically they are safe.

Key Point:	• **Fear is not based in logic. It comes from experience.**
	• **Not knowing the future is one of the most feared experiences in human life.**

We could chronicle how your childhood experiences built your emotional intellect. That is the subject of hundreds of child psychology books and not the focus of this chapter. In general, people are programmed to fear not knowing the future. Not knowing causes people to worry because they were scared by not knowing the answers to test questions in school. We have all been told to get an education or you'll be a failure in life.

Leaders, therefore, must understand that the psychological experience associated with the word change is often negative. In the Mass Production Context, the word change means something is out of control. People resist being controlled! People resist change! Mutiny and sabotage are manifestations of the fear of not knowing and not trusting the intentions of the leader.

Let's suppose that you were commissioned to sail with Christopher Columbus on his voyage around the world. You were released from prison and put on a tiny ship destined to sail over the edge of the world. How would you feel if your belief was that the world was flat? Would you be committed to go? Would you trust someone with a crazy idea?

When organizational change intends to lower cost by eliminating people, the livelihood and careers of many people are threatened. People who fear being eliminated are hardly motivated to change anything. When people don't feel secure about their future, they will be anxious, uptight, and afraid.

Transformational Change is about *creating a state of being* that has never existed before. The inescapable fact is that all journeys logically start with not knowing. The logic that justifies the journey is an attempt to provide confidence that someone knows "what we're doing." Assuming there is some trust in the leader, people can be enrolled to begin the journey. The problem is the logic file of the leader is often insufficient to answer all the questions people have about the journey. Worse yet, the logic may emanate for a strange *Context* or from *Content* experts that cannot be challenged.

Frequently people are only told, "We are going to change—don't ask questions." The logic is incomplete or deemed unimportant for them to know. I remember going to church when I was young. "Don't ask why—you're going." We learn as children to comply with authority and do what we're told without asking why. When the question why remains unanswered, people invent an answer that eases the emotional trauma of their participation.

What are the logical questions that people need answered so they can *feel comfortable* with organizational change? There are many questions with many facets, but they fall into 10 major categories:

1. Where are we going?
2. Why go? Am I included?
3. Why change what we currently do?
4. What do we need to create in order to be successful?
5. How will we deploy resources?
6. What is our chance of survival?
8. How will we be rewarded?
9. How will we be treated?
10. How will we be measured?

Consider a change initiative you have experienced. Were you able to clearly answer these 10 questions before the journey began? Most people tell me they couldn't answer a single question. They were told, "The company is having trouble and everything is going to change."

The role of leadership is to answer questions for people. The answers determine the psychological comfort of the people. It's, therefore, very logical that leaders should spend time shaping the psychological experience along with formulating the logic of the economic plan.

The Psychological Experience of No Trust

Mass Production Thinking has shaped the psychological experience of the industrial environment. As we have chronicled in other chapters, Mass Production is based upon assumptions that fundamentally separate Thinkers from Doers. The Thinkers experience the decision making process and become comfortable knowing how decisions are made. Executives, therefore, are psychologically content with change initiatives. To them, change is logical.

The Doers, on the other hand, must perform without knowing how decisions are made. They are told, "Don't ask, just do what you're told." This *Context*, applied over time, leads to a well-established compliance orientation between management and labor. The Doers are expected to trust the judgment of the Thinkers. The assumption is that decisions are made with the best interests of everyone involved. This is not always true. Labor and management disputes are highly emotional no trust issues.

The psychological experience of no trust is negative. People don't buy from companies they don't trust, nor is it likely people will follow a leader they don't trust. There are many facets of no trust behavior, ranging from mild concern to terror. Consider responding to your front door bell at midnight to find a total stranger wanting to use your telephone.

Key Point: • **Trusting someone makes you vulnerable. We have learned not to trust to retain control. To not trust is a survival tactic.**

In the Mass Production organization, no trust retains control. If management doesn't trust labor, control of decision making is retained in management. If Doers don't trust management, they retain control over the amount of cooperation they will provide. No trust prevents the forces of power and authority from being applied in an effortless manner. Operating in this way, the organization will only implement a narrow band of decisions, and customer neglect will be the natural result.

Attempts to change the trust factors between Doers and Thinkers have been resisted by both sides for years. I worked with a company that had been trying to implement employee involvement for four years. Neither side had been willing to take the first step. Doers suggested that management talked a good talk, but it didn't walk the talk. Management suggested that the Doers were self-serving and not committed to the welfare of the company. However it is expressed, no trust is a formidable barrier to organizational change.

Logic will not overcome the emotional trauma of no trust.

Key Point: • **You cannot talk yourself out of something you behaved yourself into.**

Changing the emotions associated with no trust can only be done by changing behavior. Managers must walk the talk. Until managers take some decisive action to change their behavior, Doers will not trust.

Shaping the psychological experience, therefore, is not a unilateral process. Management must begin to behave differently and Doers must take action toward new behavior. If no trust is well ingrained in the experience of the past, the initial steps toward new behavior might be very small. Don't expect Doers to embrace radical shifts in behavior. Building trust is a long, slow process.

Key Point: • **The psychological experience of past conditioning is strong. The muscle memory from the past will dominate the participants going forward**.

If this is true, Transformational Change must begin by creating new muscle memory for participants. This requires new experience in the form of new behavior. As we have said before, logic will not change emotions. Experience changes emotions. Thus, the muscle memory with Mass Production Thinking will not be easily replaced.

The Transformation of Emotions

If emotions are grounded in experience, leaders must realize that the announcement of a change initiative is a critical event. The announcement is the beginning of a *new experience* that will create a new emotional intellect for everyone involved. We have seen people seated in large auditoriums and shown video taped messages that strike fear in the hearts of everyone. We have heard industry leader speeches delivered with determination that intimidate and threaten the audience. The tactic of determined compliance with labor unions creates immediate resistance and emotional trauma.

Key Point: • **Nothing is more important than dealing with the emotions of people.**
• **People who do not trust the intent of the journey will seldom perform with enthusiasm.**
• **Recognizing that people are scared and making it okay for them to be scared is the skill of empathy.**
• **People must be enrolled in the journey, not directed to perform.**

The first step is to understand that there is an *emotional journey* ahead for everyone and the emotions will only change as the experience of the journey unfolds. Everyone will experience the journey from a different perspective and at a different rate. Therefore, the collective emotion will contain many different feelings.

The Structural View

As we have revealed in other chapters, it is difficult or impossible to deal directly with behavior. The same is true with emotions. You don't have time to become a psychologist, and it isn't possible to deal with the emotions of every individual. It is possible, however, to understand how to change the behavior and emotions of a group if we recall that behavior is a function of structure. The same is true with emotions.

Let's examine a structural view of how emotions change.

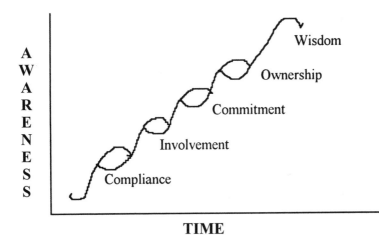

TIME

The experience of life is awareness versus time. Within our experience, we all grow an emotional intellect.[a] Our educational experience grows awareness. Obviously, it happened over a period of time. Some people are committed to life-long learning and develop very advanced levels of awareness. Others stop learning at early ages. For them, awareness is very limited.

As your awareness grows, you become more willing to accept *responsibility* for your life. This is the transition from compliance to involvement. When you accept *accountability*, you have reached the commitment level. Ownership and wisdom are very advanced as we will discuss later.

---

[a] For more information about the concept of emotional intellect, refer Daniel Goleman's book *Emotional Intelligence: Why it can matter more than IQ.*

Between each stage is a bifurcation, a knothole, or fork in the road that will require that you let go of the past to achieve the next level. Think of it as graduation from grade school, high school, and college. Not only does your awareness dramatically increase, you must let go of many old relationships and habits that brought you to that level. Consider how you may have changed your eating habits in becoming committed to a low fat diet. Awareness combined with choice is the key to change. It has very little to do with time.

The bifurcation loop is about freedom of choice. As we will discuss, many people are stuck in the loop and cannot choose new awareness for their life. This is often a tragic circumstance. People who are stuck become addicted to time. Time becomes the enemy of life, and the addiction to saving time is compulsive.

The structural view will always suggest that awareness, not time, will reveal an alternative life experience. The important organizational change agenda is to understand that awareness is the issue. You cannot defeat time.

Compliance

Assuming freedom of choice, the first structural level of emotional experience is compliance. Compliance is a common experience for everyone. We all pay our taxes, drive the speed limits, and generally obey the laws of the land. From an organizational standpoint, people report to work on time and comply with decisions made by those with authority. The *Context* of Mass Production is driven by compliance. Thinkers think and Doers do what they are told. People wait in-between being told for fear of doing something the Thinkers wouldn't want them to do.

Children are programmed to be compliant at an early age. Parents and teachers are the dominant compliance officers. Some people admit that their childhood was dominated by a compliance orientation. Many people haven't experienced true commitment to anything. They played sports because their father wanted them to play, went to college to please their parents, work to pay the bills, and don't know how to be truly committed.

The skillful application of authority and power results in compliance. People study this process. It's called management. Managers learn how to plan, organize, and control. Authority is imbedded in plans and how the organization is organized. Power is the ability to reward or punish those who comply with the plans and operate within the boundaries of the organization. Management control is about compliance.

Membership in a society, group, team, or organization brings an obligation of compliance. All groups have rules that control behavior. We have all experienced compliance and have learned to be patient with the controlling force that demands it. Something legitimate has authorized the controlling force and there is a compliance officer present to deal with offenders.

The psychological experience of compliance is neutral to negative. The emotions turn negative when the compliance officer is overly aggressive or oppressive. Seldom is the psychological experience positive in a compliance-driven environment.

Involvement

The next level of emotion is involvement. When people are free to get involved in an activity, organization, or collective process, emotions instantly change. Many people resist getting involved because it's risky. The risk associated with getting involved is accepting responsibility for making decisions.

Children who are encouraged to accept responsibility for their own lives are being asked by parents to make decisions about the direction of their lives. This is a very *defining moment* for some people. It is very pronounced when students go away to college and must make the tough decision whether to study. The compliance officer is no longer around, and students are free to make their own decisions. Many people are unprepared to be involved.

Organizational involvement requires that people accept responsibility for decision making. This is possibly the most difficult activity of organizational life. Involvement extends the authority structure of the organization to include those who have previously not been involved. A promotion to management is a move from compliance to involvement. It is a *big* step for many people. You must *be ready!*

In the Mass Production *Context*, employee involvement is risky for the employees. They have never been asked to make decisions before. It is also risky for management. Employees may make uninformed choices. The psychological experience of moving from compliance to involvement, therefore, is grounded in going from a state of neutral to negative. At least the initial stage contains fear of making a mistake.

We have all been asked to volunteer for a committee in which we were not sure we wanted to get involved. We know that with involvement comes responsibility. The initial confrontation of the choice to get involved is easy for some and difficult for others. The key is the nature of the cause or the perceived outcome to be created. If the person wants the future outcome that is to be created, the choice of involvement is easy. If not, people will decline to get involved. We have all made these choices.

Fortunately, the psychological experience of involvement turns positive for most people. The positive emotions are a *function of the ongoing experience of involvement*. We have all made the choice to get involved in situations and regret the choice. The opposite has happened as well. "The best thing that ever happened to me was to get involved in the community." One person's passion is another person's poison.

Commitment

The third level of emotion is commitment. The psychological experience of committed people is positive. They *want* what they are creating and have a passion for the process, the people, and the rewards. Commitment is a powerful emotional state. In its highest form, sustained commitment is about the *desire to be*.

Commitment is the outgrowth of a positive involvement experience. The shift from involvement to commitment is often life changing. The college student that is committed to learning can achieve great things. People get involved in the community then make a commitment to serve permanently by running for public office. Thousands of examples can be cited.

Key Point: • **The road to commitment goes through involvement. Do not confuse obedience with commitment. People cannot go from compliance to commitment without first getting involved.**

Organizations today want people to be committed. I am told everyday by executives, "I would like our people to be truly committed to the company." Within the *Context* of Mass Production, this is almost impossible to achieve. This realization frustrates executives and makes them angry. "We pay them a lot of money! They ought to be committed." Yes, they make a lot of money, but the fact is they comply with authority and seldom reach the level of true commitment.

Key Point: • **Commitment comes from creating the *desire* to become.**

The passion of commitment comes from wanting to *be* something. It grows over time until the possibility of being what you want to become appears realistic. Until the shift from possibility to realism occurs, the emotions will remain neutral at best. Therefore, the *journey to commitment* starts with compliance, proceeds through involvement, and arrives at commitment.

Ownership

Is there a psychological experience beyond commitment? There is. It is the experience of *ownership*. Many executives want their employees to act as owners of the business. Their belief is that owners act more responsibly and are accountable for the welfare of the company.

Many employee-ownership plans exist. Some work and some don't. The psychological experience of *ownership* is not the panacea that some people think.

If all employees were owners, it is still possible the company would not effectively implement change.

If we return to the structural view, owners are at a higher level of awareness than those who are in compliance, or even those who are committed. The owner is aware of the total economics of supporting the ongoing enterprise. With this awareness comes a different psychological experience. Let's consider several examples.

Just suppose you own a house. Leading up to the purchase of your first house, you were committed to having it. You *wanted* something you *didn't* have. That commitment caused you to work hard, save money, and motivated you to work long hours. When you achieved your dream, you were thrilled—for a moment. Then something happened. After you moved in, the awareness of needing to fix it up became a reality. You likely expected this reality, but as you began the living experience, you uncovered work that was beyond your initial awareness. Many people can tell you the buyer beware scenario of home ownership.

Consider the people who want to own their own businesses. Thousands of young aspiring MBAs would like to own their own businesses. We read about those who make it. The fabulous wealth of Bill Gates of *Microsoft* or Steven Jobs of *Apple* causes people to dream of starting their own business someday.

For every entrepreneur who makes it, there are thousands who fail every year. What happens? With ownership comes a new awareness of the economics of making it work. Some have a viable plan. Most are not aware of the economics of ownership.

Many people would love to own a boat, a horse, a summer cottage, or a motor home. You pick it. Once the euphoria of initial ownership wears off, the economic reality appears. For some, the psychological experience is as they envisioned. For many, the experience turns negative. Open the Sunday Classified Advertisements and observe people disposing of ownership.

To understand this phenomenon, recall Chapter 6 entitled "Structure." Owners *have* what they *want*.

	HAVE	DON'T HAVE
WANT	*A Business* *A House* *A Boat* *A Child* *A Marriage*	
DON'T WANT	*PROBLEM BOX* *"It Broke"*	

The behavior in this structure is to keep, to use, to maintain, to protect, to love, to abuse, and to take for granted. Ownership is a very positive psychological experience. However, *once the creation exists*, it only has one way to go—to the Problem Box.

This is not a pessimistic view. It is the Law of Entropy, which says that all things over time will decline, decay, deteriorate, and ultimately fail. The important business principle is *nothing fails like success*.

Key Point: • **With ownership comes awareness of the total economics.**

The economic awareness of ownership causes tension for owners. As a result, owners want employees to be committed to making the economics of the company work. Owners ultimately realize that they are dependent upon employees for the economic success of the company.

Key Point: • **A tremendous shift in the economics of success has occurred in the past 20 years. The psychological experience of ownership has changed dramatically.**

In the *Context* of Mass Production, the economics of success are dependent upon "things" doing what "things" are supposed to do. The owners own the domain of thinking. Control of "things" is built into the system, and the psychological experience of ownership is based upon predictable factors within their control.

It has now changed. The new *Context* of work requires Doers to Think, thus, the need for employees to think like owners. However, it's not that easy. Doers can't think like owners. They aren't aware of the economics of ownership, nor do many of them care.

Let's go back to the structural view. Ownership has only one place to go and that's toward the Problem Box. After something exists, the psychological experience with it will contain a predictable negative component. Consider children, marriage, house, car, or boat. It is equally true with your own business. I have seen many people who have their own business, and it's a yoke around their neck.

Key Point: • **The psychological experience of ownership isn't all positive. There is a predictable, sizable, negative burden associated with owning a business.**

Then why should employees buy into being an owner? Why should they want the burden? Worse yet, why do some companies try to lead change initiatives by promising employees ownership in the company? The tangible rewards may be enticing, but with ownership comes a predictable burden of economic responsibility and the trauma of survival and change.

Key Point: • **Continuous creating must be the orientation of ownership.**

I hope you can understand the importance of continuous creating as the orientation of owners. Once creating stops, problem solving will begin. The problem-solving structure brings blame, and the psychological contentment of ownership becomes an illusion.

Wisdom

It is important to understand that the psychological experience of life has many facets. It is impossible to achieve a constant, steady state of feeling. Feelings come from experience, and experiences have positive, neutral, and negative aspects. The psychological experience will vary accordingly.

One person lamented, "Then I'm condemned to be an emotional basket case all my life!" "How can people in the ghettoes of life ever experience any positive emotions?"

This perspective appears to be real if emotions are the result of experience. If the events of our life cause us to feel, this would be true. Fortunately, a level of awareness dispels this myth. It's called *wisdom*.

Wisdom is not about intelligence. It has nothing to do with the amount of education you have.

Key Point: • Wisdom is about awareness of the universe *and* manifestation of that awareness in your life.

The wisdom of the ages is available for everyone to know. The universal laws of life and living are well documented.

Key Point: • Knowing doesn't equal doing.

The key to wisdom is the ability to translate knowing into doing, also known as walking the talk.

Wisdom is about integrity. When your thinking, feeling, and behavior are in alignment, you have integrity. Integrity is a commitment to *be*.

Wisdom is being *unconditional* in relationships with others. A mother who has unconditional love for her child displays wisdom. It's the deepest level of love between two people.

Key Point: • Wisdom is knowing that the circumstances of your life don't make you feel. What you believe about those circumstances determines how you feel.

Wise people know that they can only control one thing: what they choose to believe about the circumstances of their life. This fact is reflected in the old parable,

> Give me wisdom to know what I can control and
> what I can't, and to know the difference.

Wisdom is knowing how to choose what to control. To the wise person, life is made up of choices. Choosing to be the creative force in your own life is a sign of wisdom.

Organizations talk about the concepts of wisdom. Unconditional guarantees appear to reflect this level of awareness. It is, however, rare that an organization walks the talk. I asked a vice president about his bank's advertising slogan, "Doing whatever it takes." The slogan was unconditional, *but* as he clarified, "only within reasonable limits."

Mass Production organizations seldom achieve a level of awareness that reflects wisdom. Many are ethical, honest, and committed to worthy values. Some achieve the awareness of commitment, yet they frequently over-promise and under-deliver to customers. The unconditional service of Nordstroms is an example of wisdom being applied throughout an organization.

Suffice it to say that most organizational change initiatives are not designed to achieve the awareness of wisdom. It is nearly impossible for people who are working in a compliance environment to comprehend the concepts in this reality. People who even think at this level are perceived as weird.

Key Point: • **The psychological experience that is most desired, even in organizational life, resides in the awareness of wisdom.**

Wisdom is a highly coveted state. Leadership courses teach how to create the awareness of wisdom in an organization. These courses are perceived as soft by most executives. The compliance orientation of Mass Production Thinking is so strong, most leaders are thankful when employees are willing to get involved.

Key Point: • **You must treat people at the level of their awareness and help them make the choice to move beyond.**

Therefore, it is urgent to understand that the *psychological journey* begins where people are located. It is unreasonable to expect workers who have been in compliance for years to be a self-directed, high commitment team overnight. Teaching the concepts of ownership and wisdom to those in compliance is like teaching calculus to grade school students. The psychological experience is a *journey*. It takes time to experience life.

Awareness is the barrier. The ghetto of life is conditioned consciousness. This is not an environmental issue. Many executives live in the organizational ghetto trying to fix people into compliance. It happens every day because of the awareness of Mass Production Thinking.

A shift in awareness is first and foremost freedom of choice. You are free to think as the wise person thinks. Many people have studied the process. The question is "Are you willing to take action consistent with this awareness?" Translating awareness into behavior is a difficult assignment for many people and organizations.

The Race Against Time

Success in business is a function of time. Failure in business is a function of time. Success and failure in life are functions of time. Your career depends on how well you manage time. Super Bowl champions manage time. A key to success in athletics is a time out. The clock stops, but time continues. A time out is artificial time imposed on real time.

We are told every day, "This is not the right time to change." In other words, "Let's wait until we have time." There is always time? Time? What is time? We waste it, use it, spend it, save it, manage it, tell it, but what is it? When did time begin? What existed before it was created? Who created it? What an amazing phenomenon.

Key Point: • **Time is an organizing mechanism.**
  • **Your cannot defeat time.**
  • **Your perception of time is the psychological interpretation of your life experience.**
  • **How you metabolize time determines how you age.**

Time flies! Time stands still! A minute on a hot stove would seem like forever. An hour with a precious person seems like a minute. Time speeds up and slows down. When you are bored, time drags. When you're in love, time stands still. Some days you have enough and others there is too little. Time is perceived by our conscious mind, processed by the brain, and metabolized by the body. Time is translated into an experience that literally determines how we age.

What would the world be like without time? Chaos! Planes would arrive and depart at will. How would you know when to be at the airport? There is no such thing as sooner or later without time. Time, as an organizing mechanism, is very useful. The psychological experience of life would be paralyzing without some measure of progression. Time provides the underlying framework for all organized activities. Without a measure of time, nothing would work as a system or perform as expected.

Key Point: • **The perception of time varies with the awareness of the person.**

Some people claim that they waste time. What do they do when they waste time? Some people say, "Nothing." Others tell me, "I do something I shouldn't be doing." Why aren't they doing the something else? "Because I'm doing the other thing." Why are you doing the wrong thing? "Because I'm lazy. I should exercise, but I'd rather watch TV." Is watching TV is a waste of time? "Sometimes it is and sometimes it isn't." Really? When is it a waste of time and when isn't it? "When something entertaining is on it's not a waste of time. When the news is on it's a waste." Really? If TV is a waste of time, why have a TV? Why not throw it away—waste it? "Because I want it." Then it must not be a waste of time to watch TV. What do you *do* when you waste time?"

This dialogue drives people crazy, but it makes the point that people link time to *doing*.

Key Point: • **When people are forced to *be*, they feel like they are wasting time.**
  • **To learn patience, learn not doing.**

Being without *doing* is a waste of time to many people. We all came into this world as human beings. We were initially loved as a being. When the psychological experience changes to *doing*, time becomes a compulsive issue for most people. When we are loved for what we do, reinforcement around being stops.

Key Point: • **When human doing masks human being, love becomes a conditional issue.**

It is important to understand the psychological experience of people who waste time. Many human beings have time-based awareness. They interpret their life experience within a finite frame of time, space, and causality. To them, life is a problem to be solved. The time-bound person is easily frustrated by slow drivers in the fast lane, people who are late, long lines, and many other barriers that impede their journey through life. Their assumption is the faster they go, the more they will have and the more successful they will be. However, somehow they never arrive. They never have enough money, clothes, fun, or enough of enough. They don't have enough time to get enough.

Key Point: • **The focus on time preempts the expansion of awareness.**

Einstein proved that time is relative. It never began nor will it ever end. We believe, however, that our lives are linear and begin to believe the same is true with time. This is an illusion. Many people fail to experience the moment of now because they believe that now is a waste of time. What *now* are they yearning for? They constantly seek the allusive moment in time when they will arrive at success. Success to them is a destination when, in fact, success is a journey. What prevents us from reaching success? It is not time. It's *awareness*.

Transformational Change is not about time. It's about awareness. To create the new reality will require acceptance of time as an organizing mechanism. Time lines are important as long as they are linked to increasing awareness. Leaders who continue to require compliance from workers are condemned to a frantic race against time.

The Bifurcation—Freedom of Choice

All of the discussion thus far assumes freedom of choice as a prerequisite for moving from compliance, to involvement, to commitment. Freedom of choice exists in our country. The Constitution guarantees that right. People are free to choose where they live and work. The *Context* within every organization contains freedom of choice.

Key Point: • **Many people unconsciously give up their freedom to choose and are unaware of having made that choice.**

The following section is very difficult to write and equally difficult for many people to accept and understand. As you read this section you must think about what I'm saying from a structural point of view and then judge whether it is true for you and your organization.

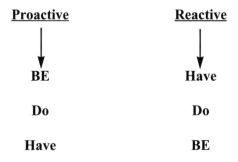

Most people live in a *reactive* orientation to life. They work to *have*. They do what they do to *have* enough money to pay their bills, live comfortably, support their family, and retire. There is nothing wrong with this approach to life. We all have a reactive orientation—some more then others.

> **Key Point:**   • *Having* **enough is the psychological driving force for many people and many organizations.**
> • *Having* **enough limits awareness to current reality.**

Having is an insatiable appetite. People who have, want more. People who don't have, want what those who have, have. Those who want more, perceive that they don't have enough, and they want what those who have enough have. We all become addicted to the vicious cycle of *having enough* and *wanting more*.

When we say the word addicted, it suggests a highly negative *Context*. It is a judgmental word that implies someone was unable to control their behavior and became addicted to a foreign substance.

> **Key Point:**   • **The structural definition of addiction is the relentless pursuit of vague or negative visions.**
> • **Not enough, as a vision, is both vague and negative.**
> • **Enough is seldom accurately defined and people don't know when it is achieved.**

Vague or negative visions frequently define the relief from pain. People relieve the pain of hunger by eating until they have enough. People smoke to relieve the stress of life, they drink alcohol to relax and socialize with friends, and they work to *have enough* money to retire someday.

Key Point: • **In the reactive orientation, people believe that** *having* **leads to being.**
• **In the addicted state, having pain leads to a pleasurable state of** *being*.

Addicted people confuse pain with pleasure. Recall your first taste of whiskey. It was harsh. It was, in fact, painful, but the pleasure of *being* a big person made the pain pleasurable. If you have ever smoked, the first drag on a cigarette was awful. People endured the pain to *be* a big shot like the rest of the gang. Over time, the pain becomes a pleasure and the habit becomes addictive.

Smoking and alcohol are obvious examples of linking the pain of *having* to the pleasure of *being*. The reactive orientation contains the slogan, "No pain, no gain." The assumption is that hard work will ultimately cause you to arrive at some vague or idealistic state of being.

Key Point: • **You can never get enough of what you don't want in the first place unless you confuse pain for pleasure.**

Consider the person we all know—the workaholic. When they were children, work was painful at first. Were you forced to do your chores? Did you enjoy homework? Work is like the cigarette. Your first encounter happened so long ago you forget the pain and now perceive it as pleasure. If it is pleasure, why does work cause so much stress? Why do so many people say, "Thank God it's Friday." Work to many people is an addictive habit in pursuit of enough.

The argument at this point is that some people really enjoy their work. I hope that is true for you. Many people have positive specific visions of what they are creating at work, and for them work is not an addiction. They are free to choose where to work and have not succumbed to the addictive process.

The truth, however, is work has become an addiction for millions of people. They are working to *have enough* and the vision that drives their relentless pursuit is vague and negative.

Like people, organizations become addicted in pursuit of vague and negative visions. The addicted organization is full of addicted people. They are all striving to produce enough profit, which will never be enough. No one cares about anything other than *enough* and enough never exists.

The addiction to enough is strong at the executive level. Senior managers put in long hours and forsake their health and family life to squeeze 1% more into this year's bottom line. Once it's over, it will be judged as the best year ever, but still not good enough.

There are hundreds of stories about executives who have tried to resolve the addiction to enough by having more of the same done faster. They are determined to solve the problem. They constantly make things go away to solve the problems.

They truly believe they are creating, not problem solving. They use the term creative solutions to pretend they aren't addicted. The proof of the addiction always shows when they fail to celebrate *having enough*.

The psychological experience of addicted people and the organizations they work in is constant worry, fear, and anger. These are the negative emotions of the present, the future, and the past. Relief from this emotional trauma is a phony bravado about when the going gets tough, the tough get going. The truth is when the going gets tough, the tough are helpless.

It is so important not to interpret this addicted state in a judgmental way. That will only deny your own addiction. We are all addicted to having enough and wanting more. We all have a Problem Box, and denying it won't make it go away.

Breaking the addiction is freedom of choice. I see people everyday who are miserable at work. I tell them to quit. Their immediate reaction is "Are you crazy?" This confirms the addiction. No, I'm not crazy, I'm just asking them to exercise freedom of choice. They are free to choose to quit, but they won't have enough money if they quit.

Jane was a young executive at a local bank. She hated her job and wanted to be a consultant. She was always angry about the way women were treated at the bank. I told her to quit. Her first question was how much money could she make if she quit. I told her, possibly none. She went into worry and fear. I told her to stay at the bank. She said she hated her job and the addictive loop played itself out again.

Jane was free to choose, but she had given up her freedom to have the pain that she confused as the pleasure of being one of the guys. Once she could see through the illusion, she quit.

Many salespeople are addicted. They tell me, "It's just a matter of price." They have been beaten with the price objection and start to confuse pain for pleasure. Price is an addiction. Nothing is just a matter of price. Everything must perform some function or fulfill some need negating the logic that it's just price.

The price addict who occupies the executive suite will devastate an organization. Nothing will ever be enough. The addicts will always be looking for cheaper, lower cost alternatives and will drive the engineering, manufacturing, and sales departments into a feeding frenzy in search of the low cost producer state. This relentless pursuit of a vague vision will strip the organization of talent. The shark pool that remains will have little chance of survival.

What if this addictive scenario is true in your organization? How would you motivate addicted people to change the organization? The organization is *them!* How would you break this addiction? Obviously, it isn't easy. I hope you can see that it cannot be done with logical declarations or a video taped message from the chairman about being world class. It takes leadership that understands how to transform the force of desire.

Reading about addiction frustrates many people. It is important for you to feel the psychological experience. I hope it made you a little angry. It is so real that it should make us all angry. The only salvation is to realize that addiction is not caused by people. It is all a matter of structure. The Problem Box addiction of many organizations is offset many times by the Outcome Box experience of creating to a clear specific vision. Increasingly today, executives are becoming aware that people are not assets. *People are people.* People have creative talent, and when they are enrolled to create, the psychological experience is invigorating, inspiring, and fulfilling. To break your addiction, learn to *create.*

The Proactive Orientation

Thousands of people have exercised freedom of choice and left the addicted organization behind. The entrepreneurial revolution is living testimony to that fact. The entrepreneur makes a conscious choice to *be* that ultimately leads to *having.* I helped Jane internalize her desire *to be a consultant.* We speculated about whether she would have enough money if she quit. Money wasn't the issue. I helped her create an accurate vision of what she wanted to become and suggested she immediately do something toward that state of being. We designed a business card that she would have if she were a consultant. The process of creating the card forced her to decide what kind of consultant she would be. The process of creating the card enrolled her in the psychological journey and the rest is history. Today, Jane is a consultant. One year after the card was created, she exercised freedom of choice and left the bank.

Wanting to *be* is the most powerful desire a person can have. People stand at the alter and say, "I Tom take thee Nancy to *be* . . ." Olympic champions decide years before the games that they want to *be.*

It is important that we not lose sight of the larger context of the process of going from being, to doing, to having. It is called proactivity.

Every executive, regardless of *Context,* wants their organization to be proactive. Everyone has a sense that the reactive firefight doesn't produce results. The firefight is the reactive *having* orientation. It is visible and frustrating. To change behavior, you must change the structure! The underlying structure that activates proactive effort is *wanting to be different.*

Transforming the Psychological Experience

We can now understand how important it is to transform the psychological experience as a part of any organizational change initiative.

Key Point:
- **People must be enrolled in a journey that is possible.**
- **The journey is to a new state of *being*.**
- **It must be safe for them to get involved.**
- **The rewards for involvement must be psychological, not tangible.**
- **The commitment level will not materialize until the experience of involvement produces a payoff.**

The fatal mistake is to define the ultimate destination in terms of *having* or *doing*. As we discussed, awareness leads to a new state of being. "I want to be an Olympic champion, doctor, or professional golfer." Doing and having are integral to being, but you must want to *be* a professional golfer years before you can walk the fairways at Augusta.

During the enrollment stage, people must see the difference between *possibilities* and *realism*. Possibilities will cause people to get involved. The realism of the journey will always appear doubtful and cause people to remain in compliance.

A *having* orientation promises people increased rewards. Profit and gain sharing are common incentives. This form of enrollment merely reverses the polarity of the force of power. Increased activity will appear, but it will not be directed at being different. A *having* orientation alone is unsustainable over a long period of time and will not transform "the Business of the BUSINESS."

Properly done, the transformational journey is defined as *creating* a new *process* to serve customers, and everyone must clearly understand their roles, not job, in that process. It is important to change the language and thinking associated with a person's responsibilities. While thousands of jobs have been eliminated in the past 20 years, roles have remained. If a person can fulfill a vital role in the process, they become an integral part of the team. The psychological experience of having a role in something inspires people to want to be involved.

The rewards for involvement must be psychological. People want to be acknowledged for their contribution. They want to know that what they do is important and really matters. If their work is defined as a role in the customer service process, their contribution to the success of organization can be clearly identified.

Never underestimate the importance of intangible rewards for performance. The biggest mistake is to drive change initiatives with tangible rewards. While money and benefits are important, the dominant reward that causes emotions to change is *feeling important*. Wanting to be important is the first step in transforming a person's desire. People *do* incredible things when they genuinely feel they are (*be*) important. When work allows people to apply their creative talent, they quickly and easily become committed.

Creating the emotion of desire to drive organizational change is not well understood. It is branded as soft stuff. Mass Production tough guys believe that a company-wide announcement of a new strategy will inspire people to achieve new heights.

Key Point: • **Organizational change cannot be declared into existence. It must be lived into existence.**

New vision and mission statements are often a part of the new strategic plan, but both vision and mission must be lived into existence. The experiential process creates the emotions. Executives should, therefore, consider what action they *will take* when announcing a new vision or mission. They must lead the psychological experience.

Enrollment Done Well

Consider what it must have been like when Mr. Iacocca announced a new vision for Chrysler. Imagine that you were an employee at Chrysler when he declared, "We must become America's car company." How would you have felt? Most Chrysler executives were cynical about the proclamation. The negative emotions reflected the realism of the past. With 600,000 cars in stock that were already beginning to rust, it was easy to be cynical. How, therefore, could Lee Iacocca communicate a vision and help people experience his commitment to achieving it? The famous story of how Lee accepted *his* car was an experiential process of communicating commitment to the journey. "Every car is my car or we won't make it."

Key Point: • **People must be enrolled, not told. Leaders must translate proclamations into personal behavior. They must begin to walk the talk.**

Lee enrolled people in his vision. He didn't ask them to accept the realism of it. He asked them to consider the possibilities. Retired executives from Ford came out of retirement to experience the possibility. Lee told the American consumer, "If you can find a better car, buy it." Knowing that Chrysler cars were the worst, he was demonstrating his commitment to his vision by asking others to get involved or get out. Many of the cynics left. The rest is history.

Enrolling people is an emotional experience. It will often appear totally illogical.

Key Point: • **Logic will not inspire people to greatness.**

Beyond the Announcement

In hindsight, it's easy to see how Lee Iacocca transformed Chrysler. Was the transformation of Chrysler an accident that just happened or was it a brilliant plan? Frankly, it was neither.

Key Point:
- **A transformational journey cannot be planned. It is an experience that happens.**
- **Enrolling people in the psychological journey is more important than the plan.**
- **Awareness of what's possible is the barrier.**

Christopher Columbus could not *plan* his journey around the world. The settlers of early America could not *plan* their journey. "Go west young man, go west!" Frankly, your life cannot be planned. Decide what you want to *be* and enroll yourself in the journey.

The key is enrolling people in a psychological journey. People need to be excited about the *possibilities* of the journey rather than the rewards after they arrive. It is a mistake to focus on *having*.

The psychological journey always begins with fear of the unknown. Leaders must not underestimate the importance of communicating the vision and demonstrating their own commitment to the journey.

Beyond the announcement, there are two ways to effectively continue the enrollment process. The first is called a benchmark, and the second is a simulation. Both accomplish similar outcomes in different ways.

Benchmarking attempts to find an existing company or organization that has already achieved a level of success similar to what you desire. Through observation of success, people can visualize the possibility of that success occurring in their organization. People are inspired by seeing that others have tried new things and have not died. The people who have achieved the success can recount the pitfalls and pain so that others can anticipate the process. Knowing that others have successfully gone before gives courage to those yet to go.

This form of emotional enrollment is still very logical and often fails to address the fear people really feel about the journey. Once again, logic does not motivate.

The second, and more effective way to enroll people in change, is to *simulate the experience*. If the journey can be simulated, the emotions associated with the journey can be experienced in a safe and nonthreatening way. If the simulation is successful, the emotional intellect of the organization will be positive as the journey begins.

Consider the journey to the moon. The astronauts went through countless simulations to experience the flight before it occurred. In this way nothing surprised them or caused them traumatic fear. The simulated experience helped them expect the unexpected.

Airline pilots spend hours in flight simulators to remain calm when faced with life-threatening experiences.

Key Point: • **If it is absolutely essential to remain emotionally calm when confronted with unexpected circumstances, simulate the experience to program the mind to remain calm.**

There are thousands of ways to simulate future experiences. A simulation is proactive practice. Can you envision a basketball team practicing last second shot situations? How can they remain calm when there is 3.7 seconds on the clock and they need to go the length of the floor and score to win the national championship? How many times must professional golfers pretend that they are making a 3-foot putt to win the U.S. Open?

Simulations take people to the future and help them experience the desired end result. While it is difficult to feel the emotions of 20,000 screaming fans, it is possible to proactively practice success until it feels very natural for it to ultimately occur.

Key Point: • **A simulation goes beyond visualizing the success. It makes the experience appear real in both logical and emotional terms.**

The organizational challenge today is to find time to proactively practice the success of becoming a mass customizer. How can this be simulated? When would you find the time to proactively practice? Is there anything that would simulate it? It might be easy to benchmark, but how could it be simulated?

The Egocentric Predicament

Let's suppose you are a hard-nosed Mass Production Thinker who has made all the mistakes outlined in this chapter. You have announced with determination that things must change. You have felt the urgency of wasting time. You have promised that *having* will lead to *being*. The intent was right, but the process was flawed.

How are you going to swallow your pride and admit you made a mistake? When you announce the revised vision and the new change initiative, how can you change the psychological journey?

This is a tough assignment facing many executives today. It is real and it's terrifying. In many cases, the bridge is burned. You were so determined last time that taking a different approach now might be perceived as failure. You cannot undo the past. The question is what now?

Transformational Leadership is not a test of will. It is not a contest to be won. It is not an ego trip. It is about changing "the Business of the BUSINESS" and transforming the organization of the existing business to support the new business. This is *not a soft agenda*. Therefore, realize that the journey ahead is much different from your last proclamation.

Key Point: • **Revised visions must reflect a *state of being*.**
                   • **It should demand that everyone create a new "Business of the BUSINESS."**

Examine your last vision. It was likely about *reorganizing the organization*. The re-vision must be about creating a new "Business of the BUSINESS." Make sure your new vision is clearly stated. "We must become America's car company." Lee Iacocca's vision was not about reorganizing the organization.

Key Point: • **Feel your own emotional enrollment in this new vision. It will be different.**

Communicate your excitement for the new vision to those who must be enrolled in the process of creating it.

Let go of the fact that you did it wrong the first time. Do it *different* this time. Think from the customer back to the business. Help people visualize their role in serving the customer and understand that they are important. Emotions will drive the creation of a new business.

Key Point: • **Ideas are awareness in bloom.**

Ask people to get involved to expand their awareness. Benchmark and simulate to create awareness. People who are aware will generate ideas about how to perform differently. It is a proven fact! It is a powerful psychological experience.

Let go of planning the journey. The Mass Production Thinker in you will want to develop a plan. Visioning replaces planning and enrolling replaces organizing. The journey will begin if people are enrolled properly. Commit to practice to develop a process.

The Psychological Journey

People love to buy! They hate to be sold! People love to create! They hate to be blamed!

Key Point: • **Leaders create the structure that defines the psychological experience that people want.**

You cannot force people to have positive desire at work. The addicted millions seldom know the joy, even at home. You must realize that the psychological experience of compliance dominates most people at work and will be an enormous barrier that you cannot remove. Only the person can remove the barrier. It is an internal issue.

Create the vision and the mission that defines a new state of *being* and ask people to *get involved* in creating it. There is no one to blame for the way it is in current reality. The conditioned consciousness of the existing culture is the result of Mass Production Thinking applied for 60 years. Don't blame yourself or anyone else for the way it is. It is time for it to *be different*.

The psychological journey will unfold. There will be emotional highs and lows. People will encounter difficulty and want to give up. Think of the settlers going west—those that gave up at the Mississippi River and founded St. Louis. Some continued the journey and settled at the base of Pike's Peak. It's now called Colorado Springs.

The only thing you can control is your own psychological journey. How far do you want to go, and can you enroll others to go along? There will be plateaus and natural resting points. "Stop and smell the roses." If you want to move on, don't blame those who are content and want to stay. Freedom to choose is not addictive. *Wisdom* is the ultimate destination.

Chapter 14
Collective Intelligence

The *Context* and Content of the business environment are changing dramatically. The new business environment is the subject of hundreds of books and articles. If you examine all that is being written, it can be boiled down to one core concept: *interdependent behavior*. What are teams, partnerships, integrated processes, networks, and seamlessness? The integrative force that creates interdependent behavior is *collective intelligence*.

Throughout this book, I have suggested that Mass Production Thinking is technologically obsolete. Mass Production manufacturing principles still work and will continue to be applied in many companies, but Mass Production organizations are not built on collective intelligence. One conclusion, therefore, is very clear—the new business environment cannot be created using Mass Production Thinking.

> **Key Point:** • **A business environment exists beyond Mass Production. Seeing the *possibility* of that environment is the prerequisite for creating it.**

The new business environment exists and is very different from Mass Production. Collective intelligence is necessary to create seamless, cross-functional processes that can customize products and services with speed. To those trained in Mass Production, this unique customized approach to doing business has tremendous appeal, but it requires that executives and managers at all levels let go of their standardized mentality. Many of the rules of Mass Production Thinking must be broken to achieve it.

Many Mass Production organizations have arrived at the bifurcation point to the new environment. Some Mass Production Thinkers can see *the Business of the BUSINESS* in the new environment. Integrated software creates networks and systems that enable companies to achieve both Mass and Customized. However, most Mass Production Thinkers believe that the new environment is a linear extension of the old, and they strategize how to reorganize the Mass Production organization to achieve it.

The new environment requires a new way of organizing the business. Interdependent behavior requires a process-based organization versus the functional approach of the hierarchical model. Cross-functional teams have been formed in many companies, yet Mass Production Thinking dominates their behavior. The ability to organize the new environment poses a major challenge to the Mass Production mind.

The interdependent relationships of the new environment require an integrated information system. Over the past 10 years, most change initiatives have succeeded at changing the electronic linkage of every company. The ability to communicate has been greatly enhanced. Yet, Mass Production Thinkers remain and determine the type and format of the communication that is occurring.

Mass Production Thinking fails dramatically in the creation of software and information systems. When information systems groups were initially formed, they were functional entities similar to manufacturing, engineering, and sales. The centralized mainframe computer system gave them functional independence and total control over the Mass Production organization. The advent of distributed systems was an enormous challenge to their ability to control the information flow of the organizations. We have seen a *siege* mentality between the systems departments and other functional groups within many hierarchical organizations. The transformation that has occurred within the systems and software environment is a classic example of Transformational Change.

If you are involved in software or information systems development, Mass Production Thinking will frustrate you. It is not possible to create software within the context of Thinkers think and Doers do. Yet, many software designers and systems engineers are constrained to live and work within Mass Production organizations.

It is fair to say that Silicon Valley was not created using Mass Production Thinking. The need for collaboration to create the hardware and software that has fueled the technology revolution is not found in the Mass Production management models. Plan, organize, and control is a useless model to high-tech companies. The new model is visualize, enroll, and align.

The interface between Mass Production and the new environment is often devastating. Mass Production managers are still in charge in most places. They are typically trying to fix the old environment. On the other hand, the information systems people are trying to create new systems. As I have chronicled many times before, creating and problem solving are very different activities. Creating takes time. The need for fixing is *now*! The difference between creating and problem-solving technologies causes enormous tension.

Let me give you an example. I have worked with many information systems people within Mass Production organizations. Many of them have been told to do it right the first time. This is an assumption within Mass Production Thinking. There isn't a software or systems person alive that can do it right the first time. Creating is not trial and accuracy—it is trial and error. The fix-it mentality of the Mass Production Thinker cannot tolerate errors.

The tension caused by the fix-it approach leads to a chicken or egg debate.

"Should we enable existing processes with technology or should we create new processes and then enable them with technology?" This is the essence of the reengineering revolution. The correct approach is to create a new process before enabling it with technology. Since Mass Production managers don't think in terms of processes, they want it fixed now. This is a *Context* issue that must be addressed at the leadership level. Does the company need to change *the Business of the BUSINESS* or *reorganize the organization*? Without an accurate vision of the desired future state, this dilemma cannot be resolved at the operational level.

The need for leadership in creating the new environment is critical. This was evident to me in working with the Information Systems Group vice president of a local company. He was frustrated and ready to submit his resignation. The president wanted the existing processes fixed with new technology—*now*! The feedback from the president to the Information Systems Group was always negative.

The existing information system had an up-time record of 99.2%. When it was up, no one heard a thing from the president or the operating divisions. When the system went down, the president would call another meeting to get things *fixed*. In addition, there was constant pressure to create a new system to support the new corporate marketing initiatives. All the new system development projects were over-budget and the budget committee wanted extensive justifications for the over-spending.

The president was a classic Mass Production Thinker. He would dream up a new profit-making strategy every week. He used negative feedback to intimidate everyone with fear of losing their jobs. He used conflict manipulation to keep the pressure on everyone. As we have discussed before, Mass Production feedback systems are based on negative feedback. When things are in control, there is no need for feedback. When things are out of control, feedback is instantaneous and negative.

The Information Systems Group was being starved for positive feedback. When I started to work with them, every senior manager had an active resume and was looking for a new job. The constant beatings from the Mass Production Thinkers had taken their toll.

I asked the vice president whether anything went well in his group on a daily basis. Frankly, he wasn't sure. All the Information Systems Group managers were confused by the question. The negative feedback had stripped them of any sense of accomplishment. They were trying to do it right the first time, and stay within the budget.

The solution to this problem was to begin to activate a *creating* orientation for the group. Everyone was deeply imbedded in the Problem Box (see Chapter 6). The shift to a creating orientation starts by recognizing that things are, in fact, going well in many ways. People must focus attention on the process of creating and believe they are making an important contribution to creating the future of the company.

I asked all the Information Systems Group management team to record one thing that went well for them the next week on a 3 x 5 card and have every employee, all 700, do the same thing. This was perceived as a waste of time, but it proved to be a very interesting process. We collected all 700 cards on Friday morning. The individual *going well* statements were in some cases minor accomplishments. Collectively, however, the statements reflected an amazing commitment to support the operations groups. The importance of the Information Systems Group to creating the future of the company became very apparent.

I suggested we send all 700 cards to the president as a testimony to the success of the Information Systems Group. If the president would not provide positive feedback to the group, the group would provide positive feedback to him. The vice president was sure he would be fired. I suggested that might be a blessing in disguise.

We sent the cards. The president called the next day wondering why he received the cards. The vice president answered, "I wanted you to know that my group is doing many things very well, and without our support, the operations groups would fail." This was a tough statement for the vice president to make.

The response from the president was typical of a Mass Production Thinker— "Yeah but, it is still not right." The vice president turned to me in total defeat. "See, I told you so."

Let me interrupt the story to remind you that Mass Production Thinkers focus on problems. The only feedback they receive from the organization is when it's out of control. They react to that feedback with corrective action. This is the dominant role of Mass Production management.

Key Point: • **A *creating* orientation must be driven by positive feedback about what's going well. Positive feedback is used to shape new behavior and encourage people to continue creating.**

Back to the story. I asked the vice president to continue extracting positive feedback from his group and send it to the president. The second week he asked everyone to record two things that went well for them that week. He sent 1,400 cards to the president. Again, the president was annoyed, but his curiosity prompted him to call me. He asked what I was doing with the Systems Group. I said, "They are creating feedback for themselves and want you to be aware they are doing some things very well. They would also like you to come and see them so they can assure you they are committed to supporting the growth objectives of the company."

The next day the president went to see for himself. Frankly, it was his first visit to the Information Systems Group facility. All previous meetings had been held in his office, which everyone referred to as the penalty box. From that visit, everything changed.

Key Point: •   **Mass Production Thinking is based upon negative feedback. The new environment requires positive feedback to create a collective intelligence.**

In defense of the president, he was correct in his assessment that the existing information system was not adequate to meet the needs of the company. However, he was seeing this as a *problem to be solved* rather than a *system to be created*. Problem-solving technology leads to a polarized approach of right and wrong. The president's communication to the Information Systems Group suggested that the existing system was wrong. The existing system was *inadequate* to meet the future, but it did a wonderful job within the *Context* of the original requirements. The president's language communicated blame, and the Information Systems Group people were feeling devalued.

Key Point: •   **The intentions of many Mass Production Thinkers are correct. The technology being applied is often wrong.**

Within a month, we succeeded in establishing a creating orientation, and the existing system was accepted for what it was—*inadequate.* It was decided that *the Business of the BUSINESS* must be changed. A vision reflecting that change was created, and the challenge of creating new information systems to support the *new Business* became a cross-functional team effort between operations and systems. Everyone could see that there wasn't a problem to be solved; instead, a new process and system needed to be created.

This sounds like such a simple and logical approach, and it is. It is not, however, easy to make this shift in orientation. The reactive, problem-solving orientation of the president resurfaced almost every day. His patience for the creating process was severely tested.

This example reinforces the fact that what you do today will determine what you will be three years from now. If you, as a leader, are fixing current reality today, your organization will likely be inadequate, obsolete, or bankrupt three years from now. Worse yet, the constant negative feedback will cause creative talent to leave the organization. You must learn to create the future every day.

Collective Thinking versus Collective Intelligence

The new business environment must be built upon a *collective intelligence.* Collective intelligence can only be created as the collective group creates. Creating takes time. Trial and error will dominate the process. Learning from errors will build the strength of the collective intelligence and permit it to achieve the desired results. This approach to organizational change is foreign to Mass Production Thinkers.

Key Point: • **The biggest challenge is not how to transform the physical environment; instead, it is how to create the collective intelligence that will transform the physical environment.**

Many Transformational Change initiatives begin by reorganizing the physical environment. Offices, desk locations, and plant layouts are rearranged. One of our clients redesigned the entire manufacturing facility into work cells before preparing the people for the change. The new environment must be redesigned to facilitate collective behavior, but creating collective intelligence must precede the transformation of the physical environment. Let the people rearrange and transform their own physical environment. This will involve them in the transformational initiative.

In the Mass Production organization, the thinking of the Thinkers is the energy source. The new environment must be built on a new energy source—*collective intelligence*.

Key Point: • **Learning is extracting meaning from experience.**
             • **The meaning of the experience leads to intelligence.**

Many Mass Production managers willingly accept the need to create collective intelligence. To them, this means holding meetings to openly communicate their thinking to the Doers. This approach helps to improve awareness, but it does not provide the hands-on experience from which intelligence is developed.

I have a client that I affectionately refer to as The Meeting Company. The managers are always in a meeting. People are perceived as important or unimportant depending upon whether they are invited to the meetings. The meetings are where the action is.

All the senior leaders of The Meeting Company have enormous stacks of correspondence on their desks and hundreds of e-mail messages to be read. If I send someone a letter, it may be months before they see it. More likely, the administrative assistant will judge the content as unimportant and either forward it to another person or file it. My follow-ups always prompt them to say, "Send me another copy."

Once a quarter, the *meeters* call the *non-meeters* together and tell them what's happening. This process is referred to as open communication. Between briefings, the non-meeters work diligently, hoping they are doing the right thing. Seldom do they know what is really going on in total. One of the non-meeters told me, "I find out more about the company by reading the newspaper. Everything is very secret within the mushroom factory."

Companies like this aspire to open communication. Employee opinion polls always reveal a need for knowing the big picture, and once a year there is a renewed commitment to communicate a vision. In most cases, what is represented as a vision is merely this year's revised strategic plan rather than a vision. Constant changes in strategy lead the non-meeters to believe that the Thinkers are totally confused and that next year will bring more of the same.

The Meeting Company lacks collective intelligence. There is collective Thinking within those who meet, but their thinking is seldom translated into intelligence. Intelligence serves as the basis of behavior. Thinking alone seldom leads to any behavioral change.

Creating Collective Intelligence

With knowledge-based work comes the requirement of creating collective intelligence to achieve results.

Key Point: • **Collective intelligence is the core capability of the new business environment.**

To create collective intelligence, you must first create the underlying structural framework.

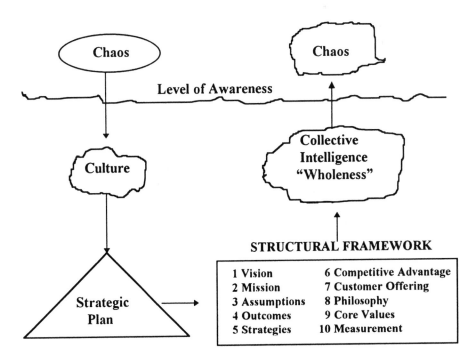

Key Point: • **The experience of creating the structural framework will cause a collective intelligence to form. The collective intelligence will be the energy force that creates cross-functional behavior necessary to serve the customer.**

Creating the structural framework should not be the work of the Thinkers alone. Transformational Leaders must involve the entire organization in creating the structural elements. When this is done properly, a collective intelligence begins to form.

It is very important to note, at this point, that Mass Production Thinkers are inherently afraid of collective intelligence. Their experience with this phenomenon is the collective bargaining process of union/management negotiations. Collective bargaining was a defensive strategy to protect workers from exploitation. Coalescence for survival is a very natural human instinct when the survival of a group is threatened. It, therefore, is very important to differentiate collective intelligence from collective negotiations.

Collective intelligence is not a new concept. In its simplest form, any meeting intends to create collective awareness and intelligence.

Key Point: • **Thinking is not the same as intelligence.**
              • **Thinking can create intelligence. There, however, are times when thinking does not create intelligence.**

It is important to understand that Thinking does not always lead to intelligence. Thinking is what you are doing as you read this book. Intelligence, however, is the assimilation, interpretation, and use of thinking.

Have you ever been asked to give someone your thoughts about a certain subject? You may be able to think about the subject, but you may not be intelligent about it. This indicates that you have very little experience with the subject. Intelligence is extracting meaning from experience. In the example of reading this book, your intelligence will develop as you apply what you have read.

Intelligence is your *conscious awareness* of the world around you. Many people wonder aimlessly through life with very limited awareness of how their own life experience contains the intelligence for success and fulfillment. This is the core concept of most self-help teaching.

Intelligence guides your behavior when confronted with the circumstances of life.

Key Point: • **People often think and nothing happens.**
                   • **People often behave without thinking.**
                   • **People often behave without intelligence.**

Behavior that results without intelligence is *experimental.* Children experiment with new behavior. Their experience with experimental behavior determines whether they will repeat the behavior. There are thousands of examples where people are accused of behaving in unintelligent ways. People observing the behavior can't believe what they see. A child is often challenged by a parent, "What were you thinking!" "How could you have done that?" "What's the matter—are you stupid?" We see thousands of examples where it appears that behavior does not reflect intelligence. Much of this behavior is experimental.

Behavior that results without thinking is *instinctive.* Let's suppose you are walking along a lake and are startled by a snake. You react without thinking. Your reaction is so fast there isn't time to think. Your actions, however, are the result of imbedded intelligence about snakes. If you have no knowledge of snakes, you would not instinctively react.

Most Mass Production managers are very *instinctive.* They often react without thinking because they have an imbedded intelligence of experience within the *Context* of Mass Production. This behavior isn't wrong, but it is often inappropriate within the new business environment.

The imbedded intelligence of most Mass Production workers is reflected in the following statements: do what you are told, work is paced by the clock, idle time is waste, time is money, and companies make money by eliminating waste. For years, most Mass Production workers have been accused of wasting time. Industrial engineers have conducted time and motion studies on all work processes to eliminate unnecessary activity. Automated systems are a constant reminder that machines can do what workers do without wasting time. Have you ever seen a totally automated warehouse? There are no Doers to waste precious time.

Now consider the likelihood that Doers will readily embrace a change initiative that asks them to spend time thinking. Their imbedded intelligence of this activity is to be punished. The same is true of Mass Production Thinkers when they experience Doers thinking. Remember the fundamental assumption of Mass Production is Thinkers think and Doers do.

It, therefore, is very important to see the importance of creating a structural framework as a prerequisite to forming the collective intelligence. By involving the Doers in the strategic thinking process, they can slowly experiment with thinking as a part of their responsibility and realize that there isn't punishment associated with the experience.

Key Point: • Involving people in the thinking process is more
              important that their contribution to the process.

It is important to note that people who have never been involved in strategic Thinking feel very uncomfortable and even frustrated with the process. They feel they have very little to contribute. It is experimental behavior for them. Don't expect them to offer brilliant ideas or masterful strategies. Their involvement in the process makes them aware of how the structure was created. Never forget, involvement leads to commitment.

Translating Thinking into Experience

The fact that Thinkers think does not guarantee implementation of the thinking. Neither does it guarantee that the thinking will result in any intelligent behavior by the Doers.

It is very common that the thinking of senior leaders is seldom known even at the middle manager level. Let me give you an example.

I was having lunch with one of my clients at a local restaurant. We noticed that the nachos and margaritas on the menu were labeled as world class. I asked the waiter why the chicken potpie wasn't world class. He said he didn't know, but it was good. I asked why it had not been elevated to world class when other menu items had been taken to that level. He said he was a waiter and didn't know why.

Ten minutes later the restaurant manager came to our table. He had been told by the waiter of my question and wanted to provide an answer.

I asked the manager what made the nachos and margaritas world class and other items were just good. He said they put expensive liquor in the margaritas and real cheese on the nachos. In other words, I asked, "The ingredients in the potpie are not expensive or real?" He was stumped. Flustered, he admitted that the world class description was something dreamed up by the Marketing Department and he was not aware of what they thought constituted world class.

Key Point: • Everyone must be aware of the strategic thinking
              of the organization.
              • Thinking must be translated into thought.

The waiter and store manager were unaware of the thinking behind the offering of the restaurant and were, therefore, thoughtless. They were unable to explain the meaning of world class offerings to customers. I suggested it was Mass Production trickery and the manager agreed.

Before our lunch was over, I asked the waiter if my question had caused him trouble with the manager. He said he was new and just doing what he was told. He wasn't expected to know all the answers yet.

If the store manager had been involved in creating the structural framework for his store, he would consciously know the customer offering and competitive advantage of his restaurant. These are two of the structural elements. If he was involved in creating these elements, world class offerings would be clearly understood and he would be able to train his serving crew in explaining that specialty to customers.

This may appear to be an absurd example. One person even accused me of harassing the restaurant employees. Remember, you are the customer and entitled to know why something is labeled world class. You would think that the thinking of the Marketing Department would be translated into the intelligence of the servers and managers to create the economic leverage that the world class enhancements intend to provide for the business. Frankly, it's rare.

Key Point: • **Creating intelligence is not merely explaining something.**
    • **People learn from experience, not by being told.**

In our restaurant example, the manager could explain to the servers that world class nachos were made with real cheese, not processed cheese. The servers could understand that explanation. However, the question remains, why does real cheese make them world class? What about the potpie? It contains real ingredients. Why isn't it world class?

Explanations of the thinking of the Thinkers often fall far short of creating complete understanding in the Doers. Frankly, many Doers don't even care about the explanations. Many workers have accused management of lying to them for years. They are immune from listening. Do you ever wonder why your children still don't understand what you have explained to them many times before? They will learn from their own experimental behavior and some day understand what you have been trying to explain.

Key Point: • **As a company begins to create the new business enviroment, everyone must enter into a process of experimental behavior.**

If we now consider the challenge of the new business environment, everyone must be involved in *thinking* and everyone must be a part of the collective intelligence. For many people, strategic thinking is experimental behavior. For others, it's very instinctive. It is important, however, that everyone experience experimental behavior to create the new collective intelligence. The first experience is in creating the structural framework.

Consider a self-directed team initiative. The behavior of the team is very experimental in the beginning. People are very frustrated that something constructive doesn't happen quickly. Frankly, it can't happen. The intelligence that leads to constructive behavior doesn't exist. It can only be created through the ongoing experience.

The instinctive behavior pattern of management poses another enormous barrier to self-directed initiatives. Asking Doers to stop doing and perform the thinking of management often slows down production output. If the Thinkers see that productivity is suffering while Doers are thinking, the Thinkers become impatient. The instinctive response by the Thinker is to *tell them the answer*, thus, negating the thinking initiative within the Doers.

It is very important to realize that the new environment is built on a collective intelligence. The first step in transforming the organization is to institutionalize collective thinking. The institutionalized thinking provides the experience from which collective intelligence forms. The imbedded intelligence of Mass Production—Thinkers think and Doers do—is a formidable barrier to success.

Visualizing Collective Intelligence

The structural framework contains thinking. The translation of that thinking into thought is the process of creating collective intelligence.

Key Point: • **The collective intelligence permits the business to behave in a thoughtful way with customers.**

The collective intelligence that supports the new business environment is very different from the *culture* that supports Mass Production. I have intentionally selected collective intelligence to refer to this level of awareness to avoid the belief that the existing culture can be changed, fixed, or somehow modified.

Key Point: • **Collective intelligence does not exist in a Mass Production organization. It must be *created* for it to exist.**
              • **Creating a collective intelligence is the key to changing the behavior of any organization.**

It is very frustrating for executives who have been *in control* for years, using Mass Production approaches, to embrace this thinking. They understand collective thinking at the senior level, but it is beyond comprehension as to how to create collective intelligence throughout the organization.

To help executives visualize the collective intelligence in their own organization, I use The Innovator Process designed by The Wilson Learning Corporation. The Innovator is a computerized process of voting using electronic keypads that show how a total group thinks about a particular subject. The

Innovator software quickly and easily records the votes from each independent keypad and projects the collective vote on a screen for everyone to see.

The Innovator Process reveals the collective intelligence of a group of people. Divergent opinions can be expressed and recognized in a safe and constructive way.

The following is a typical Innovator Map. The company represented by this map was trying to implement a high commitment work environment.

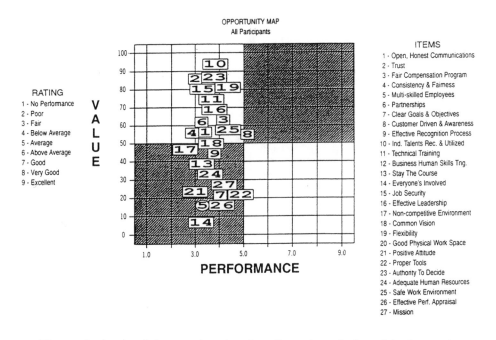

The vertical axis of the map is value; it reflects the priority of the items shown on the map. The horizontal axis is performance; it reflects the participant's perception of current performance of each element within the existing organization.

We can see from the map that Item 2, trust, is one of the high priority items, and the collective perception of performance is a 3.0

Items 1–27 reflect all the critical success factors that are necessary for the high commitment environment to become a reality. The items were identified by the participants based upon their current awareness of the situation.

Each item can be viewed in a Scattergram form. The following Scattergram is for Item 2, Trust.

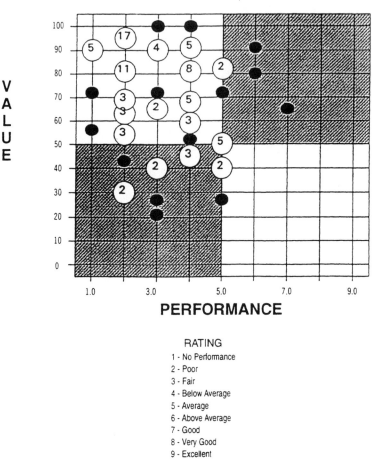

TRUST
All Participants

PERFORMANCE

RATING
1 - No Performance
2 - Poor
3 - Fair
4 - Below Average
5 - Average
6 - Above Average
7 - Good
8 - Very Good
9 - Excellent

Each dot on the Scattergram represents an individual participant's vote. The numbers inside some of the dots represent the number of participants at that location. The voting is a comparison process of rating each item versus every other item on the list.

In this case, it is very apparent that the critical success factor of Trust is very high in priority and the current performance is poor.

An Innovator session is conducted to involve people in the strategic thinking process of the organization. Remember that their involvement is more important than their contribution. The participants are asked to identify the critical success factors for changing an organization, and, most important, identify the leverage point for initiating change. In this specific situation, the people didn't *trust* the intentions surrounding the high commitment initiative; until a different level of trust was created, the high commitment initiative could not begin.

Let's look at another Scattergram.

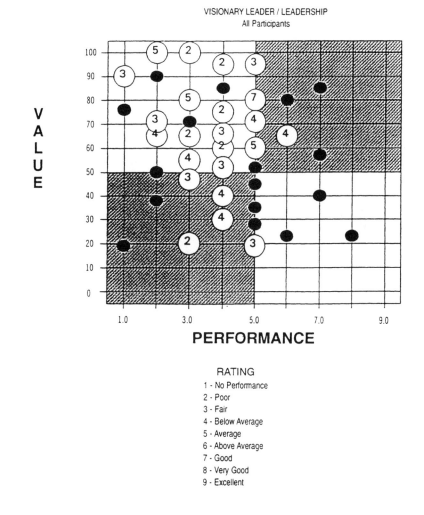

VISIONARY LEADER / LEADERSHIP
All Participants

RATING
1 - No Performance
2 - Poor
3 - Fair
4 - Below Average
5 - Average
6 - Above Average
7 - Good
8 - Very Good
9 - Excellent

This Scattergram is the perception of Visionary Leadership within a company that was in desperate need of a new competitive strategy. The collective intelligence revealed that the need for vision and leadership was very high and the current performance was low. The leader in this case thought he was visionary. He had been exhorting the need to change for over a year. He had held monthly meetings telling everyone about the competitive threats to the company. His favorite word was *fix*. His style was often intimidating and he was known as a micromanager wanting to control everything. The people weren't responding and the Innovator Map revealed the need for visionary leadership.

The message from this Innovator Map was very difficult to deliver and digest. The leader was immediately upset and visibly very angry. He could not understand why "they can't get it!" I won't recount the entire story. It is the personification of imbedded Mass Production Thinking.

After conducting hundreds of Innovator Sessions, it is very clear that leaders must involve everyone in creating the structural framework to cause a collective intelligence to form and transform the behavior of any organization. Vision in the situation described above is a structural element. This leader had an excellent strategic plan. People were aware of *his thinking*, but *his plan* was not being translated into behavior. What they needed was a vision, not a plan.

There is good news in this situation. Through the Innovator process, combined with *The Organizational Transformation™ Simulation*, the leader was able to create a collective intelligence, and the company is alive and thriving today. The senior leader still works 16 hours a day, but the collective intelligence now runs the company. It is amazing to see the difference.

It is not the purpose of this chapter to thoroughly explain the Innovator Process. The important point is to realize that technology exists that can reveal the collective intelligence of a group. When collective intelligence can be seen in visual form, people begin to understand how it impacts behavior. The Innovator software does an excellent job of revealing divergent thinking and enabling a group to create collective intelligence.

The Importance of Experience

There are many traditional Mass Production approaches to creating collective intelligence. Many Mass Production managers conclude, "We should hold regular meetings and discuss the corporate strategy with people." Every Mass Production Thinker believes that telling people their thinking is the same as creating collective intelligence. This is an illusion.

Key Point: • **Collective Intelligence is created by extracting meaning from experience.**

People learn from *experience*. The collective intelligence forms as the people experience change. To just know the thinking of the Thinkers does not help people create intelligence.

Key Point: • **Intelligence is the result of accurately extracting meaning from experience. Without experience, thinking remains a hypothesis to be tested.**

It is very important to consciously break the traditional Mass Production view about this issue. Creating collective intelligence is the most important strategic agenda facing senior leaders today. The collective intelligence translates the structural thinking into behavior. The collective intelligence is reflected in the *thoughtfulness* of the organization to the customer. The collective intelligence is the most valuable asset of the company. The collective intelligence must be valued beyond any other ingredient for success.

Leaders must be consciously aware of how daily experience builds collective intelligence. Daily successes and failures must be shared openly with the organization to create collective intelligence. Within the creating process, there is no blame. Extracting meaning from experience is a critical process in building intelligence.

Creating collective intelligence should be the perceived *purpose* of any corporate communication. In every Innovator Session I conduct, participants always identify open/honest communication as a critical success factor. Communication in the Mass Production *Context* is almost exclusively for corrective or informative purposes. Communication in the new environment must focus on how collective intelligence was effectively applied.

Key Point: • **You must first accept that creating collective intelligence is required for success.**

The collective intelligence-building process is multidirectional. Most Mass Production communication is from Thinkers to Doers. In the new *Context*, the Doers must communicate to the Thinkers—and the Thinkers must listen. Recall the example of the Information Systems Group vice president. The president was unwilling to listen to those he perceived as Doers. He was angry when they gave him positive feedback.

Frankly, it goes way beyond Thinkers and Doers. Everyone is a Thinker in the new environment. The collective thinking must involve *everyone*. In this context, *everyone is important*. Remember the waiter in the restaurant? I asked the question about world class offerings to determine whether the organization recognized the need to create collective intelligence. Obviously, it was missing in the waiter and the restaurant manager.

The Extended Enterprise

What if the collective intelligence of your organization is insufficient to create the future? What if the Thinkers don't have the answers? The terrifying truth of this reality reveals the need for partnerships with suppliers and other external sources of intellectual capital.

After you see your leadership role as creating collective intelligence, you will see the need to extend the collective intelligence beyond your own organization. Vendors have more than products and services to provide your company. A vendor organization has a collective intelligence that must be integrated into your organization. What's the price to tap that intelligence?

Key Point: • **The purpose of partnerships with suppliers is to add their collective intelligence to your organization.**

.   I was working with a large multinational company that had abandoned a vertical integration approach to supplying critical parts to their manufacturing plants. Some people had concluded, "We can buy them cheaper from a vendor." The truth, however, was that their own vertically integrated technology had become technologically obsolete and several vendors had achieved a technologically superior process of production. It was also likely that the technology within this core competency would continue to accelerate. The company made a very wise decision to abandon their vertical approach to link the collective intelligence of the supplier to theirs.

Key Point: • **The integrated supply chain creates economic leverage by applying the collective intelligence to achieve innovation.**

The new business environment is built on the logistics of an integrated supply chain. Mass Production Thinkers seek integration to lower cost. The real advantage, however, goes to those who can apply collective intelligence to achieve seamless delivery to customers. Tell all your vendors you will pay them 10% more tomorrow if they will connect their collective intelligence to yours to create seamlessness for your customers. The synergy of this type of relationship is astounding.

Seeing the collective intelligence of the extended enterprise will help you dispel the myth of the vendor mentality of Mass Production. When price dominates a buyer/seller relationship, vendors withhold the innovation contained in their collective intelligence. With technological obsolescence driving the business environment, you must extend the collective intelligence of your organization to include everyone that is vital to serving your customers. A network of *partners in process* is a collective intelligence beyond the comprehension of the Mass Production mind.

The Leadership Challenge

After leaders perceive their role as translating the structural framework into collective intelligence, everything changes in the organization. Transformational Leaders ask themselves questions such as, "I wonder if the mail clerk is aware of why we exist?" "I wonder if our salespeople are able to accurately interpret our offering to customers?" "I wonder if the servers really know what we mean by world class nachos?" The *strategic intent* of this approach to leadership is the recognition that a company is *a process designed to serve a customer* and anyone not knowing their role in the process will cause the company to fail.

Key Point: • **Corporate success is the translation of structural design into behavior.**
• **The network of collective intelligence is "the organization chart" of the new business environment.**
• **Pity the Mass Production Thinkers. They are technologically obsolete.**

Leaders must celebrate the application of collective intelligence. Leaders must see organizational success as something much bigger than bottom line results. The bottom liners fail to recognize the incredible effort required to produce results. Everyday we read of companies achieving growth and profit projections. Some reports suggest that these results happen because the Thinkers were brilliant. Mass Production models fail to recognize the role of collective intelligence in serving customers.

The Transformational Leadership challenge is to see the process of translating structure into collective intelligence. Create collective intelligence and you will be confident your organization will perform.

Chapter 15
Alignment

The complexity of Transformational Change is enormous. Many Mass Production Thinkers ask, "If it could all be boiled down to one *simple* thought, what would it be? The answer is

"Create Alignment on Purpose."

Jim Collins and Jerry Porras, in their best selling book *Built to Last*, make the following statements about alignment:

> By "alignment" we mean simply that all elements of a company work together in concert within the context of the company's core ideology and the type of progress it aims to achieve—its vision, if you like.
>
> *Built to Last,* page 202

> There is a big difference between being an organization with a vision statement and becoming a truly visionary organization. When you have superb alignment, a visitor could drop into your organization from another planet and infer the vision without having to read it on paper.
>
> *Built to Last,* page 229

> It is not the content of the ideology that makes a company visionary, it's the authenticity, discipline and consistency with which the ideology is lived—the degree of alignment—that differentiates visionary companies from the rest of the pack.
>
> *Built to Last,* page 229

> To pursue the vision means to create organizational and strategic alignment to preserve the core ideology and stimulate progress toward the envisioned future. Alignment brings the vision to life, translating it from good intentions to concrete reality.
>
> *Built to Last,* page 221

> The Builders of Visionary companies seek alignment in strategies, in tactics, in organization systems, in structure, in incentive systems in building layout, in job design—in everything.
>
> *Built to Last,* page 87

> The vast majority of your time will be spent bringing the organization into alignment.
>
> *Built to Last,* page 238

> We urge you to recast your vision and mission into a guiding context so you can get on with the most important work: Creating alignment.
>
> *Built to Last,* page 238

Based upon these statements, it appears that creating alignment is the most important work of the visionary leader.

I have asked many Mass Production Thinkers to tell me what they consider their most important work, and most of them tell me setting strategy. When I show them the statements listed above and ask them to define alignment, very few have an understanding of what it is or how to create it. Therefore, this chapter will define alignment and help you understand how it is created.

Creating alignment of behavior to achieve a purpose is a *simple* concept. It is not, however, *easy* to do. Frankly, it is the most difficult assignment a manager or leader can be given. The ultimate simplicity of this concept is not easily understood and the ability to translate a purpose into behavior will test your patience. Stay with me, and you will develop a deep appreciation for the difficulty of this part of your transformational journey.

Setting Strategy versus Creating Alignment

Let's start by understanding the difference between setting strategy and creating aligned behavior. If you look at the Transformational Change model used throughout this book, you can quickly see that setting strategy is an activity aimed at changing the structural level of the BUSINESS. On the other hand, creating alignment is an activity that intends to impact the behavioral level!

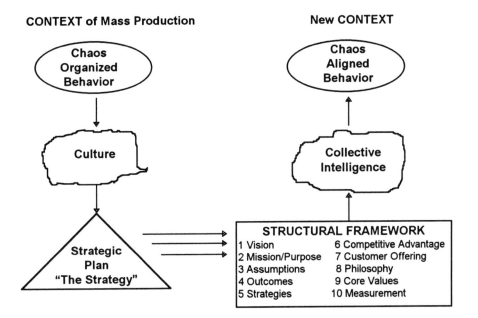

CONTEXT of Mass Production

New CONTEXT

Chaos
Organized
Behavior

Chaos
Aligned
Behavior

Culture

Collective
Intelligence

Strategic
Plan
"The Strategy"

STRUCTURAL FRAMEWORK
1 Vision   6 Competitive Advantage
2 Mission/Purpose   7 Customer Offering
3 Assumptions   8 Philosophy
4 Outcomes   9 Core Values
5 Strategies   10 Measurement

Setting strategy in the *Context* of Mass Production is the same activity as creating the structural framework in the new *Context*. Creating structure is important work.

Creating alignment is the ongoing process of unifying the behavior of every person in the organization to fulfill the purpose of the BUSINESS. Aligned behavior translates the strategic imperative of the structural framework into action. Aligning behavior is important work.

It is initially important to realize that setting strategy and creating alignment are *both* important work. If we try to establish which one is most important, we will get into a chicken and egg debate. It is true that without the structural framework, behavior likely won't be aligned, and without aligned behavior, the strategic imperative defined by the structural framework won't be achieved. For this reason, let's not debate importance; instead, understand the difference between these two leadership activities.

Setting strategy is an *antecedent*. Within the *Context* of Mass Production, setting strategy is the antecedent that defines how to deploy the resources of the organization. The strategy defines how to organize the BUSINESS. The *consequence* of setting strategy, within the *Context* of Mass Production, is controlled behavior.

Creating the complete structural framework is the antecedent that defines how the new BUSINESS will function. The collective intelligence will decide how to organize the BUSINESS. The consequence of collective intelligence is aligned behavior.

This can be illustrated by the Transformational Change model as follows:

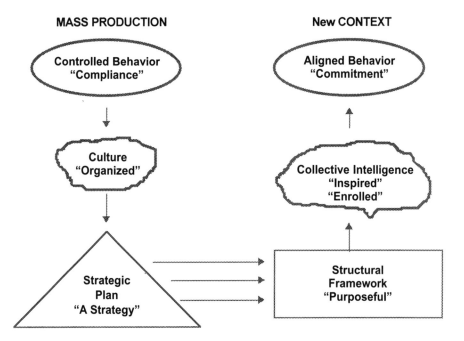

There are many definitions for strategy and alignment, but the first difference between setting strategy and creating alignment is to understand that strategy, in whatever form, is an *antecedent* and alignment is a *consequence*.

An *antecedent* is the thinking that precedes behavior. If you think about going on vacation, you will determine where, why, when, and how to go. All these questions are generally answered before the actual behavior of going. Planning leads to efficient behavior during the vacation. When everything goes as planned, you feel organized and in control.

The same is true in business. Most companies have a strategic plan that contains the thinking of the Thinkers. The work of management is to translate that thinking into behavior. If the plan leads to the desired results, executives feel as if they are in control.

A consequence is the behavior that results from thinking. If the course of action is well thought out, the behavior can be both efficient and effective. If the thinking contains a clear answer to the question why, the resulting behavior within a group of committed people will be aligned.

Controlled Behavior versus Aligned Behavior

The second difference between setting strategy and creating alignment is the motivation contained in the resulting behavior. The emotional content of behavior can be very different depending on the *antecedent*. Let's suppose you ask your teenage son to mow the grass. You have provided the antecedent of what you want done. Telling him what to do does not determine his emotional engagement. The motivation associated with the behavior is determined by the answer to *why*. The why associated with mow the grass can be "because I said so" or "so that we can play golf this weekend." The motivation switches from *compliance* to *commitment* and from *external direction* to *self*-direction.

> **Key Point:**
> - **Strategy answers the questions what, how, and when. The consequence of strategy is controlled behavior. Controlled behavior occurs out of compliance with authority.**
> - **Purpose answers the question why. The consequence of purpose is aligned behavior. Aligned behavior occurs out of commitment to achieve the purpose.**

Mass Production Thinkers are experts at telling people what, how, and when to do things. Most strategic plans focus on defining these issues. The answer to the question why is assumed to be to make a profit. The ultimate reward for the Mass Production manager is to have *things organized and under control*. The emotional engagement of people who perform *under control* is *compliance*.

The End Results of Strategy versus Alignment

The third and possibly the most important difference between setting strategy and creating alignment is the end results achieved. Most strategy-based organizations become very tactical and functionally independent. Mass Production Thinkers always complain about the "silo mentality" within their organizations. The functions of manufacturing, engineering, and sales all have different "what's" to do. Knowing what to do does not guarantee that everyone will be operating on the same "why."

Let's return to your son and your grass. You can tell him to mow the grass, but he won't trim around the trees. He may not put the mower away. He likely won't think to water the grass or be concerned about trimming the shrubbery. Concern for the well being of the entire landscape, over time, is yours. All he knows is the *what* at the moment. The *why* of maintaining the continuous beauty of *your* home is not his responsibility.

Mass Production organizations suffer a similar fate. I have had countless conversations with executives who wish people would accept responsibility for the success of the whole company. They want them to act like owners. The culprit appears to be the willingness of the people, but the truth is that setting strategy only leads to controlled behavior. Behavior that is in control will be organized, obedient, and efficient, but once the *what* is done, the Doers will wait until authority tells them what to do next.

Key Point: •   **Behavior that is organized and controlled is based in compliance with authority**.

On the other hand, aligned behavior is the *consequence* of a very clear understanding of purpose.

Key Point: •   **Purpose answers the question why we exist in terms of customer expectations.**
            •   **Purpose serves as the antecedent for aligned behavior.**
            •   **The purpose, not a person, contains the authority to act.**
            •   **Fulfilling the purpose of the BUSINESS requires cross-functional cooperation.**
            •   **Aligned behavior is called teamwork.**
            •   **Aligned behavior is done with commitment.**

Aligned behavior can exist within the *Context* of Mass Production, but the term alignment is not generally used by Mass Production managers. In fact, the most common perception is that the act of organizing is the same as creating alignment. Most managers believe that once the strategy is set and the organization is organized, that aligned behavior will occur. I hear statements like,

"Everyone knows the budget and what's expected of them in order to achieve our goals."

"We've taken great pains this year to develop our strategic plan. We've held extensive meetings across the company to be certain there is no confusion about our focus. We can't be all things to all people and we are determined to stay focused on our core business."

"We must become the low cost producer. We are committed to being an operationally excellent company. Everyone is clear that we must achieve world class service to survive."

These statements, and many like them, suggest that behavior will be aligned because budgets, goals, and strategies have been set and communicated to all the employees. The executives that make these statements exude a determined confidence that the organization is in control and will comply with the strategic plan!

Key Point:
- **Alignment is not controlled behavior to achieve the strategy.**
- **The strategy defines how the BUSINESS will deploy resources.**
- **The budget defines the control limits of how money can be spent.**
- **The budget does not define the purpose of the BUSINESS.**
- **Aligned behavior intends to fulfill the purpose after the resources are deployed.**

I can't tell you the number of times I have encountered confusion on how to create alignment of behavior. Mass Production Thinkers believe that increasing determination creates alignment. This is an illusion. Increasing determination leads to a highly autocratic environment. While control and compliance increase, the effectiveness of the organization generally decreases. Creative people do not work well in an autocratic environment and will leave to find a place where their talents are appreciated. One human resource vice president expressed it to me as, "The beatings continued until all the talent left. All that remained were those who were in compliance with the latest directives."

Key Point:
- **The acts of organizing, setting strategy, and budgeting are not the same as creating alignment.**

Therefore, before we begin to examine alignment, don't confuse controlled behavior with aligned behavior. Controlled behavior is in response to *what*; aligned behavior is in response to *why*. Mass Production Thinking is based on telling the Doers what to do. The imbedded muscle memory of Mass Production Thinking is a formidable force that prevents creating alignment.

Organization versus the Business of the BUSINESS

The final difference between setting strategy and creating alignment is how the Mass Production Thinker and the Transformational Leader differentiate between *the Business of the* BUSINESS and *the organization of the* BUSINESS.

Key Point:
- *The Business* of the *BUSINESS* is what the BUSINESS does in service of customers.
- The organization of the BUSINESS is a process that intends to efficiently and effectively decompose the tasks and responsibilities of the BUSINESS to serve customers.
- Aligned behavior fulfills the intention to serve customers as defined by the purpose.
- The purpose defines the *Business of the BUSINESS.*

Every Mass Production BUSINESS has been organized. The act of organizing creates a process of executing *the Business of the BUSINESS.* The act of organizing distributes authority within the process. People are inserted into the organization and given responsibility and authority to execute *the Business of the BUSINESS.* The intent is to make the process of executing the Business efficient and effective. If the resulting behavior efficiently and effectively fulfills the promise that the BUSINESS makes to customers, the behavior is aligned on purpose.

Confusion starts when managers began to refer to the organization of the BUSINESS as the BUSINESS. The organization of the BUSINESS is represented in pictorial form by an organization chart. This suggests to many people that the organization is the BUSINESS. "We have a tremendous organization" or "Our organization is committed to serving customers" are common statements you might hear. There is nothing wrong with these statements, but over time people begin to confuse the organization as the BUSINESS and the organization as the people. Ask any executive who is talking about the organization what they mean by the term organization and you will likely get an explanation about the goodness or commitment of the people who are involved in the BUSINESS.

Key Point:
- The organization is a process. It is *not* the BUSINESS.
- The organization is *not* the people. People can come and go, but the organization, the process, remains unchanged.
- The organization is a process. It is not a *thing*.

The word *organization* is a noun and when used in this context implies that the organization is a *thing*. The organization chart is a visible manifestation of *thingness*. The organization chart contains the names of people holding positions of authority, and many Mass Production Thinkers see people as valuable assets or things.

Many of my clients ask why it is important to make this distinction between the organization as a process and the BUSINESS as an entity. It only matters if you are trying to change something. You must be clear about what you must change. If you change the organization of the BUSINESS when you should be creating a new *Business of the* BUSINESS, you will make a devastating mistake.

Think about how Mass Production Thinkers act when the performance of the BUSINESS begins to suffer. To them, it's either the plan, the organization, or uncontrolled things that are to be blamed. If the organization and the people are perceived as *things*, the people and the organization will likely be changed to bring performance under control. How many change initiatives have you experienced that started by reorganizing the organization and eliminating things? The call goes out to be lean and mean.

Key Point:
- **Major performance problems stem from the fact that *the Business of the BUSINESS* is obsolete.**
- **It is an illusion to believe that reorganizing the way the BUSINESS is organized will create a new *Business of the BUSINESS*.**
- **The new Business must exist before it can be organized.**
- **Transforming the organization is about creating a new *Business of the BUSINESS*.**

It is very important to understand that the organization is not the BUSINESS. IBM is IBM, Ford is Ford, and McDonald's is McDonald's. The way they are organized does not define the BUSINESS. Likewise, how they are organized does not define the *Business of their BUSINESS*.

Finally, the organization is not the people. The proper view is that the organization is the process of executing the *Business of the BUSINESS*. If the existing process does not serve customers in a way that is competitive and sustainable, then it may be necessary to transform the *Business of the BUSINESS*, reorganize the organization, or create alignment of behavior. All three options must be considered, and it is important to know the difference in these three activities.

Key Point:
- **Creating alignment is not about reorganizing the organization.**
- **Aligned behavior is different from controlled behavior.**
- **Aligned behavior is a consequence of *intention*. If the intention is not clear, the behavior that follows will be chaotic.**

If you are confused by all this double talk, it is intentional. Transformational Change is a very complex and confusing issue. Transformational Leaders must be very clear about why, what, and how to change. If you merely change your clothes every day and forget to take a bath, the relief of the smell will only be temporary. Mass Production Thinkers get very frustrated with what they believe is a semantics issue. It is very common for Mass Production Thinkers to make tragic mistakes by believing they can transform the organization of their BUSINESS by setting a new strategy.

Creating Alignment

The illusions of Mass Production Thinking are clearly ones of *Context* and process. Creating Alignment on Purpose is neither a new concept nor is it a buzzword approach to organizational change.

Let's begin our understanding of creating alignment by recalling the definition of alignment:

Key Point: • **Alignment is the unified behavior of every person in the organization to fulfill the purpose of the BUSINESS.**

The alignment of behavior within the organization (the behavior within the process) is determined by the purpose for which the BUSINESS exists. The organization of the BUSINESS was created to *effectively and efficiently execute the Business of the BUSINESS*. Thus, the purpose of the organization is the same as the purpose *of the BUSINESS*.

Key Point: • **Transformational Change is about changing the alignment of behavior within the organization to pursue a new *Business of the BUSINESS*.**
• **The new *Business of the BUSINESS* may still contain elements of the old Business.**
• **Mass Production Thinking will not be a part of the new organization of the BUSINESS.**
• **The alignment of the behavior within the organization prioritizes the work that flows through the process.**
• **Aligned behavior is authorized by the purpose.**
• **The purpose distributes authority within the organization to facilitate efficiency and speed of customer service.**

To help you visualize this issue, let's step back and look at how a BUSINESS is formed and how alignment occurs.

When an entrepreneurial BUSINESS is formed, the BUSINESS does not have an organization. The process of executing *the Business of the BUSINESS* resides in one person. The person can be very organized in his own behavior, but an organization does not exist until entrepreneurs add people to the process of executing *the Business of the BUSINESS*. After they add people and distribute authority to these people, they can then refer to their organization.

While the one person entrepreneurial BUSINESS does not have an organization in the beginning, the BUSINESS does have a purpose.

Key Point:
- **The purpose of the BUSINESS defines why it exists.**
- **The purpose establishes the fundamental intent of the Business of the BUSINESS.**
- **The purpose of the BUSINESS defines what the *Business of the BUSINESS* will do for customers.**

The purpose of any BUSINESS is to help customers get what they want. Many people mistakenly believe that an entrepreneur starts a BUSINESS to make a profit. While making money is an important *objective* of every business, *the Business of the BUSINESS* is not defined by profit. There is a great quote from *Built to Last* concerning this issue:

> PROFITABILITY is a necessary condition for existence and a means to more important ends, but it is not the end in itself for the visionary companies. Profit is like oxygen, food, water, and blood for the body; they are not the point of life, but without them, there is no life.
>
> *Built to Last*, page 55

I have worked with many people who want to start their own BUSINESS. The vast majority don't feel they have enough money or can afford the risk. The fear is real because their initial purpose is about making money. Starting a BUSINESS does not, however, start with money. It starts by defining *the Business of the BUSINESS*. After the idea exists as to what *the BUSINESS* can do for a customer, then and only then, can the financial requirements and risk associated with starting the *BUSINESS* be determined.

Key Point:
- **Purpose defines *the point of the Business of the BUSINESS*. It is not about profits.**
- **The objective of the BUSINESS is to make a profit.**

After the purpose is defined, the entrepreneur becomes committed to creating *the BUSINESS*. Having a purpose, however, does not guarantee that *the BUSINESS* will be successful. The purpose merely defines *the Business of the BUSINESS*.

In the beginning, entrepreneurs often feel like one-armed paperhangers. They must juggle many balls. They have too much to do and not enough time. While the behavior within *the BUSINESS* may not be organized, it is typically aligned to fulfill the purpose of serving customers. The Alignment on Purpose prioritizes the efforts of entrepreneurs to fulfill the promises they make to customers.

Key Point:	• **Alignment is about translating the *intent* of the BUSINESS into behavior.** • **Alignment may exist within unorganized effort.** • **Alignment may exist within organized effort.** • **The customer can feel the alignment of the BUSINESS.** • **Doing business with an aligned BUSINESS that is also organized will be seamless and effortless.** • **Aligned behavior intends to fulfill the promise inherent in the purpose.** • **Alignment is not a function of time.**

If you have been an entrepreneur, you will understand the difference between alignment and organized. Alignment is a function of *purpose*. It is the consequence of a predetermined intent to serve the customer. It is not about the efficiency or organization of the effort. Alignment is also not a function of time. The behavior of an entrepreneur may be very slow and methodical.

Let's suppose the entrepreneur's BUSINESS grows and begins to add additional people to serve customers. *The alignment of intent* now becomes a major issue. Alignment is easy to sustain if the purpose of *the BUSINESS* has been clearly defined.

Key Point:	• **Alignment is unified behavior to fulfill the purpose of the BUSINESS.**

We have all experienced small BUSINESSES that are known for excellent customer service. Regardless of whether it's a product- or service-based BUSINESS, everyone fulfills their role in the customer service process. Alignment of behavior within a small BUSINESS is rather easy to create. The owner communicates the intent of the company up front and everyone is committed to fulfill their role in the process. The behavior of the BUSINESS is aligned.

As *the BUSINESS* grows, the alignment of behavior within the customer service process can easily become misaligned.

Key Point:
- **Misalignment begins when people within the customer service process loose sight of the customer.**
- **Misalignment will exist if the purpose of the BUSINESS isn't clear.**
- **Misalignment will exist if the purpose of the BUSINESS is incorrectly defined as "to make a profit."**
- **Misalignment will exist if people only know the task they are to perform.**

It is easy to keep the customer in view within a small BUSINESS. There are precious few customers available and everyone is aware of how important they are to success of *the BUSINESS*. The most common cause of misalignment is rapid growth and taking it for granted that everyone knows the purpose of the BUSINESS.

I have seen many entrepreneurial BUSINESSES experience rapid growth and suffer from misalignment of intent. Being an entrepreneur does not guarantee that you consciously know how to create alignment.

Suffice it to say misalignment is very common. Many people are hired to perform specific tasks and their contract with *the BUSINESS* is to trade time for dollars. In many situations, new employees are told the function of their job, but are seldom told "why they do what they do" in terms of the customer. It is implied that customers must be served, but the specifics of how that is to happen are often vague.

Let me give you an example. During a recent sales training seminar, we were interviewing the facility engineer in a large hotel. He was responsible for maintaining the heating, air conditioning, plumbing, and guest service equipment in the hotel. He had 6 maintenance people and 20 housekeeping staff under his supervision. We asked him if he received many guest satisfaction complaints. He confirmed that he did, and that there had been an increase in complaints recently. We had experienced terrible cooling and food service problems in the room we occupied. The maintenance person responsible for adjusting the cooling was apathetic to our needs and the coffeepots in the room were frequently empty.

We asked the facility engineer how he oriented new employees into the process of serving customers. He said, "I tell them what to do." When we asked whether the new employees were told *why* they do what they do, he said, "They should know that they are here to serve customers. We are a hotel and people should know that." He left alignment of intention to chance. We also asked him why the coffeepots were frequently empty. He said, "Replenishment of the coffee is not my responsibility." His approach to customer service was totally reactive and typical of a Mass Production Thinker.

In this case, we could feel the misalignment of the organization. We had to call three different managers to get what we wanted. It was our responsibility to align the organization to meet our needs.

> **Key Point:** • **Creating and sustaining Alignment on Purpose is the most important work of every BUSINESS.**

Every Mass Production BUSINESS struggles with this issue. Writing vision and mission statements and preparing a strategic plan do not create alignment. The work of creating alignment is the ongoing effort of managing the consequences of "why" and it is very difficult work for every manager and leader.

I hope you can envision how both small and large BUSINESSES that exist within the *Context* of Mass Production become very misaligned. The reality is that Mass Production organizations are *organized* to be functionally efficient and effective. While the manufacturing, engineering, and sales functions intend to serve customers, the truth is, their behavior is influenced more by how they are measured than by the purpose of the behavior. Everyone agrees that alignment should occur, but agreement does not guarantee it will happen. If the functional groups don't have a common purpose, misalignment will be the common customer experience.

No Alignment

It is important to insert a brief, yet important, point about creating alignment.

> **Key Point:** • **Alignment assumes the free will of the people to engage in purposeful behavior.**

Many Mass Production Thinkers quickly polarize issues and assume that misalignment means no alignment. This is not true. No alignment would be characteristic of slavery or conscription where the free will of the participants doesn't exist. While working for some managers might feel like no alignment, you are always free to quit your job. If you continue to work in an environment that is constantly misaligned, I would suggest that you reevaluate your own personal alignment mechanism. I discussed this issue in Chapter 13, "The Psychological Experience."

Alignment to Survive and Grow

Aligned behavior to fulfill a purpose is a powerful force. It can be achieved to fulfill two very important personal and organizational agendas: survival and growth.

Alignment to Survive

Just suppose you are in a crowded building and someone yells "FIRE!" Everyone will immediately act. This panic stricken behavior is instinctive, unconscious, and often dangerous. Someone must, however, announce that the building is on fire and seek to evacuate the building. The behavior of the people in this instance would be for the *purpose of survival*, but the behavior within the process of evacuation would be random and very misaligned. It's a free for all. The survival instinct of every individual dominates their behavior.

Let's suppose, however, that before the fire there had been a well-planned and rehearsed fire drill and everyone had practiced evacuation. The purpose of aligning behavior in this case is *survival*. A fire alarm would cause people to immediately react, and, hopefully, their behavior would follow the orderly evacuation process. The behavior is *aligned*.

Key Point:
- **Alignment to survive is unified behavior in anticipation of an unwanted circumstance.**
- **The unwanted circumstance is generally described as an accident or a *crisis*.**

The fire drill creates alignment in response to an anticipated, unwanted circumstance—a fire. A fire drill is one of many examples where people proactively practice the alignment of behavior in anticipation of a crisis.

Key Point:
- **Behavior is a series of choices. Choices can be made consciously or unconsciously.**
- **Behavior is aligned when everyone consciously chooses to behave in response to the same answer to the question "why?" and everyone knows their role in the process for achieving the desired end result.**

Our military preparedness would be an excellent example of aligned behavior in anticipation of unwanted situations. The drill sergeant creates aligned behavior by the troops. While military behavior is very disciplined and in control, the behavior should be perceived as aligned because the purpose of National security is always clear.

The Army, Navy, Marines, and Air Force all proactively practice together to create alignment between the Forces. Winning the Gulf War is an excellent example of superior technology applied by an aligned organization.

> **Key Point:** • **An organization, proactively aligned on purpose, is a formidable force.**

It's easy to understand Alignment on Purpose in the context of a crisis. People must know their role and their relationship to others in the process. They must also understand that should the anticipated crisis occur, their emotions would be very different than during the practice sessions. One of the keys to success is to simulate the anticipated situation often enough so that people will remain calm during the actual event. Periodic fire drills simulate the real thing in hopes that people will "feel in advance" the comfort and confidence of aligned behavior.

The alignment of behavior in response to a crisis must begin with the purpose of the response. In the case of a military response, the purpose is the *survival* of a Nation. In the case of a fire drill, it's the *survival* of the building inhabitants. The alignment of a paramedic squad with an emergency room is about the *survival* of a trauma patient.

It is amazing to think about all the people who have given their own lives to rescue or protect the lives of others. The purpose of aligned behavior in response to a crisis often requires personal sacrifice and even death of those seeking to help others survive.

> **Key Point:** • **Alignment of behavior to achieve a purpose is a powerful force. Commitment to fulfill your role in the process can require personal sacrifice and even death.**

Because the personal sacrifice potential of crisis alignment is very real, all survival teams take time to *practice* and simulate the crisis. Rescue squads and emergency teams spend hundreds of hours practicing their roles to perfect the process of survival. Consider what your health and safety would be like if the process behind 911 was misaligned?

> **Key Point:** • **Alignment is achieved by practice for a purpose.**

It is important to realize that the *purpose* must drive the *process*. If the *purpose* is clear, the *process* to achieve the *purpose* will be well defined. If the purpose is vague or not properly defined, the *process* will be random at best.

> **Key Point:** • **Practice in anticipation of unwanted circumstances reveals prevention strategies.**

If people anticipate how accidents can occur, they will develop strategies for preventing accidents from happening. Companies purchase fire alarms, install sprinkler systems, build guardrails along embankments, and require workers to wear hard hats on construction sites. Many companies require employees to wear safety glasses to prevent eye injuries. Aligned behavior isn't optional to *survive*.

Organizational Alignment to Survive

In many Mass Production organizations, the purpose that is used to align behavior is *to survive*. Executives conduct fire drills on how to handle crises. There is an orderly process of controlling overhead and meeting quotas to meet planned objectives.

Key Point: •   **The budgeting process is a simulation to avoid a crisis.**

Many companies are run with precise measures to avoid a crisis. Performance is reviewed at the end of each month to be certain the company is on plan and expenses are under control. The organization is constantly realigned to avoid the crisis. The strategy sessions are extensive. Market research and competitive intelligence are very advanced skill sets. The war room is well equipped to avoid the crisis.

Key Point: •   **Avoiding a crisis is the vision of many Mass Production organizations.**
                                      •   **To survive is the only desired future state of being in many Mass Production Thinkers minds'.**

Even in the best run companies a crisis can occur. Unwanted circumstances can cause the organization to face extinction. Many Mass Production Thinkers use the threat of a crisis to align behavior. One organization that I worked with several years ago had a leader that was always saying, "Remember, s--- happens." Everyone was led to believe that a crisis could occur at any moment if costs were not controlled and quotas met. The crisis orientation became an addiction.

Alignment in the crisis-driven organization is highly protective of scarce resources. The culture often becomes altruistic with high levels of determination to work hard to prevent the crisis from occurring. Many executives tell me, "It's a constant firefighting drill around here!"

There are always casualties in crisis-driven organizations. There are those who "can't stand the heat" and won't commit to "lay down their lives for the company." Life in the crisis-driven company becomes very imbalanced. Many personal lives have been ruined in the process.

Alignment in anticipation of a *profit crisis* is very difficult to achieve. The Doers often aren't willing to sacrifice their own welfare to *make a profit* for the company. Mass Production Thinkers, who drive organizations with a crisis mentality, frequently intimidate everyone with loss of job security. Some even threaten to move the company offshore. The negative vision is "If we don't lower cost, we will all be out of a job."

It is important to realize that it is almost impossible for crisis-driven Mass Production Thinkers to declare that the threat of a crisis is over. Keeping the threat of a potential crisis alive gives them job security. If the potential of a crisis didn't exist, many Mass Production Thinkers wouldn't know what to do.

Crisis-driven organizations are often confronted with "wanted circumstances." Rather than a crisis, the business environment presents an opportunity to grow. If the company is programmed to merely survive, it will fail to properly pursue the growth opportunity.

An amazing thing happens when crisis-driven companies are confronted with a growth opportunity. The crisis Thinker is very cautious and linear. Growth projections are generated based only on past experience. While there is cautious optimism about the future, the *purpose* of growth remains "to make more profit."

Another response to growth opportunities is "If it ain't broke, don't fix it." When times are good many Mass Production Thinkers believe they have only arrived at a time before the next crisis. Things are currently fine and they resort to developing slightly more aggressive plans. Consider what it is like to work for an executive whose vision is to *be fine* between crises.

Several years ago, the president of a local bank asked me to help his senior management team develop a strategic plan for the coming year. He was a crisis Thinker. At that time, the bank was having the best year ever. Profits were at an all time high. Alignment on making a profit was strong. The bank was growing in linear form and everyone had very little zeal for developing a new plan. There wasn't a crisis against which to respond. When I suggested they should develop a strategic vision rather than a strategic plan, the president was openly hostile. He was confident they had a vision—to be the most profitable bank in the land— and his only interest was to rethink their strategy.

Key Point: • **When confronted with a growth opportunity, the organization that is aligned to survive will cautiously rethink the existing strategy and remain risk averse.**

Many Mass Production Thinkers are known for being very cautious and risk averse. They are very logical. The bank president had just increased loan projections 40% in anticipation of a strong market forecast, but the operating expense budget was only allowed to increase 5%. All of the salespeople were told to attack the market with determination. The president held alignment meetings to be certain everyone knew the opportunity for growth was here and confirm that everyone was to work smarter, not harder. The truth, however, was that the behavior of the organization was still aligned to survive, and everyone perceived the 40% projections as unrealistic and stupid.

Alignment to Make a Profit

Mass Production Thinkers bristle at the suggestion that alignment to make a profit is merely a survival strategy. Recall the statement from *Built to Last.*

> PROFITABILITY is a necessary condition for existence and a means to more important ends, but it is not the end in itself for many of the visionary companies. Profit is like oxygen, food, water, and blood for the body; they are not the point of life, but without them, there is no life.
>
> *Built to Last*, page 55

Making a profit is an important *objective*. Without profits the organization will die. It is important to realize, however, that alignment to make a profit will only produce prevention strategies and risk-adverse behavior. There is nothing wrong with prevention strategies. Installing traffic lights and railroad crossing signals are all worthy endeavors, but this behavior is in response to anticipated unwanted circumstances.

Key Point: • **Companies that are aligned to make a profit will consciously erect limits to customer service.**

A new fast food restaurant had opened locally that specialized in ice cream. When I read that they were struggling financially, I decided to try their offering. I drove up to the drive through menu board. It was impressive. Beautiful pictures of large ice cream cones and banana splits were illustrated. I ordered a single dip of Oreo ice cream in a wafer cone. I was told the price was 99¢ and "please pull around."

The attendant extended the cone through the window and simultaneously held out the 1¢ change. I reached for the cone then quickly withdrew my hand. The cone didn't look like the picture on the menu board. I asked, "Why doesn't the cone have as much ice cream as the picture on the menu board?" She said, "That is all the scoop holds." When I told her I could get a much larger cone at a lower cost at a competitive restaurant, she said, "They'd go broke giving away so much ice cream."

Because there weren't other cars in line, I asked her, "What's the purpose of your job?" She was totally confused and asked, "Do you want the cone or not?" I told her I'd take it if the amount of ice cream matched the picture on the menu board. She said, "I can't give you any more than what the scoop holds." I drove off leaving the cone behind.

The next day I wrote the company and told them that their profit problem was the result of over-promising and under-delivering to customers, and they lacked Alignment on Purpose. Two weeks after the incident, I was invited to meet with the vice president of operations. He was rather defensive and wanted to know why I asked the crewmember the purpose of her job. I told him I wanted to test the alignment of the organization. I had read that they were having profit problems and I wanted to know if the organization was properly aligned. He then offered that their restaurant was very well organized and the crewmember did exactly what she was suppose to do. "You make money in the fast food business by portion control. If we gave away extra ice cream on every cone, we'd go broke!"

He used all the buzzwords. People were crewmembers, they were empowered, and they had attended extensive teamwork training. He then asked, with an intimidating tone, "What would you suggest?" I suggested that the amount of ice cream on the cone should look like the picture on the menu board.

He said, "We'd go broke doing that."

Key Point: • **Alignment to make a profit is based on survival.**
              • **Alignment to make a profit always leads to over-promised and under-delivered customer service.**

In six months, the company declared bankruptcy. The excuses were many, but the vice president was quoted in the newspaper as saying, "It is difficult to get good help."

Take time to ask people who are serving you what is the purpose of their jobs? Start to accumulate the answers. When a company is aligned on make a profit, the answers are based on the survival instincts of the organization. Listen carefully to the answers. You will be told an incredible array of "we can't do that" answers to very simple requests. The essence:

"We can't do that or we'll go broke."

The Illusion of Profit Alignment

The behavior in most Mass Production organizations is "under control" to make a profit. It comes from years of budgeting and living within the budget. The assumption is that the customer will be served if the company makes a profit. Mass Production organizations further assume that the future is a predictable extension of the past and that the purpose of the organization is to make a profit.

Profit alignment experts are called managers, and good managers are rewarded with promotions and bonuses based upon bottom line results. The problem with this approach is that very few people actually know how a company makes a profit. The server at the ice cream store only knew not to give more than the scoop holds.

Profit alignment processes have very sophisticated mechanisms that constrain employees from going beyond preestablished control limits. I worked with the claims department of a large insurance company. The claims adjusters had very narrowly defined limits for settling claims. As long as a claim fell within those limits, the adjuster was free to settle the claim. As inflation caused the costs of repairs to escalate, the limits were constantly being challenged by customers. The constant hassle with the control limits cost the company dearly in customer retention. The senior leaders responded to this dilemma by creating a new strategy. They reorganized the organization to lower cost to "compete on price" in an effort to keep and attract customers. This strategy failed to recognize the need to change the alignment of the organization.

The company frequently performed miracles when there was a major disaster. During the aftermath of hurricane Hugo, the company was recognized by its policyholders for the superior way that adjusters handled the claims. The vice president of claims asked me why they were known for customer satisfaction after the Hugo disaster and could not create that same level of satisfaction in the normal course of doing business. The answer is very simple. In response to Hugo, the adjusters were Aligned on Purpose. During normal times, the adjusters revert to the alignment of *make a profit*. The vice president didn't understand the word alignment.

I told him the issue was the force of authority. During normal times, the adjusters were authorized to say *yes* within predetermined cost control limits. If the cost of a settlement fell beyond the limits, the adjuster would say *no* and had to seek approval to say *yes* from a higher authority.

In processing the claims associated with Hugo, the limits were relaxed and the adjusters were authorized to say *yes* within the limits of what they thought was right for the customer. If they wanted to decline the claim, say *no*, they had to seek approval of a higher authority. The reversal of the force of authority changed the alignment of the adjusters.

I told the vice president to try reversing the *yes/no* decision-making process being used with the adjusters during a normal workweek. Let them say *yes* when they think the settlement is fair for the customers, regardless of the limits. Trust them to make good decisions just as they did after Hugo. If they want to decline the settlement, they must seek your approval to say *no*. His response was "We'd go broke if we did that," the same response as the ice cream executive.

Key Point: •   **Alignment to make a profit is about survival.**

Creating Alignment on Purpose is a terrifying thought for Mass Production Thinkers. The profit alignment mechanism is well imbedded in the organization. If Alignment on Purpose is suggested before a new structural framework is created, the immediate response is "We'll die if we do that."

The truth is, it is impossible to achieve profit alignment. It is an illusion to believe it will ever happen. In fact, the make a profit approach will always cause severe misalignment of the customer service process.

Key Point: • **Profit is a measure of success not the purpose for being.**
• **If everyone has different ways of measuring success, alignment will be impossible to achieve.**

Profit is a measure of success. Every functional group within an organization has measures for success and impacts the bottom line of *the BUSINESS* differently. Let's return to the insurance company. The sales agents are responsible for top line revenue. To an insurance agent, there isn't any risk that shouldn't be written. The Underwriting Department is responsible for evaluating the risk of the business the agents want to write. An underwriter protects the bottom line by accepting only select risk customers. It is, therefore, impossible to achieve profit alignment between Sales and Underwriting. In the scheme of how each department is measured, "more for one" is "less for the other." This creates conflict, and customers are caught in the middle of the conflict. In fact, this happened to me.

My insurance agent wrote a new homeowners and auto policy for my wife and me. We paid one-half the premium the day we bought the policy, and the agent told us we were covered. Fifteen days later we received a letter direct from the Underwriting Department declining our policy. When I called our agent, he was unaware of the letter. He checked with Underwriting and sure enough, we were not a select risk. He was baffled as to why, but the decision by Underwriting was final. He was later told by the company not to write any more business in rural areas that don't have fire hydrants.

The point is the customer will eventually experience the misalignment of the make a profit measurement mechanism. Somehow the "scoop doesn't hold enough ice cream" or "you aren't a select risk." It's crazy, but it happens.

The "yeah, but" debates always escalate at this point. Mass Production Thinkers will justify the profit alignment approach with all the logic that is within them. Tenacious battles rage and determined executives prepare highly detailed charts and graphs that show employees how what they do impacts the bottom line. This creates fear within the customer service representatives of violating the rules. In profit-aligned organizations, the customer service representatives are always prepared to tell the customer why they can't have what they were promised.

Let's look at one more example of profit alignment that failed to satisfy a customer. On a recent flight to the West Coast, the airline provided an in-flight movie. After the preview was shown, the flight attendants came down the aisle selling headsets for $4.00. I had already seen the movie, so I declined.

The gentleman to my right bought the headset and prepared to watch the movie. He was in the window seat in front of the bulkhead and had trouble seeing the screen. After a half-hour, he got a kink in his neck and gave up trying to watch the movie. He wanted his money back, but the flight attendants were busy serving beverages. He fell asleep and waited until the movie was over to asked for a refund. The attendant said, "There cannot be any refunds once the movie is over, sorry."

On final approach, the flight attendant sat in the bulkhead seat right in front of us. We were face to face for the next 10 minutes. After brief chitchat about his job, I asked him why the airline couldn't refund the gentleman's money. His answer was, and I quote, "You know those airline executives, they want all the green stuff they can get." This is obviously a profit alignment answer. He had neither a justification for his behavior nor a good answer to the question. Rather, he blamed the executives of the airline for being greedy.

Key Point:
- **Doers have a difficult time choosing purposeful behavior when the aligning force is to make a profit.**
- **Customer requests are often against the rules and outside the control limits.**

If the airline was aligned on purpose, the flight attendant would have easily refunded the money. He would be as clear about the value of entertainment on board as he was about serving free beverages. He shouldn't refund anyone's money after they legitimately watched the movie, but he should have easily recognized the man's dilemma and refunded his.

Is this too much to expect? The obvious answer is of course not—yet many Mass Production organizations seldom take the time to align the organization on *purpose*. The imbedded thinking of Mass Production is strong. The alignment of *make a profit* is a powerful survival strategy that controls the behavior of the organization.

Alignment to Grow

The business agenda today has a strong growth orientation, and executives everywhere are looking for the magic pill, the killer strategy, and a new vision for success. Mergers and acquisitions abound. This frantic behavior reminds me of the gold rush days of early American history.

The business opportunities today are enormous. A world of abundance is available to those who can see the opportunity through the correct lens. The key is to accurately define the growth opportunity and understand the leadership agenda.

The Characteristics of Growth

Growth has many interesting characteristics and principles. There are, however, three principles of organizational growth that you, as a Transformational Leader, must understand:

Key Point:
- **Growth is invisible while it is occurring.**
- **While growth appears linear, as measured in financial terms, growth creates exponential complexity in personal relationships.**
- **Growth is inversely proportional to effort. The more effortless the ecosystem becomes, the faster growth will occur.**

Let me give you several examples to illustrate these principles.

Children grow. We know they are growing. We can measure their height and weight in linear form, but we can't see them grow. The linear measurement of height does not explain the exponential changes in personality and maturity. In addition, as much as you, as a parent, would like to control their personal growth, the harder you work at controlling it, the worse it gets.

Growing a garden is a similar experience. I plant corn seeds and nothing appears to happen. Within a week plants appear. I watch the plants and can't see them grow. Several weeks later, the corn is knee high. Somehow, the plants grew, but I could not see it happen. As the plants grow, weeds appear from nowhere. The care and weeding accelerates, requiring effort on my part, but the ecosystem within which the corn seeds grow is effortless.

Key Point:
- **People who are external to the growth process must provide protection and nourishment and be patient while growth is occurring.**
- **While the linear measurement of growth is important, the ultimate quality of the crop is the most important measure of success.**
- **Growth occurs in phases. It is important to know when to plant and when to reap.**
- **Growth requires preparing the environment for effective results to be achieved.**
- **Accelerated, uncontrolled growth is often fatal.**

Using the child and garden metaphors, it is easy to understand these concepts. Think for a minute about our prior discussions of setting strategy versus creating alignment. If we are to understand how to create alignment for growth, it is important to recognize that aligned behavior is within the growing organism (the child or the plants) and not within the gardener or the parent. Setting the strategies of how big a garden to plant and how many children to have are very different activities than creating alignment within the object of growth.

For some reason, Mass Production Thinkers have a difficult time with the concept of growth. The metaphors of nature and life don't seem to apply to business. Yet, all the concepts and principles listed above are equally valid when applied to organizational growth.

Mass Production Thinkers are obsessed with linear measures of effort. I have worked with many managers who evaluate growth by looking at the numbers. To them, the height of the corn is more important than the yield of the crop. How many annual meetings have you attended where the focus was on linear increases in sales and profit and customer satisfaction was never mentioned?

The Mass Production Thinker always defines growth in numerical terms. One executive told me recently, "We need to be a billion-dollar company in two years." I asked him, "What does that mean in terms of customer satisfaction?" He had not considered the question.

Growth to numbers people is linear and simply a matter of deploying more resources. The assumption is that there is a market for the company's products, and an increase in market penetration will cause the company to grow. A linear extension of current reality always dominates their thinking.

Growth to Mass Production Thinkers is always about effort and intelligence. They constantly say, "We need to work smarter, not harder," but they don't know how to translate working smarter into reality. Smarter generally means to have a better strategy and less hard means to increase cross-functional cooperation. I have never had a Mass Production Thinker tell me that working smarter, not harder had anything to do with creating Alignment on Purpose. Their answers are always about better thinking behind the effort.

The Mass Production Thinker is programmed to achieve growth using cause and effect logic. The *Context* of Mass Production is built on the assumption that growth can be planned and controlled. General Motors used planned obsolescence as a growth strategy for years. If customer behavior can be controlled, a predictable market will sustain growth. The mechanistic models of Mass Production Thinking are well known.

The new global business opportunity is not a linear extension of the Mass Production model. The three characteristics of growth will be present. Growth will be invisible and rapid. The relationship complexity will be exponential, and growth will occur on effortless networks.

Think about these three factors. Forget the details of how to create Web pages or logistics systems. Are you able to accept living and working within this

Context? Do you know how to manage something you can't see, measure, or control? I hope you can feel the need to Align the organization on Purpose.

In the new business environment, you must embrace the paradox of effortless and effectiveness to grow. I don't know any person alive who is *smart* enough or *tough* enough to *figure out* how to *force growth to happen*. The exponential complexity of relationships is beyond *control*. It is impossible to *organize* a dynamic network of people. It is an illusion to believe that growth can be achieved by planning, organizing, and controlling *things*. Mass Production Thinking no longer contains the answers to the global growth agenda.

The key is to focus on *effortless relationships* with customers. The economic agenda today is driven by speed and responsiveness. Quality is a given. *The Business of the BUSINESS* must embrace the context of Mass Customization. The economic leverage of standardization is gone. Everything can be customized by the richness of the information it contains.

Information networks extend the reach of information and transport rich messages to even Third World countries. Can you see the growth? No, it is invisible, but you know it's happening as you read. The Mass Production Thinker in you will be frustrated if you aren't getting your fair market share *now!* Visit the board room at any financial institution tomorrow. The feeding frenzy of the Mass Production Thinkers is something to watch. The gold rush is on.

Aligned on Purpose

For your BUSINESS to participate in the new business environment, you must create Alignment on Purpose. The relationships that are needed to be a player in the new environment likely don't exist today. Mass Production relationships are adversarial and built on no trust. New relationships must be created.

Key Point: • **You can't talk yourself out of something you behaved yourself into.**

You created adversarial relationships through years of alignment to make a profit. You can't say you're sorry and expect forgiveness. The buyer-beware belief runs deep. You can't call yourself a partner and get married to your customers tomorrow. It takes time to behave in new ways.

Key Point: • **The new behavior of your organization must be Aligned on Purpose.**

To behave your way out of the Mass Production mess you are in, you must change the alignment of the new behavior. For new behavior to be effortless and effective, you must clearly define *effective*. Making a profit for your company is *not* the definition of effective as perceived by customers today. Customers today want it *their way*, and there are plenty of entrepreneurial businesses out there to give it to them that way.

Purpose must define why the BUSINESS exists, and the process of fulfilling that purpose must be carefully designed. If this work is properly done, Alignment on Purpose can be achieved. It is not easy, but it does guarantee that *the Business of the BUSINESS* will be effortless and effective in serving customers.

Creating Alignment on Purpose

Let's now consider how to create Alignment on Purpose. Let's assume that the *Context* of the Business environment has changed. In other words, *the Business of your BUSINESS* must somehow embrace Mass Customization. Let's further assume that most of your senior leaders are Mass Production Thinkers and your accountant is content reporting financial alignment every month. The company is profitable within the current context and a crisis does not yet exist. How can you change the alignment?

Creating a new *Business of the BUSINESS* while simultaneously running the old organization is the ultimate Transformational Leadership challenge. You must be very clear about what you are doing. If the preceding discussion about purpose doesn't make sense and you still believe the need is for a new Mass Production strategy, please don't proceed.

If, however, you are committed to creating a new *Business of the BUSINESS* that will be Aligned on Purpose, there are six specific steps to creating alignment. I will outline each step. Many of the actions have been the subject of previous chapters.

Step One

The first step in creating Alignment on Purpose is to accurately interpret the future growth opportunity facing your BUSINESS. Ask yourself the key question:

Has the *Context* changed?

Mass Customization, enabled by technology, is here to stay. If your organization is anchored in Mass Production Thinking, you must challenge your leadership team to create a clear, specific vision of the future rather than merely developing new strategies. Visualize *the Business of the BUSINESS* 5 to 10 years in the future. Don't concern yourself with how the BUSINESS will be organized until you can see *the Business of the BUSINESS*.

As I have said many times before, begin by creating the new architecture, a new structural framework for the BUSINESS. The structural framework contains the vision and the purpose that will serve to ultimately align behavior. In addition to the vision, the senior leaders should identify the assumptions that must change for growth to occur. Be careful of the assumption that *the Business* will serve customers if it makes a profit. Also, and equally important, clarify the competitive advantage that will produce growth. The Mass Production Thinkers will believe that the company can win the competency game. This is an illusion. Remember, the issue today is effortlessness. This simple fact, alone, demands a capability based competitive advantage.

Everyone must be involved in creating the structural framework. Involving the entire organization in the architectural process is the first step in creating Alignment on Purpose.

Key Point: • **The involvement of people is more important than their intellectual contribution. The process of involvement begins to align behavior.**

Please don't underestimate the difficulty of this first step. Let me give you an example. Four years ago the chairman of a major international company announced that their old organizational form was obsolete. During his presentation to all the senior managers he said, "We need to transform the organization," and "We need a new vision." Both were accurate statements. Four years later, they still have not defined a vision, and the company is aggressively reorganizing the organization. What should have been a Transformational Change initiative turned into a centralization and downsizing spiral. Profits remain strong because hundreds of jobs have been eliminated. Hundreds of highly talented people who could not stand the heat have left. The Mass Production Thinkers that remain are more determined than ever to win the game by standardizing the product offering. It is an illusion to believe that the organization is being transformed. The truth is that the alignment on make a profit is stronger than ever, and the psychological experience throughout the organization is compliance.

Step Two

The second step is for senior leaders to immediately change their own *behavior*. Mass Production Thinkers are programmed to Think and they don't believe that their own behavior must change. This is an illusion. Don't ever forget—*you cannot talk yourself out of what you behaved yourself into.* The senior leaders must demonstrate transformational *intention* in behavioral form.

There are thousands of ways to demonstrate intentions, but nothing is more important than involving everyone in creating the *structural framework*. Listen to the input, and take action to validate the ideas contained in the input.

Key Point: • **The psychological experience of a Mass Production organization is compliance. Senior leaders must involve the Doers in the thinking.**

It is difficult for the Thinkers to involve the Doers in the thinking process. It is equally frustrating for the Doers. They don't know how to think the thinking of Business, and they frequently feel intimidated by the Thinkers. The key is to ask the Doers to examine the customer experience and suggest ideas as to how it can be improved or transformed. Don't ask the Doers to translate anything into financial terms. Focus them on connectivity and Alignment on Purpose opportunities.

During this step, I always suggest that teams of people be asked to visit customers and determine how well the promise of the organization is being fulfilled. The teams always uncover the over-promised and under-delivered scenario of the old Mass Production process. Ask the teams to figure out how to create a new customer service process.

The input from the teams will always contain an "oh ain't it awful how" perspective about the current customer service process. Shift them to a creating orientation by asking them to suggest ideas as to how it can be *different*. Do not use words that end in "ER." Linear improvement is always possible, but look for new *Context* and new Content.

Another key is to become visible to the Doers after you ask them to get involved in creating the structural framework. You will need to shape their thinking with vision and assumptions about change. If you truly intend to value the input of everyone, you must find ways for them to present their ideas to you interactively. This is obviously an enormous task, but nothing is more important than creating alignment.

Step Three

The second step will begin to uncover the need to change the customer's experience with your BUSINESS. The customer experience is defined by the purpose. Therefore, the third step is to declare that the behavior of the new *Business of the BUSINESS* must be Aligned on Purpose. If you are creating a new *Business of the BUSINESS*, you must create a new customer service process. A new process will be required to fulfill the mission and purpose as defined in the structural framework.

Key Point: • **A process designed to serve a customer is not the same as customer service.**
             • **The purpose answers the question "Why do we exist?" and creates alignment within the new customer service process.**

During this step, cross-functional teams can identify how the entire customer service process must work to fulfill the purpose of the *new Business*. If the *new Business* must be seamlessness or be based on customer partnerships, the behavior within the process must be Aligned on Purpose.

Key Point:
- **Involving the people in creating the structural framework leads them to the awareness that their own behavior must be Aligned on Purpose.**
- **When they define their own role in the customer service process, they will do it with commitment.**

Every person in the organization must be able to understand their *role* in serving the customer and translate that *role* into the daily behavior of their job.

Key Point:
- **The *Business of the BUSINESS* is about helping customers get what they want.**
- **The organization of the BUSINESS is the process of serving customers effectively and efficiently.**
- **Alignment of behavior is about making the customer service process seamless and effortless.**
- **The strategy of the BUSINESS is about deploying the resources of the BUSINESS in such a way as it competes effectively and produces a return on the investment for the owners.**
- **Making a profit is one measure of success.**

I hope by now you can see the difference between setting strategy and creating alignment. Senior leaders must be very clear about these two issues. It is foolish to believe that people will serve customers when the alignment is to make a profit. If the purpose isn't clear and the customer service process is not clearly defined, it will be impossible for alignment to occur.

In the book *Built to Last*, Jim Collins and Jerry Porras give many examples of companies that are Aligned on Purpose. Nordstroms, Disney, Boeing, Hewlett Packard, Proctor & Gamble, Marriott, and many others are cited. It is not the purpose of this book to validate the process; rather, it is to help you understand that the barrier to creating Alignment on Purpose is Mass Production Thinking.

Step Four

The fourth step is to institutionalize practice time. Change doesn't just happen. Everyone must *learn to behave differently*. You must continue to run the old *Business* simultaneously while creating the new Business. Learning must be an integrated process of extracting meaning from experience. Everyone must experience change in new behavioral ways. The trial and error environment will challenge everyone, especially you, to let go of old beliefs and try new things.

Once you realize that the old *Business of the BUSINESS* will not stop while you create the new *Business*, you will recognize the need to *institutionalize practice time*. The new *Business* cannot be created while you are fighting the fires of the existing Business.

To begin to institutionalize practice, I suggest that everyone commit one hour a week to practice new behavior. Meet in small groups to create cross-functional awareness of how the *process of serving customers* is working. Determine if the current process is aligned or misaligned. Examine the *intentions* of all the participants. Ask a lot of *what if* and *just suppose* questions about the purpose of *the BUSINESS*. Examine customer interactions that go well. There are many instances where the current organization performs well. Recall the insurance adjusters after Hugo. Ask why it works sometimes and why, in other instances, it doesn't work. Be aware of the invisible forces that affect behavior.

Key Point: • **Don't blame people. Look for misalignment of purpose and how the process is not designed to fulfill the promise.**

As people begin to try new behavior, be aware of the risk they run in breaking the rules of the old organization. New purposeful behavior may appear to be opposed to the make a profit strategy of the past. Recognize the intent is to create new alignment.

The process of creating alignment is dynamic. Some people will easily move from the compliance orientation to a high level of commitment. Others will resist. This shift is not easy. Remaining in compliance is comfortable for many people. It's safe to be told what to do and remain in a functional job.

Key Point: • **The most difficult step in creating alignment is to ask people to accept responsibility for customer satisfaction.**

Many people are so far removed from the customer, that they don't believe that what they do has any direct impact on customer satisfaction. They know how to control an expense or process a piece of paper, but they have never been asked to think about how their behavior fulfills the purpose of the Business.

Those who are close to the customer, such as salespeople and direct customer support people, can easily accept responsibility for customer satisfaction. However, they can be very cynical about the rest of the organization's willingness to change. Sales people in a Mass Production organization find it harder to sell their own organization on serving customers than it is to sell customers. The over-promised, under-delivered scenario has played itself out many times.

Key Point: • **Many people have the will to win, but only a very few have the will to prepare to win.**

Change doesn't happen just because the economy is strong or an executive wills it to happen. The people must prepare to change. This takes a commitment to *practice new behavior*.

One company president I encountered had just announced a reengineering initiative to grow his company. He wanted to grow to $100 million within the next five years. At the time of his announcement, the top line revenue of the company was $32 million. The company was a very conservative family-owned BUSINESS that had never achieved more than a 12% growth in any of the past 20 years. Yet, the president willed that reengineering shall happen. Three years later, the reengineering effort was declared a disaster. The company had lost market share and was struggling to achieve $25 million in sales.

Key Point: • **Change today is about connectivity.**
• **People must practice being connected.**

Change and growth today are not about size. It's about *connectivity*. Remember that growth brings exponential complexity in relationships. It takes time to make all the connections. Growth is about creating networks for information flow that are way beyond the hierarchical model. Intranets and Internets enable people to communicate and grow their awareness. Awareness translates into possibilities. A creating orientation leads to growth.

The alignment within the new Business environment is about effortlessness, seamlessness, responsiveness, and speed. It is *not* about financial controls. Alignment within this new environment is about the purpose of serving customers. Customers today are able to buy what they want from many different *channels of communication*. The expectations of customers regarding speed, responsiveness, and integrity have been totally transformed in the past 20 years. This transformation requires a new form of organizational alignment.

Key Point: • **To compete within the new *Context* of today's information-based environment, the behavior of the organization must be Aligned on Purpose.**
• **People must practice being Aligned on Purpose.**

The president referred to above had read *Reengineering the Corporation*, by Michael Hammer and James Champy. He thought that reengineering was about making the existing organization more profitable. Reengineering is about creating a new customer service process and aligning the behavior within that process to achieve a new way of doing business. He would not allow people time to practice new behavior. The reengineering effort was perceived as a strategy to maximize family wealth, and employees became very cynical about growth.

Key Point: • **Teamwork is the proactive alignment of behavior.**
              • **Teams practice.**
              • **How you practice really matters.**

Creating Alignment on Purpose requires that people practice *being aligned*.

Step Five

The fifth step is to *track positives* by asking, "What is going well?" Creating Alignment on Purpose is a dynamic process. It cannot be declared to exist. Alignment must be created through the ongoing experience of organizational life.

In my Transformational Leadership course, I teach managers and leaders to track what is going well. If customers are being satisfied, the customer service process is working well. It may be a conscious or unconscious act, but the key is to elevate everyone's awareness to a conscious level.

When a customer interaction goes well, Alignment on Purpose happens. Managers should ask the team how that success was created. Does everyone consciously know how they contributed to the success? The person who sweeps the floors should know their role in the process.

Likewise, when a customer interaction doesn't go well, the failure should be viewed as a *process failure*, not a people failure. If the customer service process doesn't function as expected, somewhere the behavior was not Aligned on Purpose. People should be able to examine process failures without blame. "The process failed, let's find out why." When people can see their role in the customer service process, they place importance on what they do, and they feel fulfilled by their work.

Mass Production Thinkers will quickly point out that the *work ethic* today is low. "People are lazy and need to be directed." They see customer service problems as people problems and are constantly trying to control people to achieve results.

I'll be the first to admit that there are many people who have worked for years in the Mass Production *Context* of Thinkers think and Doers do what they are told. They wait between steps of the process and often fail to see the whole process. Their *condition consciousness* is based in *fear*, and it poses a formidable barrier to change.

Tracking positives provides balance to the negative feedback mechanism of Mass Production. Employees must create a new process of serving customers.

Because the new process doesn't exist, it serves no purpose to focus on the aspects of the old process that don't work. However, it may make sense to incorporate what's going well with the old process into the new process.

The absolute key is to eliminate blame. If people who are previously Doers are asked to participate in thinking, they must be safe in their participation.

Step Six

Stop thinking in steps. Creating Alignment on Purpose is not linear. The simultaneousness of it all is enormously complex. The simplicity of Transformational Change is that people will align their own behavior to fulfill the purpose if the Mass Production Thinkers will let go and allow it to happen.

The Terrifying Truth

The issue of creating Alignment on Purpose scares most Mass Production Thinkers. Frankly, it is a concept that is perceived as "that touchy-feely stuff," and many executives reject the notion.

I could tell you about Carl, Rick, Dave, Gregg, Harry, Bob, Ed, Chris, and Jim, who to this day reject the notion. Literally thousands of executives are committed to win the Mass Production game by achieving the low cost producer status. Some of these executives have Junior behind their names. They earned their stripes by watching their fathers demand alignment on financials. Many of their companies are doing well, but they are slowly losing creative talent and the cry for teamwork is getting louder every day.

The terrifying truth is that we, as customers, have choices, and we don't have to buy a General Motors car. People don't have to buy the products and services of your company either. There are lots of restaurants and airlines. The choices are also customized. Never forget the teller is the bank, the server is the restaurant, and the flight attendant is the airline. The last person in the customer service process must know their role and be Aligned on Purpose or you, as a customer, won't be satisfied.

One senior leader when confronted with this truth denied that it was true. He called the customer service representatives in his organization "minimum wagers." When I suggested that they must be trained to fulfill their role in the customer service process he said, "We don't train those people, they might leave." What? "They are minimum wagers and if they were given training to expand their skills, they would leave and get a better job." My response was, "What if you don't train them and they stay!" He was furious. At that time, he was in a highly regulated business where customer service was not a priority. Today, that has all changed, and his company is spending millions trying to create Alignment on Purpose.

Key Point: • It's not a matter of *whether* to Align on Purpose; instead, *when* will you do it.

The acid test is to be a customer of your own company for a day. Ask yourself how it feels. Can you feel the alignment or is the customer service process an accident at best.

The Challenge Ahead

Never in our modern history has the need for Alignment on Purpose been more important. As the Mass Customized *Business of the BUSINESS* continues to unfold, the most important work of leadership will not be setting strategy; it will be to create Alignment on Purpose.

It is impossible to imagine how the global networks, operating simultaneously in different time zones, can function unless there is Alignment of Purpose. People must make decisions based upon information available to them on computer networks. Face-to-face interaction may never occur. Choices of how to behave within the organizational context will be made by people with very different financial expectations.

Key Point: • The age of control is over. The era of Alignment on Purpose has arrived.

Very few people know how to make this happen. There are models and metaphors within our existing *Context* to draw from, but we must think about the leadership challenge as never before. Creating the structure that defines the expected behavior is an enormous challenge. Charisma alone is insufficient to meet the challenge. Welcome to the era of Transformational Change.

Chapter 16
Self-Awareness

This chapter is about you, personally. If you are like most business people today, you are deeply imbedded in a Mass Production organization. You work for Mr. Mass Production Thinker personified. Old Harry isn't going to change. He not only doesn't know the term Mass Customization, he wrote the book entitled, *When the Going Gets Tough, the Tough Get Going.* Your organization has tried all the buzzwords in attempts to keep pace with competition. The reengineering effort produced some change, but the bottom line results are still *not good enough.* Harry is on the rampage again, and the rumor today is another reorganization will be announced soon.

Actually, the change in the information network was exciting at first. The challenge of learning new technology was fun until the number of e-mail messages went beyond your ability to respond. The number of meetings has accelerated and doing *more with less* has everyone bewildered. You concluded several months ago that *this isn't it*, but you are so busy there isn't time to think about changing jobs. It just isn't fun. The empowerment initiative is turning into insanity. The touchy-feely stuff is running wild again.

This scenario takes many forms, but the common thread is that Mass Production Thinking dominates most organizations and it isn't going to change anytime soon. It matters not whether you are dealing with Old Harry or a new CEO who has vowed to change the culture. The muscle memory of Mass Production Thinking is strong.

You have concluded that the organization isn't going to change fast enough for you to realize your potential. You are feeling *burned out* and *still shining.* During a recent leadership seminar, you were reminded that

A journey of a thousand miles starts with but a single step.

You have read this parable many times and you know it contains an enormous truth. You must act—do something—to change your situation, but you aren't sure what that single step would be for you. You have read Harry's book and are somewhat convinced that you are tough and can tough it out.

The Fear of Falling

A great friend of mine, David McNally, wrote the terrific book *Even Eagles Need a Push: Learning to Soar in a Changing World*. In that book, David uses the metaphor of the mother eagle teaching her baby eaglets to fly. She must eventually push them out of the nest, *trusting* they will fly. David makes the following point, however, on behalf of the baby eaglet:

Why does the thrill of soaring start with the fear of falling?

What a profound statement. As I thought about this statement, I realized that it had happened to me. I had been with the Trane Air Conditioning Company for 17 years. It was a comfortable nest. Then, without warning, my job was eliminated. The Trane Company bought the Air Conditioning Division of General Electric. In integrating the two distribution channels, it made sense to close the existing Trane warehouse system. All nine Trane Distribution Center managers, like me, were suddenly kicked out of the nest. We could not believe what had happened.

As we flew home from the termination meeting, we all felt like we were in free fall. Then, something very interesting happened. I realized that I was prepared to fly, and I spread my wings and flew.

Key Point: •   Are you prepared to fly? Is it *time* for you to soar?

Many people have been pushed out of the nest by mother corporation in the past 10 years. The illusion of lifetime employment has been dispelled. If you were fortunate enough to experience soaring after the fear of falling, you will relate to most of this chapter. For those of you who crashed, I'm sorry. It hurts to be pushed out with no explanation other than your job was eliminated. If you are still trying to please Mr. Mass Production Thinker, maybe it's time for you to soar.

As we have discussed many times before, most action within the *Context* of Mass Production Thinking is directed at *solving the problems* of current reality. Let's return to my experience at Trane. General Electric wanted to sell its Air Conditioning Division because it wasn't making a profit in that business. The Trane Company bought the ailing division as a defensive move to thwart an unfriendly takeover. Both companies were trying to *solve the problems* of current reality. Neither company had a true vision of the future.

Let's suppose for a moment that mother eagle sees her baby eaglets as *problems*. They are growing too large for the nest. They are placing increasing demands on her for food—demands that she can't fulfill. She's frustrated by the situation and decides that the solution is to kick them out of the nest.

Can you *feel* the difference in *problem solving* and *creating?* Problem solving is useful if there is a problem to be solved. Confusing the need to create something that doesn't exist as a problem to be solved is the single biggest reason why Transformational Journeys fail.

Key Point:
- The mother eagle knows that the eaglet's destiny is to be an eagle.
- To *be* an eagle is *not* a problem to be solved.
- To help the eaglet to fulfill its destiny, the mother eagle must take action when it's time for it to fly.
- For you to be a *leader* is *not* a problem to be solved.
- For you to be an *entrepreneur* is *not* a problem to be solved.
- The comfortable nest of Mass Production Thinking is obsolete. It's time to leave the nest. The only relevant question is are you prepared to soar?

The First Step

The absolute first step in your Transformational Journey is to make a conscious choice to *be different*. The frustration you currently feel is making you aware that there is a gap between who you *are* and who you want to *be*. Also, if your destiny is to *be* something more than you *are*, you must take action soon.

Key Point:
- You must begin by expanding your awareness of what's possible. The *nest* of Mass Production Thinking is very familiar and comfortable.

Accept the fact that you are a Mass Production Thinker. It is the way you have been programmed to think. It isn't wrong to think that way. I hope that by now you realize that the world ahead will require that you think and behave in a different way.

Key Point:
- Choosing to be *different* in the future is risk free.
- Your destiny is to be *different*. Make the choice today.

Throughout your life, you have been confronted with many Transformational Change opportunities. You have been transformed from a child to an adult, from a worker to a manager, from a parent to your child's best friend. All these transformations begin with a conscious choice. They are not problems to be solved. If you want to *be different* as a person, a leader within an organization, a parent, or an entrepreneur, the first step is to *choose to be different*. Transformational Change does not start by quitting your job or accumulating more possessions.

What you currently *have* is irrelevant. (Remember, you arrived with nothing and you will depart with nothing.) What you currently *do* is irrelevant. You can keep what you *have* and continue *doing* what you *do*, but *having* more and *doing* the same things faster or better are insufficient to produce the future you desire. You must want to be *different* at home, at work, in your life, or on the playground.

Key Point:
- **The journey of 1000 miles does not start by having enough money or better time management. It starts by wanting to be *different*.**
- **Wanting to be *different* will expand your *awareness* to what's *possible*.**

Defining Different

Many people want to *be different*. Very few people are satisfied with who they are. Every executive I have worked with over the past 15 years has had a desire for their company to *be different*, and that desire always translates into a personal desire to be different. When I ask people what *different* looks like, their visions are typically vague or idealistic.

Key Point:
- **The inability to accurately define a vision will prevent you from making the choice to *be different*.**
- **Mass Production Thinking will limit you to a better, bigger, faster, or smarter version of your existing reality.**

Most Mass Production Thinkers have a difficult time visualizing a future state of *being*. They tend to define their existence in terms of *doing* or *having*. Therefore, begin by sorting yourself into three distinct piles. It is easier to think about the ultimate result in terms of (1) what you want to *know*, (2) what you want to *do*, and (3) how you want to *feel*. When people do this, the view when seen from the perspective of current reality is very *complex*, your emotions always contain a high level of *anxiety*, and the journey always appears *difficult*. We can illustrate this as follows:

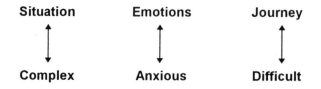

Situation	Emotions	Journey
↕	↕	↕
Complex	**Anxious**	**Difficult**

These three states are the starting point for every Transformational Journey. Obviously, if you want to be different, you must change current reality. You cannot accomplish this by doing more of the same. You must, therefore, start by defining what *different* looks like. Initially you may not know. You likely don't have a picture of *different* in your mind. Maybe you want to play basketball like Michael Jordan or play golf like Tiger Woods. These pictures are vague and idealistic, and they cause most people to return to the comfort zone of enduring the problems of current reality. The Mass Production Thinker in you will easily be convinced that the end result you are after is to *have more* by working smarter, not harder.

Because an initial picture of *different* is difficult to formulate and often perceived as unrealistic, think about the desired future state in terms of the situation, emotions, and journey. Ask yourself what would you want it *to be*? Because your awareness of what's possible is limited, the answers are likely about *simple, fulfilled*, and easy.

I think it's fair to say that everyone would like their life to be *simple, fulfilled*, and *easy*.

These three dimensions of human behavior are

Take a moment right now and think about yourself in these three dimensions—thinking, feeling, and doing. Sort or separate yourself into these three components. Don't worry about how they are connected or how they work. Within your current *awareness*, ask yourself what are you thinking, doing, and feeling right now. For example, you may be reading this book, thinking about getting a snack and feeling fulfilled because you are reading a great book.

Please, don't try to be religious or metaphysical about what I'm asking you to do. Make it simple. Get to know yourself in these three forms. It is amazing to realize that you can be thinking about something totally unrelated to what you are doing. For example, right now I am writing and thinking about playing golf.

> **Key Point:**   • **Recognize how instinctive your behavior has become and how random and chaotic your thinking can be.**

While you are in this thought pattern, recall the last time you were angry with a child for doing something you thought was stupid. Remember when you said, "What were you thinking?" and they looked at you with a blank stare. The truth is, they weren't thinking; they were just doing.

> **Key Point:**   • **Doing becomes instinctive and is often totally unrelated to a person's thinking at that moment.**
> • **Consider how accidents occur.**

As you begin to think about yourself in these three components, ask yourself which area do you currently like most and which area would you like to change? Some people want to go back to school to *know* more. Others have a strong desire to *do* something different. Many people are compulsive about *feeling* and find relief in the addictive habits of nicotine and alcohol. It is important to realize that these self-awareness components do not define a state of *being*, but they are useful to expand your self-awareness and understand how you really function day to day.

Now, think about a specific desire to *be*, such as losing weight to *be* thin. Sort the process of dieting into these three piles. Ask yourself, do you *know* about weight loss? Have you *done* something to lose weight? Did it work? Can you tolerate the *feelings* associated with dieting? Losing weight is a problem-solving activity. It is important to recognize which part of yourself you must change when the agenda is to *solve* in order to *be*.

> **Key Point:**   • **Eating becomes instinctive.**
> • **Instinctive behavior can become compulsive and addictive.**

Consider the process of saving for retirement. Do you *know* about saving and investing money? Are you *doing* something every month to prepare for retirement or are you compulsively spending all that you earn? How do you *feel* about your current retirement program?

Now, think about your retirement program as something to be created rather than a problem to solve. Be honest with yourself. Do you really *know* how to *think* about saving and investing, or is the field of money *complex?* Is what you are *doing* really related to retirement, or are you just trying to beat the taxman? Are you confident you will have the retirement income you want? Most people spend what they make. They buy a big home and luxury car and invest in 401Ks and IRAs to save taxes. The point here is not to judge your current habits; rather, challenge yourself to *be retired* and consider what conscious choices you would want to make today to achieve that reality.

Key Point:
- **Most people don't do what they know they should do.**
- **People who think they know, actually don't know.**
- **Instinctive behavior patterns repeat themselves over and over again.**
- **The intention to change is often present. However, the comfort of the nest and the fear of falling are formidable barriers to change.**

Now, think about *becoming* a professional golfer, an entrepreneur, or a concert pianist. Most people quickly tell me they are way beyond *being a professional*. They realize that they failed to make the choice *to be* years ago. Furthermore, their current reality doesn't contain enough time, money, or resources to afford the journey at this point in their lives. I understand that you likely missed the boat the first time. Just suppose you could rewind the clock, how would you start *to be a professional?* What would you need *to think, to feel,* and *to do*, and when would you need to begin to make the choices to *be?* What do people who are professionals *think, feel,* and *do*, and when did they make the choices to *become a pro?* Did it just happen?

Now think about what you have just said to yourself in terms of *thinking, feeling,* and *doing*. It is obviously unrealistic to be anything if you don't know how to begin the journey.

Key Point:
- **Think about it.**
- **What would it take for you to be on the Senior Golf Tour when you turn 50?**
- **What would it take for you to own your own business?**
- **What would it take for you to be something *different?***

At this point, many people feel the hopelessness of their current situation. They wish they had made different choices when the time to choose was there, but they accept the fact that they didn't. The most important realization is that *becoming* takes time, and the first step is a conscious choice to *be*.

Key Point:
- **The journey may not be about you.**
- **You may be in a position today to help someone you love make the choice to** *be.* **Your role as a Transformational Leader is about the followers.**
- **Helping other people make choices is the ultimate role of a leader.**

In this context, think about the organization where you work. Sort the thinking, feeling, and behaving parts of your business into piles. The Thinkers are at a strategic planning retreat thinking. The Doers are in the factory doing, and the touchy-feely stuff has likely been stripped away. Can you see the Mass Production organization in this way? Can you see how instinctive everyone's behavior, including your own, has become? Can you see how all the *thinking, doing,* and *feeling* won't lead to anything different unless there is a conscious choice to *be different?*

Key Point:
- **The comfort zone of Mass Production Thinking is based upon highly instinctive behavior patterns.**
- **People instinctively behave within the control limits established by the rules.**
- **To be** *different* **you must break the rules which are based in obsolete thinking from the past.**

When people are asked why they do what they do, I often hear, "That's the way we've always done it around here." Breaking the instinctive behavior patterns of Mass Production Thinking is a very difficult process.

Now think about choosing to *be different* within your organization in terms of *simple, easy,* and *fulfilled.* Consider the model used throughout this book.

Simple: **Create a structural framework.**
            – Answer 10 key questions for people.
Easy: **Create collective intelligence.**
            – Let everyone get involved.
Fulfilled: **Align behavior.**
            – Fulfill the purpose.

The structural framework will break the random, chaotic thinking patterns within the organization. Involving everyone in the thinking process will challenge them to think about how they make choices. Conscious choice leads to aligned behavior.

Now repeat the process for yourself.

Simple:	**Create a structural framework.**
	– Answer 10 key questions for yourself, starting with what you want to *be*.
Easy:	**Create collective intelligence.**
	– Share your vision with key people who can help you. Create a network that can support your journey both emotionally and economically,
Fulfilled:	**Align your behavior.**
	– Stay on purpose. Be aware of how what you want to *be* serves other people.

The Mass Production Thinker in you will resist. "Change should be hard work. It can't be that easy."

Key Point:	• **Never forget effortless–effectiveness.**

I hope you can feel the Transformational Leadership challenge ahead. Your Transformational Journey does not start by figuring out the complexity of the world, working harder, or having a phony attitude to trick yourself into believing that everything is fine.

Key Point:	• **A Transformational Journey is not about fixing current reality. It is about wanting *to be simple, easy, and fulfilled.***
	• **A Transformational Journey is not about defeating *time*. It is about making choices to be and building awareness of how to *become*.**
	• **A Transformational Journey is not about being tough. When the going gets tough, the tough are helpless.**
	• **A Transformation Journey is about changing the instinctive behavior patterns of your old game.**

Nothing is more important than understanding that Transformational Change is about wanting to *be different*. Mass Production Thinking is based upon the concept of separating thinking from doing and stripping the touchy-feely stuff out of your life. This level of awareness will not permit you to *be different* in the future. Mass Production Thinking is technologically obsolete.

Making Choices

Now that you have made the choice to be *different,* you must begin to make additional choices to bring different into existence. Said another way, you must begin to break the instinctive behavior patterns of your old game. It is important to note that you may not have an accurate vision at this point. Everything may be vague and idealistic. Don't forget you are a Mass Production Thinker and you will instinctively define the future in terms of *more* or *better.* Let it be that way. The only question for now is do you start to transform yourself by *thinking* something, *doing* something, or *feeling* something?

Go back to your thinking about *becoming* a professional. After the choice to *be* a *professional* is made, the aspiring professional begins the journey by *doing* things independent of *thinking.* The *thinking* typically resides in a person who encourages them *to do* without *thinking.* We can illustrate this as follows:

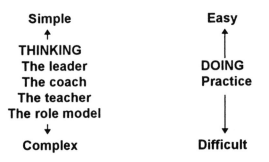

Simple	**Easy**
↑	↑
THINKING	
The leader	
The coach	**DOING**
The teacher	**Practice**
The role model	
↓	↓
Complex	**Difficult**

Every professional will tell you about their leader, coach, teacher, or mentor who was responsible for them *being* what they are today.

> **Key Point:**   • **In the beginning, a choice to *be* must be translated into choices to *do*. The thinking behind the choice may be unknown by the performer.**

Consider the baby eaglets. They are likely very surprised by the choice made for them by their mother. They have a fear of falling until they realize they can soar.

It's a well-known fact that many children are forced *to do things* because their parents want them to *be* something. I coached Little League baseball and had several kids on my teams who didn't want to play baseball. They were on the team because their dads wanted them to play. For the most part, this was the exception. Most kids wanted to play, and many of them already had a professional idol.

Children at early stages of *becoming* are very impressionable and they all need the positive vision of a role model. The picture of the role model, doing what they do, serves as a behavior model for many children. It is very common for children to imitate the behavior of Michael Jordan or Tiger Woods.

The role of the coach is equally important. The coach must help the child learn to play the game within the rules and with the proper technique. The child is very dependent upon the knowledge and thinking of the coach. The child, however, must practice to develop their skills. The coach cannot do it for them.

It is easy to see how a piano student is dependent upon the music teacher and aspiring golfers like Jack Nicklaus had Jack Grout to teach him how to play. Everyone must be inspired to begin by an outside influence.

Key Point:
- **The separation of thinking from doing is unavoidable in the beginning.**
- **The separation of knowing from doing cannot be permanent.**
- **Doing builds knowing. Knowing builds the ability to think.**

The aspiring professional ultimately arrives at a level of learning that requires the integration of knowing with doing. The leader, coach, teacher, or mentor must let go of telling the student everything they know and help their students extract meaning from their own experiences. The professional performer must ultimately understand the complexity of their profession and be able to perform instinctively.

Key Point:
- **You will not arrive at Carnegie Hall if you can only play the piano by ear.**
- **Mass Production Thinking is based upon a permanent separation of thinking from doing. It is an illusion to believe you can be a professional without integrating knowing, and thinking, with doing.**

Let's now suppose that the performance of a professional is slipping. Where do they turn for help? A professional golfer turns to the coach, and a doctor might turn to other colleagues. In every case, the professional is willing to ask for help from someone who can diagnose behavior.

For the professional, the choice to ask for help is easy to make. All professionals have learned to accept coaching.

Key Point:
- **When doing suffers, coaching is essential.**
- **When coaching suffers, a change in *Context* is essential.**

What happens when the coach doesn't know, but thinks he knows? We've all seen coaching failures. When the knowing is not working, generally the *Context* is wrong. A new coach always brings a fresh new approach to the situation. A change in *Context* can produce immediate results with struggling performers. What is perceived to be a lack of talent within the performers, is often a *Context* issue within the coaching staff.

Key Point:
- **Mass Production Thinkers always believe that poor performance emanates from a lack of talented performers.**
- **The *Context* of senior management knowledge is never the problem.**
- **Asking for help is a sign of weakness for many Mass Production Thinkers. *Fake it until you make it* is a common management theme.**
- **A shift in *Context* at the leadership level can produce immediate results within the performers.**
- **Mass Production Thinking no longer contains the *knowing* to change the performance of the information-based *doing* environment.**

It is very important to realize that your ability *to think* is impaired because the knowledge base of Mass Production is obsolete. You actually may not know how to think, and your doing within the *Context* of Mass Production has become instinctive. Changing this situation is not easy.

The Learning Dilemma

Many people stop learning at some point in their adult life. Fortunately for some, life-long learning is a value. However, most Mass Production Thinkers stop learning sometime in their business careers. They believe they have mastered Mass Production management and their management behavior becomes instinctive. We all know the know it all.

Key Point:
- **Adults expand their knowledge and develop their ability to think by extracting meaning from experience. Most people aren't good at doing that.**

We all know the definition of insanity: repeating the same behavior and expecting different results. We see it applied in business every day. People manage their departments the same way, day after day, expecting to produce different results. Why can't people change their behavior? Let's not kid ourselves by being nice or polite. Many people run companies, conduct sales calls, and serve customers using techniques that have been declared obsolete for years.

I was recently asked to help a senior leader who still threatens to take people out behind the woodpile. There's hell to pay for making a mistake in his department. What's even more terrifying is that he is an information systems executive and believes people can do it right the first time. The problem is not the behavior of the people who work for him. The problem is Mr. Mass Production Thinker is unaware that the *Context* has changed.

True learning requires experimental behavior and the ability to extract meaning from the experiment. How many times did Edison experiment before he invented the light bulb? Experimental behavior, however, must lead to meaning. If you experiment with teambuilding and it doesn't work, you must understand why it didn't work.

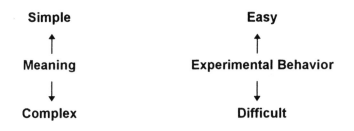

The trial and error behavior of the entrepreneur is experimental behavior. Many entrepreneurs have experimented with Mass Customization and have developed an extensive base of *meaning* on which to grow the business. This knowledge is generally very different from the knowledge of large Mass Production organizations. Entrepreneurs have learned to inspire and empower people to perform. They have learned to break the instinctive habit patterns of the Mass Production *Context*.

The entrepreneur poses no threat to the market penetration mind-set of the Mass Production Thinker. When Mass Production Thinkers are confronted with entrepreneurial results, they pass them off as niche players. "Wait until they grow-up. They'll learn!" In other words, the Mass Production Thinker already knows. Thirty years of industry experience has taught them how to get results— plan, organize, and control. I know executives who continue to believe that standardization leads to competitive advantage.

Key Point: • **Learning is extracting meaning from experimental behavior. New knowledge can result from reading a book, but learning may not occur.**

There is a very important distinction between learning and knowledge. Learning is a dynamic process of extracting meaning from behavior. Knowledge can be acquired without an association with behavior. The Mass Production Thinkers have read the books about teamwork and empowerment, but they cannot do what they have read. A person who puts their hand on a hot stove learns that the stove is hot. Reading about a hot stove does not confirm what hot means.

Transformation of Awareness

I hope by now it is becoming clear that your Transformational Journey requires new awareness, and new awareness comes from extracting meaning from experience. As you experience working for a Mass Production Thinker, you must realize how limiting the *Context* of Mass Production Thinking is.

Key Point: • **It is not your boss that limits you from achieving your potential—it is the Mass Production Thinking within you and your boss.**

When I was in free fall from my experience with The Trane Company, I realized that I was prepared to soar. I was easily able to transcend the fear of falling and feel the exhilaration of being free. I wasn't aware at that time why I felt so free, but looking back on it now, I realize that I had learned four very important principles early in my career with Trane. I attended a *Counselor Selling* class, taught by Larry Wilson, where I learned:

1. There is a world of abundance available to those who believe that their purpose is to help people buy rather than to make a sale.

2. I cannot fail if I can learn from my mistakes.

3. I am not my behavior. No one can reject *me*. I am invulnerable if I am unconditional with myself.

4. I will always succeed if I play win-win.

I had been teaching these principles to my Trane dealers for 10 years and had internalized these principles into my own self-awareness. I was very fortunate to work in the Consumer Products Division, which had embraced many nontraditional approaches to doing business. When the General Electric decision was announced, I realized that I was now free to *be* an eagle. There was a world of abundance out there, and I was free to soar.

Many people know of these four principles, but Mass Production Thinking is based upon a totally different view.

Key Point: • **Knowing who you *are* is at the core of every Transformational Journey.**

Again, it is not my purpose to tell you who you should *be* or suggest a religious or philosophical way for you to think about who you want to *be*. However, there is a consistent message within all religious and philosophical contexts:

Key Point: • **You must start by knowing yourself to change who you *are*.**

As illustrated in the following figure, there are consistent levels of personal awareness:

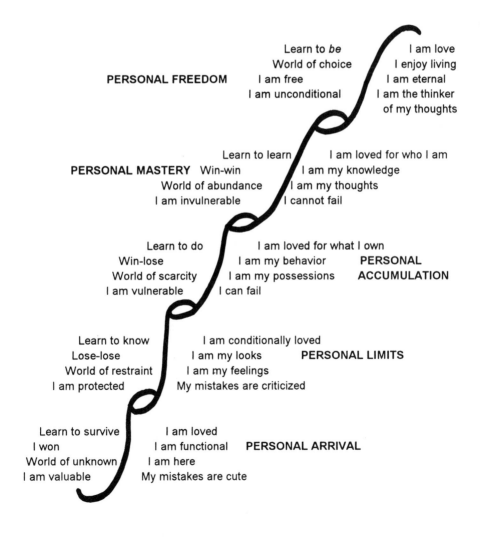

Learn to *be*
World of choice
PERSONAL FREEDOM   I am free
I am unconditional

I am love
I enjoy living
I am eternal
I am the thinker
of my thoughts

Learn to learn
PERSONAL MASTERY   Win-win
World of abundance
I am invulnerable

I am loved for who I am
I am my knowledge
I am my thoughts
I cannot fail

Learn to do
Win-lose
World of scarcity
I am vulnerable

I am loved for what I own
I am my behavior   PERSONAL
I am my possessions   ACCUMULATION
I can fail

Learn to know
Lose-lose
World of restraint
I am protected

I am conditionally loved
I am my looks   PERSONAL LIMITS
I am my feelings
My mistakes are criticized

Learn to survive
I won
World of unknown
I am valuable

I am loved
I am functional   PERSONAL ARRIVAL
I am here
My mistakes are cute

As you study this figure, I hope you can see the simplicity of personal transformation. Obviously, it is not easy to grow your awareness because it comes from extracting meaning from the experience of life.

Take a moment, right now, and think about your life. Babies are at the Personal Arrival level of self-awareness. The bifurcation point begins when the babies begin to walk and continues through the terrible twos.

For many years, young people live within limited awareness imposed upon them by their parents. During that time, school is about learning to know. Students are graded on knowing rather than meaning. Young children are reinforced for knowing their ABCs. It doesn't matter whether they initially know the meaning of the letters.

Teenagers begin to test the limits. They experience tremendous tension, breaking out of the limits imposed upon them by their parents. When you were 16 and able to drive a car, you became aware of the enormous potential *to have and do* beyond the boundaries of walking or riding a bike. Most people remain in a Personal Limits orientation until they graduate from high school. Graduation from college marks the beginning of the Personal Accumulation level of self-awareness.

The awareness in the Personal Accumulation level is exciting and fun. People learn to do. Armed with the knowledge from the schooling years, people begin their careers. People begin to define who they are by what they own and what they do. Many people attach their own self-worth to an athletic team. They live or die based upon the success of a sports team. The personal identity of the accumulation phase is all about *enough*. It is easy to see the accumulators. I am always reminded of the saying, "You can tell the men from the boys by the price of their toys."

Many people never transcend the Personal Accumulation level of awareness. Frankly, they deny that any other level of awareness matters.

Beyond accumulation are the Personal Mastery and Personal Freedom levels. These levels of awareness are often labeled as religious and psychologically weird. The accumulators believe that they must leave their possessions behind to achieve these levels of personal existence. This is an illusion. While you will attach less value to accumulating after you reach these levels, it is totally appropriate to own things and enjoy the tangible world around you. The important shift is to realize that tangible possessions no longer define who you *are*.

Key Point:
- Mass Production Thinking is the imbedded awareness of the Personal Accumulation level.
- Mass Production Thinkers try to keep the Doers within the AWARENESS OF LIMITS.
- The battle between management and labor is about accumulation of *enough*. The Personal Accumulation phase of self-awareness will not drive the new business environment.
- A shift in personal awareness must be driven by a desire to be *different*. Accumulating more possessions will not transform your awareness.

For now, think about your current awareness. Don't label yourself wrong for the way you *are*. You have experienced life in a very normal way. If it's time to change, it's simply a conscious choice to be made and an exciting journey to undertake.

You should also be aware that there is a positive and negative aspect of every level of awareness. The positive accumulators are often very philanthropic. Negative accumulators are always compulsive about time. To them time is money. They become very arrogant and flaunt their possessions. These people are the great pretenders. They always pretend to be more than they *are* based upon what they own.

The positive level of Personal Mastery is a quiet self-confidence that can coach, counsel, and guide other people to consider achieving success beyond possessions and compulsive use of time. People who are masters of self reflect integrity. They walk the talk and don't boast about their accomplishment. Behavior and possessions don't define who they *are*. The negative aspect of Personal Mastery is the holier than thou scenario. These people often condemn human possessions and become cult-like in pursuit of loftier ideals. The negative level of Personal Mastery is often accused of being psychologically weird and nonfunctional in the business world.

The study of self-awareness is a fascinating process. I hope this brief discussion will prompt you to consider the importance of your own self-awareness as you begin to transform your life and *the Business of your BUSINESS.*

The Awareness of Mass Production Thinking

It is important to note that many people who have reached Personal Mastery run Mass Production organizations. Leaders who achieve the Personal Mastery level of self-awareness lead dominating organizations. If you read *Built to Last*, you easily see the difference in leadership awareness between the visionary and comparison companies.

Mass Production Thinking is based upon the self-awareness of Personal Accumulation. The dominant views are

- A world of scarcity—The strategy is to accumulate enough because there is only so much to go around. "Bigger is better."

- People are their behavior—To control behavior, control people. Managers are necessary to establish limits and boundaries within which behavior is permissible. "What you see is causing all the problems."

- Failure comes from mistakes—To survive, minimize mistakes. "Do it right the first time."

- Learning is about doing things right—The knowledge of right and wrong resides in management. "Knowledge is power and must be withheld from those who Do."

Mass Production Thinking reinforces a level of self-awareness that is well below Personal Mastery. When Mass Production Thinkers are confronted with Personal Mastery concepts, they reject them as being that touchy-feely stuff. Others call it New Age thinking and immediately suggest that it won't work in the business world.

I see many people apply Mass Production Thinking to their personal lives and relationships. The results are always devastating. Remember, Mass Production Thinking strips the touchy-feely stuff out of the organization, and it will cause you to have an oppressive family life as well.

Key Point: • **It is virtually impossible to live two lives. Your orientation at work will rule your life at home**.

Today, things have changed. It is possible to be *fulfilled* by what you do. You are no longer constrained to live and work in the monolithic Mass Production assembly line of large corporations. To change jobs so you can apply your creative talent is not a blot on your résumé. "Do what you love and love what you do." This advice has been known for years, but millions of Mass Production Thinkers and workers have been convinced they must endure the pain of a miserable job in pursuit of *enough*. For many people "Thank God it's Friday" will continue to be their mantra.

Where are you on the self-awareness scale? How would you start to transform yourself? The first step is not to quit your job. Rather, begin today to define the reality of the world around you in a *different* way.

Personal Mastery

The transformational challenge for the Mass Production Thinker is to understand Personal Mastery. You likely know that this type of thinking exists, but you haven't learned to live at this level. If you are like most Mass Production Thinkers, you have dabbled with participative management. During your performance review, you have been reminded that autocratic management styles are nonproductive in today's business environment. A 360-degree feedback survey likely revealed your strengths and weaknesses, and you are aware that you are perceived by many people as a good manager.

All the Mr. Nice Guy aside, Personal Mastery is not about being nice to people. It is about being the creative force in your own life. It is not about accumulating anything or how well you can fix current reality. It's about learning to learn how to create. I have talked throughout this book about *creating* and I trust that that message is clear.

Personal Mastery also requires that you embrace two additional views about your existence: the world of abundance awaits the invulnerable self.

The World of Abundance

The new business environment is living proof that there is a world of abundance out there. Technological obsolescence and Mass Customization are creating new opportunities for you to apply your creative talent every moment of every day. Even more important, it's not going to stop or go away any time soon.

The manifestation from nothing to everything begins in conscious awareness. The first step is to be aware of the following key points:

Key Point:
- **Everything already exists. It's just in a different form than you currently desire.**
- **You must learn to transform everything into everything**.

This is strange advice to most people. They have been programmed to clean their plates because there isn't enough. The survival of the fittest concept in nature suggests that there is only so much and those who are the fittest and toughest will survive. There isn't anything wrong with this level of awareness, and it is sound advice when you are climbing mountains and hunting big game animals.

If you are to transcend the Mass Production level of awareness, you must begin by being aware that everything exists. To my knowledge, we are not yet importing anything, other than the energy of the sun, from outer space. It's all here on earth. It may be in a different place, owned by a different person, and in a different form than you currently desire, but *everything* is available to you. For example, from where did all the cars and buildings that you see around you come? Did the Pilgrims bring them over on the Mayflower? Did the Native Americans have them stored in their homes? Of course not. Everything we have today was created from what appears as nothing. The world of abundance exists all around you and is waiting to be transformed by your creative talent.

It is amazing how well our free enterprise system operates in this regard. Consider the abundance around you and how well the Mass Production process has performed until now. This reality always prompts the Mass Production Thinkers to declare, "If it ain't broke, don't fix it."

> **Key Point:**
> - **Mass Production Thinking isn't broken.**
> - **Mass Production Thinking doesn't need to be fixed.**
> - **The world of scarcity awareness that is inherent to Mass Production Thinking will severely limit your ability to *be different*.**

Mass Production Thinking is based upon a world of scarcity mentality. It limits organizations to achieving low cost producer status. It stifles creativity and prevents innovation from occurring. If you are fulfilled by that level of personal challenge and contribution, keep doing what you do.

> **Key Point:**
> - **The entrepreneurial revolution is living proof that the world of abundance exist and that creative people thrive when they are free to create something from everything.**

When you can break the functional fixation of Mass Production Thinking, you will be free to create new possibilities within the world of abundance. If you are currently constrained by the world of scarcity, you will work hard to protect what you have, steal market share from those who have it, and convince the Mass Production Thinker you work for that you are working smart enough to keep your job.

How limiting is this level of awareness? Think about all that is being created as you are reading this paragraph. Feel your urge is to stop and go get your share. If you believe there is only so much out there, the tension you feel emanates from your scarcity mentality. We all have it. We were programmed for years to believe it.

> **Key Point:**
> - **Relax! The world of abundance will be there tomorrow. The ability to create everything from everything won't go away.**

Your Transformational Journey is that simple. You can be free of the constraints of accumulating enough. Enough is everywhere. It's all around you. Transformational Change isn't about getting enough; rather, it is about what you want to *be*.

The shift in awareness from scarcity to abundance is simple, but it is very difficult for most people to make. Most people only see the mess on their desk and the clutter on the streets. They are working to get it organized or make it go away. Recently, I was in the office of a highly successful organization that has reached a major plateau in its growth. The senior leaders were frustrated by lack of time management skills. They were trying to squeeze another hour out of every day. Many of their desks were piled high with papers, reports, periodicals, and miscellaneous debris. They were convinced that continued success was a function of making the mess go away and better time management. The story is too long to relate, but the world of scarcity was alive and well in their minds. When I asked them what they were creating within all that mess, they were stumped. They were focused on making the mess go away and being more efficient to accumulate enough.

Key Point:	• **Relax! The mess isn't the issue.**
	• **The mess is the abundance from which everything can be created.**
	• **Do you know what you want to *become* and have the ability to create that reality out of the mess?**

From a very practical standpoint, do something today to be aware of the world of abundance. For the next 10 days, consciously be aware of your interaction with businesses that facilitate your existence. How do you feel when you must settle for the standardized, one size fits all approach of the low cost producer? Be aware of your expectations for low cost and high quality in a customized way in almost everything you want. Be aware of the incredible variety that is available to you. Where is all this stuff coming from? Is there a world of scarcity or a world of abundance out there? Do you need to hurry and accumulate enough? Where would you put it all if you got it?

Key Point:	• **You must begin today to transform your thinking to be *different* in the future.**
	• **Doing more with less, faster and better leads to exhaustion.**
	• **If more of the same defines what you want to *be*, do more of the same.**
	• **If you want to be *different*, begin by seeing the abundance that has been provided to support your journey.**

The Invulnerable Self

After you are able to see the world of abundance, you will begin to relax. You will realize that your agenda for today is not about accumulating enough; instead, it is about creating what you want *to be*. You will begin to experience an amazing transformation of how you define who you *are* and how you want to live your life.

People who are on a constant journey in search of enough will define who they are by how much they accumulate. Let's suppose you have just finished eating dinner and say, "I'm full." Subconsciously you have told yourself "you are enough food." This is a strange way to think about such a simple statement, but the truth is you have linked "full" with "I am." Consider the person that wins a lottery jackpot and they say, "I'm rich." Once again the "I am" is defined by "enough money." How many times have you said, "I'm tired," "I'm angry," or "I'm bored?" Think about the *enoughness* of all these statements.

Worse yet, how many times are children told they are lazy, stupid, worthless, or bad, during their childhood? Think about the *enoughness* of these statements. All the implications are that the child is their behavior or intelligence.

Think about adults in the work environment. Ask your peers to finish the statement, "I am _____." For example, I am a salesperson, manager, programmer, secretary, receptionist. It is very natural for all of us to define who we are by what we do.

Many people finish the statement "I am" with "not bad." This answer is a negative vision of what they aren't, rather than who they are.

Another common answer to the statement "I am" is "fine" or some reflection of how you feel. "I am angry" or "I am frustrated" are statements that link who we are to how we feel.

There is nothing right or wrong with this way of defining who we are. It is very useful and very conversational to communicate in this way. This approach, however, does prevent people from achieving higher levels of potential in life. The self-awareness of limits and accumulation run deep.

Some years ago, I played golf with the son of a very famous person. At that time, he was 35 years old. After nearly every shot, he would agonize about the imperfection of the shot and say, "You dummy." After I heard him say you dummy at least 15 times, I asked him why he said that to himself. He was surprised by my question and asked, "Say what?" I told him he said you dummy after almost every shot, and he asked, "I do?" He was actually unaware of his habit. His father was a hard-charging athletic person, and he ultimately admitted that his dad called him a dummy every time he fumbled the ball or made an error.

What if you want to *be different?* Is *different* defined in terms of thinking, doing, or feeling? Or is *different* merely a state of *awareness?*

Transformational Change is seldom about changing what you do for a living. Many people who are accountants, bankers, salespeople, and managers want to do something different. They believe they must change their profession to find enough or feel fulfilled. They don't realize that what they must change, first, is simply how they define who they are.

Key Point:
- **You are not your behavior.**
- **You are not your feelings.**
- **You are not what you own.**
- **You are not your body.**
- **You are the thinker of your thoughts.**
- **You are invulnerable.**

Remember the old adage, "Sticks and stones may break my bones, but words will never hurt me?" Who are you? You are *you*. You are a human *being*. You are in your body somewhere. You are able to think, and do, and feel, but *you are you*.

This is a very strange level of awareness for most people, but after you grasp this reality, you can begin to take charge of your own Transformational Journey. You can *be* anything you want to *be* if you define who you are as a human *being*. If you believe you are a human *doing* or human *having*, you will struggle in search of *enough*.

Key Point:
- **The Transformational Journey starts from the inside. You must begin to think *differently* to be *different*.**

If you want people to love you, you must *be* lovable. Love is a state of *being*, not a state of having or doing. Start today to be kind, effortless, and happy. If you wait for something outside yourself to make you happy, you may be miserable for a long time. *Be happy* today and see what happens. *Be effortless* tomorrow and see what happens. Learn from the experience. How do people respond? The Mass Production Thinker in you will believe you must be tougher and more efficient. You will try to wring every ounce of work out of every minute of the day to get enough done.

Key Point:
- **Experiment with new states of *being*. You will be amazed at the results.**

After you experiment with being lovable, effortless, and happy for a month, you will realize how *different* life is. There is a world of abundance for those who can see it. You will begin to see how *efforting* and anger limit you. Watch how the hard-charging Mass Production Thinkers try to control the world around them. Listen to the blame and fear it produces. Observe how people who comply with their commands lack the desire to create beyond the limits of authority. Can you see how it all starts with your perception of *yourself?* If you aren't enough, you will believe you must take it from others. If you are vulnerable, you will always be at risk when relating with others. If you aren't lovable, you will try to force people to love you.

The truth of this reality is always revealed on the deathbed of life. When people who are dying are asked what they would have done differently if they had it to do all over again, they always talk about *being* different. Seldom would they spend one more day at the office to make enough money. Their desire is always about a higher level of self-awareness.

Personal Freedom

The Transformation of self-awareness is not complete until you declare that you are *free*. The wisdom of the ages has always suggested that there is a universal consciousness that makes us all one. At this level of awareness, everything dissolves into an unconditional state of being *human beings*.

We all know about this level of awareness because there are many religious teachings that suggest we should live in this state. The Golden Rule, for example, is a principle of oneness. Be unconditional with your neighbor as you would like them to be unto you. The principle of unconditional love for your children is a concept that many parents have embraced throughout the ages.

The unconditional level of human awareness is very rarely achieved within the *Context* of Mass Production. Everything about people is conditional. You will feel the strain of "What have you done for me lately?" every day. The end-of-the-month numbers bring the conditional awareness of not enough into vivid focus.

I have facilitated many strategic visioning sessions with executives who truly want to break the vicious cycle of month-to-month thinking. They can visualize the need for an unconditional customer focus, but they are unaware of the shift in self-awareness that is necessary to make this change occur.

To break the oppressive short-term focus of Mass Production Thinking, you must shift to a world of abundance view. I distinctly remember how that view enabled me to focus on my customers' needs and let go of making enough sales to keep my job.

Key Point: •   Beyond Personal Mastery lies the real opportunity of Personal Freedom.

The ability to *be free* starts within your own awareness. If you unconditionally love yourself as a human *being*, you will create a life-long relationship that is not dissolvable. You can conditionally correct your behavior as you experiment with life, *but* your unconditional state creates the bond with yourself that lasts forever. If you always define who you *are* in terms of enough, you will never experience true freedom in your life.

It is very difficult for Mass Production Thinkers to embrace this reality and apply it in their business lives. The separation of Thinkers from Doers drives a permanent stake in the heart of this concept. Mass Production Thinkers believe that people who think this way are not tough enough to be in top management positions.

Key Point:
- **The new environment demands unconditional awareness.**
- **What are partnerships that last other than an unconditional commitment to *be*?**

My purpose is not to justify the thinking and existence at any level of self-awareness. You must make your own choices. However, I must make you aware that your own awareness is the dominant opportunity for starting your Transformational Journey.

Bloom Where You Are Planted

I hope you are ready to begin your own personal journey to *being different*. The transformation of the Mass Production Thinker in you is not about quitting your job. You don't need to start your own business. You can begin today by making a conscious choice to *be different*. You can bloom where you are right now.

Key Point:
- **Make it simple. Choose to be the master of yourself.**
- **Make it fulfilling. Relax, it won't hurt.**
- **Make it easy. Let go and be effortless.**

I offer you the following checklist:

🖎 Recognize the world of abundance within your current situation.

🖎 See yourself as the thinker of your thoughts. Be fascinated by who you really are. Look in the mirror and perceive that you are in there somewhere behind your eyes. Wiggle your toe. You are not a toe, but you wiggled it. Where are you inside your body?

🖎 Be effortless every day this week. Don't push back on those who push you. Their awareness is very limited. Remember, you can't fail if you extract meaning from the effortless experience.

🖎 Begin to create a vision for yourself as a Transformational Leader.

- Define the purpose of your work. What do you do in service to customers? Feel the simplicity of helping customers get what they want.

- Involve everyone that works for you in understanding their role in executing *the Business of the BUSINESS*. Be patient (effortless) with those who don't know or don't care. Realize that their Personal Awareness is either Limits or Accumulation.

- Link what you do into the competitive advantage of the *BUSINESS*. You are a competency. How your work unit interacts with the rest of the organization is a component of capability.

- Visit with other people in the customer service process that you don't know or with whom you have a difficult relationship. Be unconditional in talking with them. Respect them as human beings. They are likely trying to defeat time to get enough. Be fascinated by the way it *is*.

- Ask yourself and your work unit to spend one hour a week to create the future. Consciously suspend the firefighting and begin to create. Feel how strange it is at first.

- Be deterministic. Take action today toward a new level of awareness and determine tomorrow what you will do next. Stop trying to figure it out.

- As you attend meetings with the Mass Production Thinkers, listen for the polarized views about enough. Listen for predictions as to when enough will arrive. Suggest that enough already exists, it's just in a different form. Ask yourself the tough question, "Why are we doing this?" What is the purpose of the organization?

- Track positives everyday. Ask what's going well before tackling the Problem Box of your existence. When you experience the hopelessness of the Problem Box, ask yourself a *just suppose* question. Be aware of the importance of vision in creating the future.

- Begin to help those you love make choices to *be*. Be especially effortless with teenagers. They are in a very difficult state of awareness. They will always experiment with new behavior to test the limits of their awareness. Help them see the difference between being, doing, and having.

- Feel the Personal Mastery starting to build within you. You will begin to feel the power of desire. Be aware of how you make choices. Your choices will be purposeful and your ability to create will increase exponentially.

⚮ Be effortless when mistakes are made. Extract meaning from the mistake. When things don't go well, understand how Mass Production Thinking was the culprit.

⚮ As you watch television, listen for the polarized views of those who want to defeat time to get enough. The conflict of polarized thinking will come from the right and from the left. The cultural perspectives will be very visible. Realize how structural change always leads to a new collective commitment.

There are many approaches to transforming your self-awareness, but none is more important than *blooming where you are planted*. Also, never forget, when the going gets tough, the tough are helpless. *Command and control* works in the military, but it is a useless skill in the new business environment.

Key Point:	• **Self-awareness is the key to personal transformation.** • **Make it simple.** • **Make it fun.** • **Make it effortless.**

Stop trying to control others for you to be successful. Start with yourself. You don't need to make an announcement to anyone other than yourself.

The Transformational Leadership Challenge

To *be* a Transformational Leader within the new business environment, you must ultimately change the self-awareness of everyone within the organization. This is not easy to do.

Key Point:	• **There is a world of abundance out there. It is now global. For those who can *create*, there are enormous opportunities ahead.** • **You are invulnerable. You are not what you do. People are people; they are not assets. If you want the culture to *be different*, start by respecting everyone as a human being.** • **You can create a business that is Aligned on Purpose. Win-win can define what you do, or don't play. The world of abundance will sustain those who can embrace this commitment.**

- **You cannot fail if you can extract meaning from mistakes. Learning is the key for all successful people**.

These four key points will test your commitment to change. You will quickly find resistance at almost every level of the organization. In working with the vice president of marketing for a major international company, I was emphatically told, "I don't want my people thinking this way." He was convinced that thinking this way would make his salespeople weak and customers would take advantage of them. To this day, his company continues to struggle. Their major competitor is well on the road to Mass Customization.

Key Point:
- **Mass Production Thinkers are too busy trying to get enough and defeat time with the promise that they will be fulfilled after they have enough.**
- **Beware: Mass Production Thinkers over-promise and under-deliver.**

Get to know *yourself*. Stop the facade and phony bravado. Choose to *be different*. Most important, recognize that your old game won't inspire those who must follow your lead to achieve the self-awareness that is fulfilling for them.

Chapter 17
The Journey

There are as many ways of seeing the world as there are points on the globe. Recall the parable of the blind man observing an elephant by alternately feeling the leg, the tail, and the ear.

Key Point: • **A fly without wings is not a walk. It's still a fly.**

The *Context* of the new environment is truly global. The observation point may be Europe, Asia, or the United States of America. Information technology has made any parochial or provincial view obsolete. In this *Context*, Mass Customization defines the new reality. Every organization must embrace the paradox of Massive Customization to meet the challenges ahead. To think any other way is technologically obsolete.

The paradox of global and local is the same as Mass and Customized. Every company must be able to think of itself as local and global. Every restaurant is challenged to consider tastes from around the world in service of local customers. How many Italian, Mexican, Chinese, and French restaurants are there in your city? The truly provincial perspective is very limiting.

The Mass Production Thinker typically thinks within a paradox of either/or. This type of thinking causes the organization to oscillate between mutually exclusive extremes. Almost every large company has gone through the thinking of centralization and decentralization. The new reality is that all large businesses must be both centralized *and* decentralized. This inescapable reality is obvious when we embrace the *Context* of local and global.

Key Point: • **The leadership challenge is to be able to perceive that all things, including every person, every object, and every event, are potentially something *different* than their current reality. Seeing the possibility of this potential is the driving force for Transformational Change.**

Nowhere is the *Context* of the new environment more visible than in the world of professional golf. The ratio of the size of the playing field to the actual measurable goal is enormous. The size of the course is massive; the size of the 18 little cups is very small. Driving the ball over massive distances matters, but in the end, the 300-yard drive counts as much as the 1-inch putt. No one player dominates the game, yet all the players are dominant. Rewards are achieved for victory; however, the nonvictorious are rewarded. The regulated system is highly self-regulated. The integrity of the entire system preserves the integrity of each player.

In golf, there are no moving targets. All shots must consider the relative distance between current reality and the intended target. Without the picture of the end result, the game does not make sense. A professional golfer does not need to be "at war" to defeat the course. Effortless effectiveness is rewarded.

The target in the new business environment is the customer. There is a massive playing field when you see the global market. If you focus on the size of the playing field, you will miss the significance of the actual measurable goal–serving each individual customer, one at a time. Let go of the bigger is better mind-set. Focus on customization with each customer within the massiveness of it all.

Never forget the principle of effortless effectiveness. The massive global market will tempt the Mass Production Thinker within you to increase *efforting*. It's easy to resolve the paradox of effortless effectiveness with customers when you recognize that you are one. Consider that you are the customer of your own company and recognize that there is no need to be "at war" with yourself.

Finally, realize that the caddie does more than carry the bag. The caddie must think and the player must do. In golf, the roles of thinking and doing are integrated. The choices are made as a team. A failure to recognize that talent must be intelligently applied is a failure to resolve the paradox that Thinkers think and Doers do.

Beyond golf, many models and metaphors explain the new reality. Many of them have been used to explain interdependence before. The leverage of economic individualism has been exhausted. You cannot cut cost and arrive at prosperity. As I said before, "Fixing weaknesses will not arrive at excellence."

Many executives tell me, "You don't understand, I'm not the problem." They tell me how the people aren't motivated or the work ethic just isn't there any more. I will remind you one more time, Transformational Change is not about solving a problem. You must learn to *create* the new environment for yourself and for your company.

Never forget, the behavior of water is dependent upon the structure of the land and the invisible force of gravity. We give the water the name of the structure–a stream, a brook, a lake, or a muddy pond, but water is water. Likewise, people in your organization behave based upon the structure and the invisible force of *intention*. You can call people lazy, idiots, stupid, minimum wagers, or any other demeaning name you choose. Water is water and people are people. Calling people valuable assets will not motivate them to perform. Value the diversity that the new environment presents. It is not a problem to be solved; instead, it is a new mentality to be created.

The first step is for *you* to choose to *be different*. You must declare that "it's over." The Context of Mass Production Thinking is burned out. You cannot *be* what you want to *be* by accumulating more. You can begin today to transform yourself. Do something today to experience *being different*. Experiment with letting go of control. It's not a sign of weakness. Learn to *be* effortless. Ask the Doers what they think. You will be amazed that they have ideas of how to create *different*. Good luck.

Bibliography

Adams, Scott. *The Dilbert Principle*. HarperBusiness, 1996.

Adizes, Ichak. *Corporate Lifestyles: How and Why Corporations Grow and Die and What to Do About It*. Prentice Hall Trade, 1998.

Adizes, Ichak. *The Pursuit of Prime: Maximize Your Company's Success with the Adizes Program*. Knowledge Exchange, LLC, 1996.

Barker, Joel Arthur. *Discovering the Future: The Business of Paradigms*. ILI Press, 1989.

Barker, Joel Arthur. *Future Edge*. Wm. Morrow & Company, 1992.

Barlett, Christopher A. and Sumantra Ghoshal. "Changing the Role of Top Management: Beyond Strategy to Purpose." *Harvard Business Review*. 94601 November 1, 1994.

Belacso, James A. and Ralph C. Stayer. *Flight of the Buffalo: Soaring to Excellence, Learning to Let Employees Lead*. Warner Books, 1993.

Blackwell, Roger D. *From Mind To Market*. HarperBusiness, 1997.

Block, Peter. *Stewardship: Choosing Service Over Self-Interest*. Berrett-Koehler Publishers, 1993.

Chopra, Deepak M.D. *Ageless Body, Timeless Mind*. Harmony Books, 1993.

Chopra, Deepak. "The Higher Self." Audio tape.

Collins, James C. and William C. Lazier. *Beyond Entrepreneurship: Turning Your Business into an Enduring Great Company*. Prentice Hall, 1992.

Collins, James C. and Jerry I. Porras. *Built to Last: Successful Habits of Visionary Companies*. HarperCollins, 1994, 1997.

Covey, Stephen R. *The 7 Habits of Highly Effective People: Powerful Lessons in Personal Change*. Simon and Schuster, 1989.

D«Aveni, Richard A. *Hyper-Competition: Managing the Dynamics of Strategic Maneuvering*. The Free Press, 1994.

Davis, Stanley M. *Future Perfect*. Perseus Press, 1987, 1996.

Davis, Stanley M. and Meyer, Christopher. *Blur*. Addison-Wesley, 1998.

De Bono, Edward. *Serious Creativity: Using the Power of Lateral Thinking to Create New Ideas.* HarperBusiness, 1992.

De Bono, Edward. *Sur/petition.* HarperBusiness, 1992

Deming, W. Edwards. *Out of the Crisis.* Massachusetts Institute of Technology, 1982, 1986.

Dertouzos, Michael. *What Will Be: How the New World of Information Will Change Our Lives.* HarperCollins Publishers, 1997.

Drucker, Peter R. *Innovation and Entrepreneurship.* Harper & Row, 1985.

Drucker, Peter F. "The Theory of the Business." *Harvard Business Review.* 94505. September 1, 1994.

Fisher, Robert and Willaim Ury. *Getting to Yes: Negotiating Agreement Without Giving In.* Penguin Books, 1983.

Fritz, Robert. *The Path of Least Resistance: Learning to Become the Creative Force in Your Own Life.* Fawcett Book, 1984, 1989.

Fritz, Robert. *Creating.* Fawcett Book, 1991.

Fritz, Robert. *Corporate Tides: The Inescapable Laws of Organizational Structure.* Berrett-Koehler Publishers, 1996.

Gilmore, James and B. Joseph Pine II. "The Four Faces of Mass Customization." *Harvard Business Review.* 97103. January 1. 1997.

Goldratt, Eliyahu M. *Theory of Constraints.* North River Press, Inc., 1990.

Goldratt, Eliyahu M. and Jeff Cox. *The Goal: A Process of Ongoing Improvement.* North River Press, Inc., 1986

Goleman, Daniel. *Emotional Intelligence: Why It Can Matter More Than IQ for Character, Health and Lifelong Achievement.* Bantam Books, 1995.

Guaspari, John. *Theory WHY.* Amacom, 1986.

Hagel, John III. *Net.gain.* Harvard Business School Press, 1997.

Hammer, Michael and James Champy. *Reengineering the Corporation: A Manifesto for Business Revolution,* HarperBusiness, 1993.

Hammer, Michael and Steven A. Stanton. *The Reengineering Revolution: A Handbook.* HarperBusiness, 1995.

Handy, Charles. *The Age of Paradox.* Harvard Business School Press, 1994.

Harvey, Jerry B. *The Abilene Paradox–And Other Meditations on Management.* Lexington Books, 1998.

Hickman, Craig R. *Mind of a Manager, Soul of a Leader.* John Wiley & Sons, 1990.

Iaccocca, Lee. *Iacocca, an Autobiography.* Bantam Book, 1984.

Imparato, Nicholas and Oren Harari. *Jumping the Curve: Innovation and Strategic Choice in an Age of Transition.* Jossey-Bass Publishers, 1994.

Johnson, Barry Ph.D. *Polarity Management.*HRD Press, Inc., 1992.

Johnson, Spencer M.D. and Larry Wilson. *The One Minute Sales Person.* Wm. Morrow & Company, 1984.

Kaplan, Robert S., and Norton, David P. *The Balanced Scoreboard.* Harvard Business School Press, 1996.

Kotter, John P. *A Force for Change: How Leadership Differs from Management.* The Free Press, 1990.

Land, George and Beth Jarman. *Breakpoint and Beyond: Mastering the Future–Today.* HarperBusiness, 1992

Lebow, Rob. *A Journey Into the Heroic Environment.* Prima Publishing, 1995.

Leider, Richard J. and Shapiro, David A. *Repacking Your Bags.* Berrett-Koehler Publishers, 1995.

Lewis, Jordan D. *Partnerships for Profit: Structuring and Managing Strategic Alliances.* The Free Press, 1990.

Lewis, Jordan D. *The Connected Corporation: How Leading Companies Win Through Customer-Supplier Alliances.* The Free Press, 1995.

Love, John F. *McDonald's: Behind the Arches.* Bantam Books, 1986.

McNally, David. *Even Eagles Need A Push: Learning to Soar in a Changing World.* Transform Press, 1990.

McNally, David. *The Eagle's Secret.* Delacorte Press, 1998.

Maynard, Herman Bryant Jr. and Susan E. Mehrtens. *The Fourth Wave: Business in the 21st Century.* Berrett-Koehler Publishers, 1993.

Miller, Danny. *The Icarus Paradox: How Exceptional Companies Bring About Their Own Downfall.* HarperBusiness, 1990.

Monden, Yasuhior. *Toyota Production Systems: An Integrated Approach to Just-In-Time.* Industrial Engineering and Management Press, 1993.

Murphy, Michael. *Golf in the Kingdom.* The Viking Press, Inc., 1972.

Nora, John J., C. Raymond Rogers, and Robert J. Stramy. *Transforming the Work Place.* Princeton Research Press, 1986.

Peppers, Don, and Rogers, Martha, Ph.D. *The One to One Future.* Doubleday, 1993.

Peters, Tom. *In Search of Excellence: Lessons from Americas Best-Run Companies.* Harper & Row, 1982.

Peters, Tom. *Thriving on Chaos: Handbook for a Management Revolution.* Alfred A. Knopf, 1987.

Pinchot, Gifford and Elizabeth Pinchot. *The End of Bureaucracy and the Rise of the Intelligent Organization.* Berrett-Koehler Publishers, 1993.

Pine, B. Joseph II. *Mass Customization: The New Frontier in Business Competition.* Harvard Business School Press, 1993.

Pine, B. Joseph II, Bart Victor, and Andrew C. Boynton. "Making Mass Customization Work." *Harvard Business Review.* 93509. September 1, 1993.

Sculley, John and John A. Byrne. *Odyssey: Pepsi to Apple, A Journey of Adventure, Ideas, and the Future.* Harper & Row, 1987.

Senge, Peter M. *The Fifth Discipline: The Art and Practice of the Learning Organization.* Doubleday, 1990.

Sink, D. Scott, William T. Morris, and Cindy S. Johnson. *By What Method? Quality and Productivity Improvement.* Industrial Engineering and Management Press, 1995.

Stalk, George Jr., Philip Evans, and Lawrence E. Shulman. "Competing on Capabilities: The New Rules of Corporate Strategy." *Harvard Business Review.* 92209. March 1, 1992.

Tapscott, Dan and Art Caton. *Paradign Shift: The New Promise of Information Technology.* McGraw-Hill, Inc., 1993.

Taylor, T Alex III. "How Toyota Defies Gravity." *Fortune.* December 8, 1997.

Tichy, Noel M. and Devanna, Mary Anne. *The Transformational Leader.* John Wiley & Sons, 1986.

Ulrich, Dave and Lake, Dale. *Organizational Capability.* John Wiley & Sons, 1990.

Watson, Gregory H. *Business Systems Engineering: Managing Breakthrough Changes for Productivity and Profit.* John Wiley & Sons, 1994.

Wilson, Larry. *Changing the Game: The New Way to Sell.* Simon & Schuster, 1987.

Wilson, Larry. *Stop Selling–Start Partnering: The New Thinking About Finding and Keeping Customers.* Oliver Wight Publication, Inc., 1994.